WITHOUT CHILDREN

WITHOUT CHILDREN

THE LONG HISTORY OF NOT BEING A MOTHER

PEGGY O'DONNELL HEFFINGTON

SEAL PRESS

New York

Seal Press

Hachette Book Group

1290 Avenue of the Americas, New York, NY 10104

www.sealpress.com

@sealpress

Printed in the United States of America

First Edition: April 2023

Published by Seal Press, an imprint of Perseus Books, LLC, a subsidiary of Hachette Book Group, Inc. The Seal Press name and logo is a trademark of the Hachette Book Group.

The Hachette Speakers Bureau provides a wide range of authors for speaking events. To find out more, go to www.hachettespeakersbureau.com or call (866) 376-6591.

The publisher is not responsible for websites (or their content) that are not owned by the publisher.

"Advice for Former Selves," by Kate Baer, and "The electrician sings 'Easy Love' in the kitchen while fixing my light," by Joy Sullivan, were reprinted with permission from the authors.

Print book interior design by Amy Quinn.

Library of Congress Cataloging-in-Publication Data

Names: O'Donnell Heffington, Peggy, author.
Title: Without children: the long history of not being a mother / Peggy O'Donnell Heffington.
Description: New York, NY: Seal Press, [2023] | Includes bibliographical references and index.
Identifiers: LCCN 2022045141 | ISBN 9781541675575 (hardcover) | ISBN 9781541675568 (epub)
Subjects: LCSH: Childlessness. | Childlessness—Social aspects. | Women—Psychology. | Interpersonal relations—Psychological aspects.
Classification: LCC HQ755.8 .O336 2023 | DDC 306.85—dc23/eng/20221114
LC record available at https://lccn.loc.gov/2022045141

ISBNs: 9781541675575 (hardcover), 9781541675568 (ebook)

LSC-C

Printing 1, 2023

To my chosen family, for giving me a world.
To my little family, for giving me a home.
You know who you are.

Advice for Former Selves

Burn your speeches, your instructions,
your prophecies too. In the morning when
you wake: stretch. Do not complain. Do not
set sail on someone else's becoming, their voice
in your throat. Do not look down your nose
at a dinner party, laughing: *If only they didn't
have so many children.*

Revision is necessary. The compulsory bloom.
When you emerge with crystals in one hand,
revenge in the other, remember the humble
barn swallow who returns in the spring. If not
for her markings, another bird entirely.

—Kate Baer, from *What Kind of Woman*

CONTENTS

AUTHOR'S NOTE

WE HAVE A TERM FOR WOMEN WITH CHILDREN, WHICH IS MOTHER. What we don't have is a great term for a woman without children other than "a woman without children"; we can name her only with a description of what she does not have, or what she is not (i.e., a non-mother). For some, this is a problem that runs deeper than semantics. "I don't want 'not a mother' to be part of who I am," Sheila Heti's narrator muses in her 2018 book *Motherhood*, "for my identity to be the negative of someone else's positive identity." Heti suggests the term "not not a mother": For women without children, it could be a rejection of the negative identity, "not 'not a mother.'" For mothers, the double negative cancels itself out and they become, simply, a mother. This, Heti writes, is a "term we can share."[1] I find this suggestion delightful in theory, but it is also—at least for the purposes of writing a nonfiction book—a little bit impractical.

Not having the right words to describe the state of not having children was, as you can probably imagine, a bit of a challenge for the book that follows, which is a lot of words about the state of not having children. Wherever possible, I have tried to avoid labels that carry specific political or cultural baggage: barren, certainly, but also infertile and even, where I could, childless.

Instead, I've tried to describe people as they lived: a woman "without children" or "who did not have children," who "was not a mother" or "experienced infertility" or "chose not to have children." However, the part of my training as a historian that I have tried hardest to cast off is my discipline's enthusiasm for torturing the English language. In some cases, you just need an adjective or a noun, and in those cases I have usually gone with childless and childlessness, which are the most common and widely used terms available.

Since it emerged in the early 1970s, the alternative "childfree" has risen in popularity, eagerly adopted by those who have chosen a life without children. Many see it as a positive reframing, an antidote to the deficiency the term "childless" implies. The emergence of "childfree" is part of the history this book tells, and to employ it more widely would be both anachronistic and potentially confusing. It would also run counter to the experiences of many women in this book, who may have wanted children and would have chosen to have them if various factors in their lives had been different, who tried and were unable to have children, or who experienced their reproductive choices as so constrained that they never really felt they had a choice in the first place.

The sociologist Adele E. Clarke has observed that "we need legitimating vocabularies for not having biological children—both 'childless' and 'childfree' are already inflected/infected. We need an *elaborated vocabulary* for making kin and caring beyond the 'pro- and anti- and non-natalist,' and that does not use the binary-implying word 'choice.'"[2] I agree wholeheartedly, but I don't have the right words either. The fact that we lack good terms for a life lived without children—that it is on us to explain and define and invent words for this sort of life, a life that has never been uncommon and is becoming increasingly common— is part of why I wrote this book in the first place.

INTRODUCTION

WE'RE NOT HAVING CHILDREN

THE HISTORY DEPARTMENT'S BABY CEREMONY TOOK PLACE ON A Thursday afternoon under the fluorescent lights in the Clausewitz Library, located in the windowless basement of one of West Point's oldest buildings. Its walls are lined with black-, green-, and gold-bound tomes about military strategy and history, and the center of the room features clusters of glossy leather chairs appropriately uncomfortable to read them in. The Clausewitz serves as a quiet study space for the academy's students and a venue for faculty meetings and award ceremonies. But on that afternoon, we were using it as a place to celebrate fertility. "We are a very successful department," the faculty member at the front of the room said, mostly joking but also a little bit not. "How do you measure a department's success? By the number of new historians we produce for the world." He gestured to the roomful of babies and toddlers, who ate Goldfish and tried to wriggle loose from the arms of their mothers, most of whom were my colleagues' wives.

I arrived at the United States Military Academy at West Point on the Fourth of July in 2016, a fitting date to breach the gates of the forbidding granite fortress perched on the west bank of the Hudson River. Just six weeks earlier, I'd donned a set of blue-and-gold velvet robes to receive my doctorate at the University of California, Berkeley. I'd taken a teary and devastatingly hung-over red-eye flight from Oakland to Boston, with all my worldly possessions—including, for reasons I cannot explain, an IKEA trash can that I still have—packed into two large duffel bags that I commandeered from dear friends. In Boston, I ate a hot dog at my sister's holiday barbecue, loaded the bags into a used Ford Escape I'd managed to buy on the internet, and drove south and west, diagonally across Connecticut and into the lush green forests and spiky granite peaks of New York's Hudson Valley.

The year I spent teaching history at West Point was full of jarring experiences. My students had to stand when I entered the room. After seven years of teaching classes shod almost exclusively in Birkenstocks, I was supposed to check that their shoes had been properly shined. Most alarmingly, given that I was twenty-nine years old and had recently found my first gray hair, they had to call me "ma'am," a farewell to my youth that punctuated every statement they made and every question they asked. I learned that Army officers, some of whom were my fellow history professors, engage in elaborate rituals involving hats and saluting. They can't stand under umbrellas. In the early days, I got a lot of mileage out of Berkeley-to–West Point jokes.

The Army officer corps is "demographically urban but culturally rural," one captain told me, when I was still too new to understand what he meant. When I went to the first "ladies' coffee," a regular social event for the handful of women faculty members in the History Department and our colleagues' wives, I started to get a better idea. As we sipped drinks and nibbled on baked goods, woman after woman introduced herself to the room by listing her husband's name and her children's ages. When it was my turn, I said that I was just starting to feel ready for the responsibility of keeping a houseplant alive. The laughter that followed was generous, but it also made clear just how much distance there was between our lives.

On paper, you wouldn't think there would be much distance at all. The women sitting around the room were college educated, mostly white, and at least middle class, not entirely unlike the women in the graduate program I'd just completed or the women I knew from college. But those women and I had come to our thirties thinking of motherhood as, at most, an afterthought, something we might get around to eventually, once we'd done all the other things we'd wanted to accomplish or felt we had to do. One friend joked that we were waiting to have a "going out of business" sale: one kid before the clock strikes forty. I was still trying to figure out what to do with my face when a woman my age told me she was pregnant: Was this a terrifying, potentially life-altering mistake? Or were we celebrating? These thirty-year-old officers' wives were pregnant with their third.

I walked out into the warm fall evening with my mind buzzing from sugar and wine, still thinking about this divide. The writer Sheila Heti has since observed that mothers and non-mothers are in "a civil war." She asks, "Which side are you on?"[1] In the years since that evening, the questions that interested me were less about which side I should be on, and more about how there came to be sides in the first place. I found myself wondering how having or not having children became the defining aspect of many women's identities, separating them across a gulf that yawns wider and wider as the years go on, and then—*bam!*—through a definitive act of biology, fixes them forever on either side. We're all familiar with the trope—unflattering to everyone and repeated past the point of cleverness in television, movies, and books—of a group of mothers primly discussing diapers and bath time while the childless outcast sits in the corner, usually drinking heavily.[2] In a scene from the Netflix series *House of Cards*, a presidential candidate's wife chats with Claire Underwood, who is both the sitting First Lady and the running mate on the opposing ticket. "Do you ever regret it, not having children?" she asks Underwood. Underwood looks pointedly at the door the woman's young son had stomped out a moment earlier, after interrupting their conversation to loudly demand juice. "Do you ever regret having them?" she responds.[3]

Mothers and non-mothers can't even talk to each other, popular culture tells us in articles with titles like "5 Things People Without Kids Just Don't Understand," "I Didn't Lose Friends After Having Kids. I Just Moved On," and "Can Mothers and Childless Women Ever Truly Be Friends?"[4] In my own life, I have felt a creeping distance between myself and mothers my age—like the women at the ladies' coffee, but not only the women at the ladies' coffee. Women I got graduate degrees with, drank too much whiskey in bars with, ran marathons with, have been transformed, literally overnight, into Adults, with Real Responsibilities and Meaning in Their Lives. Meanwhile, I have remained a child, failing to feed myself properly on a regular basis, killing houseplants, and indulging in wild, hedonic pleasures like going for a run every morning and having a clean living room.

As I turned it over in my mind, I slowly came to realize that we feel this divide because we're supposed to. The battle lines of the motherhood civil war were given to us as the birthright of people born with female reproductive organs. Women, a swaggering Napoleon Bonaparte told his confidante Gaspard Gourgaud, "are mere machines to make children."[5] On our side of the pond, the expectation that people sexed female at birth would become mothers was forged by a long history that sought to make reproduction into white American women's primary civic contribution, and the nuclear family into her only natural home. At the same time, various American politicians, thinkers, and cultural figures reinforced that thinking by characterizing women who did not have children as deviant, broken, unfeminine, unpatriotic, even—when they were white—traitors to their race. These efforts date back at least to the late eighteenth century, during and after the Revolutionary War, when the wives and daughters of patriots were transformed into "republican mothers," who served the infant nation by birthing and raising its next generation of citizens, bathing their progeny in American civic virtue and spoon-feeding them American morals.[6] In 1873, the US Supreme Court made it official. "The paramount destiny and mission of women are to fulfill the noble and benign offices of wife and mother," Justice Joseph P. Bradley wrote in a concurring opinion to a ruling that allowed states to prevent women from becoming lawyers. "This is the law of the creator."[7]

Unlike most laws in today's polarized political landscape, this one has broad bipartisan support. "The most important job any woman can have is being a mother," Ivanka Trump said in a 2016 video for her father's presidential campaign.[8] In a commencement address to Tuskegee University's 2015 graduating class, First Lady Michelle Obama pledged her personal allegiance to Bradley's law: "Being mom in chief is, and always will be, job number one."[9] Hillary Clinton will probably go to her grave still apologizing to Democrats and Republicans alike for the time she said there was more to life than baking cookies and being a full-time mom.[10]

The *New York Times* has repeatedly published op-eds in recent years that accuse Americans who do not have children of not "affirming life" or refusing to have "radical hope."[11] Ross Douthat, the conservative pot stirrer on the *Times* opinion page, has dispensed with persuasion altogether: "More babies, please," he demanded in 2012.[12] In March 2019, Senator Mike Lee, a Utah Republican, stood up in the Senate chamber to offer "the solution to so many of our problems, at all times and in all places: fall in love, get married and have some kids."[13] Republican politician J. D. Vance lamented in the summer of 2021 that the Democratic party has "become controlled by people who do not have children," who, he argued, do not have a "personal indirect stake" in the future and therefore cannot be trusted to make decisions about it.[14] Even Francis, "the most liberal pope ever," told a crowd gathered at Saint Mark's Square in 2015 that "the choice not to have children is selfish."[15] Francis—a man who, in a more literal sense than most, chose his other passions over parenthood—has repeatedly expressed his dismay at young people who prefer adopting pets to having children, a phenomenon he sees as an alarming "cultural degradation."[16] Fox News anchor Tucker Carlson wholeheartedly agrees. "Having children means less time for vacations and spin class, where the real meaning in life resides, right?" he asked on air. "I mean, have you ever seen anything more selfish, decadent, and stupid?"[17]

Though few of them say it out loud, it is mostly women's selfishness, decadence, and stupidity that concerns them. It is, of course, equally possible for a man to live his whole life and produce no children, and if fewer women are having children, presumably fewer men are fathering them. But a man who produces no children is not usually identified with that lack. "Women's status as child bearer has been made into a major fact of her life," Adrienne Rich writes in her 1986 classic, *Of Woman Born: Motherhood as Experience and Institution*. Unlike *non-mother*, "the term 'nonfather' does not exist."[18] This isn't to say that men face no pressures and expectations about families. The sociologist Alice Rossi has observed that a man's arrival into adulthood is defined by his ability to support a woman and the children she would have.[19] But the pressure to produce the children who need providing for, and the blame for failing to do so, falls entirely on women.

Today, we benefit from the wisdom of Black, queer, and Indigenous feminist thinkers who have taught us that "mother" is best used as a verb, not a noun: mother is something that you do, not something that you are. The social scientist Stanlie M. James argues that radically expanding the definition of mothering and who can do it—so adoptive parents can mother, and so can men, gay couples, trans people, nonbinary folks, teachers, neighbors, friends—is the key to transforming our society for the better.[20] As James frames it, mother*ing* need not have anything to do with a uterus producing a child, or even with whether the person doing the mothering has a uterus or identifies as a woman. bell hooks called this "revolutionary parenting," stripping gendered associations from her term altogether.[21] But for much of the history this book tells, gendered associations reigned supreme: people cared very much about uteruses and what people who had them did with them. The Venn diagram of "women" and "people designated female at birth" would have been a circle, in terms of how society viewed them, and everyone in that circle would have been expected to become a mother, regardless of what she wanted from her life: who she wanted to be, whom she wanted to love, and what she wanted to prioritize.

Throughout history, some undoubtedly found ways of opting out of marriage and/or childbearing because they were not sexually attracted to men, or because they did not want to take on what were traditionally women's roles, or because they did not identify as women. Others may have done so because they had no interest, sexual or otherwise, in the particular man their parents or community expected them to marry and have children with. (The notion that romantic love or sexual attraction were necessary requirements for heterosexual marriage and baby making is a relatively recent invention.[22]) Still others may have done so because they wanted to be scholars or pilots or judges or tennis champions and, at least until very recently, combining motherhood and professional ambitions just didn't seem possible. Whatever their reasons, all of them would have paid a social price. Today, a cis woman who has prioritized her career over children, a lesbian woman who cannot afford fertility treatments, and a trans woman who does not have a uterus have equally failed to undertake the biological act of reproduction that has come to define our gender. Despite our preferences and identities and anatomies, in this, and in the social price we pay, we are united.

Millennial women are failing to undertake this particular biological act en masse. We're gunning for the highest rate of childlessness in American history, or at the very least, the highest rate of childlessness since the unlucky generation that lived their fertile years during the Great Depression.[23] American women's expected lifetime fertility is around 1.7 children per woman, far below the replacement rate of 2.1.[24] Adoptions are down too: the annual number of adoptions in the United States fell more than 17 percent between 2007 and 2014 and has continued its downward slide ever since.[25] Overall, nearly half of millennial women, the eldest of whom are in their early forties, have no children, and an increasing number of us don't ever plan to.[26] "Thinking about the future," a 2021 Pew survey asked American nonparents aged eighteen to forty-nine, "how likely is it that you will have children someday?" Forty-four percent of them said "not too likely" or "not at all likely," a sharp increase of seven percentage points from a 2018 survey, when 37 percent answered that way.[27]

The phenomenon of falling fertility is not solely an American one, of course. The lowest fertility rates in the world are in East Asia: in South Korea, women average 0.8 births in their lifetime. In Singapore, it's 1.1.[28] Fertility in several southern European countries has also dropped low enough to cause alarm: in Greece, Italy, and Spain, women average around 1.3 births. Many of these countries have responded with policies expressly designed to encourage people to have children, and to have a lot of them. In Japan, where the fertility rate has dipped to 1.3, the government has been particularly creative, instituting "family weeks," during which parents are not allowed to work past 7 p.m., and throwing state-sponsored parties where young people are encouraged to fall in love, have sex, and marry, in whatever order. Over the past decade, the French government has spent significant sums to encourage births, funding policies for extended maternity and paternity leaves, tax breaks and other financial incentives, in-home childcare, day care, and stay-at-home allowances for mothers who prefer to take time off from work while their children are young. In France, at least, there is some evidence that these policies are working—if not to increase births, then at least to slow their decline. The French fertility rate is falling—1.83 in 2020, down from 1.89 in 2018 and 2.03 in 2010—but more slowly than elsewhere, and it remains the highest in Europe.[29]

The United States has been slow to institute policies that might encourage people to have more children—aside from trying to limit access to contraception and criminalizing abortion—but that hasn't stopped us from freaking out about the fact that many Americans aren't. Each spring, the US Department of Health and Human Services releases a report tallying up the total number of babies born the previous calendar year and breaking down the data by mother's age, race, and location. Each spring, from 2015 to 2021, that number was lower than the year before. News in the spring of 2022 was mixed—the number of babies born in 2021 was slightly higher than in 2020, but still down significantly from 2019—and it didn't stop the avalanche of panicked articles and stump speeches and social media posts that have now become a yearly tradition.[30] American women are having fewer children, they report. Families are smaller; childlessness is on the rise. These pieces all ask the same question: Why? Why are today's young women screwing up the one really basic function of our mammalian bodies? Why are they ignoring the imperatives of their biology, refusing to do their part in continuing the human species, denying their parents the joy of having grandchildren? Why are they missing out, seemingly choosing to miss out, on something so many people say gives their life its meaning? *Why* are young American women not having babies?

Theories, of course, abound. The least generous explanation for the modern childless woman usually concludes, simply, that she cannot be bothered. She is (we are) too selfish, the story goes, too greedy, too shortsighted, and too into her (our) job(s). As women moved out of the private sphere and into the workforce, heading to factories, offices, hospitals, and board rooms, this theory goes, they began to prioritize career ambition and professional success over motherhood. Women are *choosing* to have no children, in other words, because they want other things—lattes, degrees, careers, vacations, definitely avocado toast—more than they want kids.

More generous explanations focus less on our feminism or our coffee habits, and more on the colder, harder economic realities young Americans actually face. At the risk of overstating the obvious, it costs a lot of avocado toast to send your kid to day care for a month. A *New York Times* survey in 2021 concluded that reproductive decisions were closely tied to jobs, money, and the desperate struggle many millennials have faced to gain even a tenuous foothold in the rapidly eroding middle class. An accompanying county-level inspection of births nationwide found that fertility has dropped dramatically since 2009, not just on the coasts or in cities or blue states like you might expect, but in most counties: red and blue, wealthy and poor, urban and rural, across the nation. For those of us who graduated from college into the Great Recession, as I did, or weathered it from the small, unstable dinghies that are early career jobs, wanting to feel economically and professionally stable before signing up to provide for a new human isn't simply a preference. Many young women see prioritizing their careers as nothing short of necessary for survival.[31] We have all gotten the timeworn advice to just have a baby because, even if the finances or logistics look impossible now, "it will work itself out." What may once have been encouraging words of wisdom now ring hollow to many in a generation that has seen firsthand what it looks like when things very profoundly do *not* work themselves out: When Lehman Brothers declared bankruptcy on the morning of September 15, 2008, dragging the global economy into a yearslong death spiral, millennials were twelve to twenty-seven years old. In the spring of 2020, when the COVID-19 pandemic forced Americans onto the unemployment rolls in numbers not seen since the Great Depression, they were twenty-four to thirty-nine.[32]

As COVID-19 spread across the country and lockdowns pushed us into our homes, demand for over-the-counter and prescription birth control soared in the United States and around the world, quickly outstripping the national and global supply.[33] Four in ten American women told the Guttmacher Institute that the pandemic had caused them to change their plans about when and if to have children, or to reduce the number of children they planned to have.[34] Phones at abortion clinics rang off the hook throughout the pandemic's first year, in part because a number of states ruled abortions to be "nonessential" services under lockdown, causing spillover to clinics in neighboring states, and in part because, as women told abortion providers repeatedly, the ongoing crisis meant that "having a child right now isn't best for them."[35]

But while the crisis was global, its effects were unevenly spread, cushioned or not by economic stability and status. The pandemic years saw a drop in births among Black and low-income women, the people hardest hit by the economic downturn that accompanied the virus. Meanwhile, a small-but-not-insignificant slice of wealthier American women—the ones who found themselves working from home and saving money they'd normally have spent on restaurant tabs and vacations—saw the pandemic as an ideal time to get pregnant and did so in greater numbers than they otherwise might have.[36] Births were down overall during the pandemic, but they were up in the white middle and upper-middle classes. Hannes Schwandt, an economics professor at Northwestern University, observed, "It could well be that this is the first time in a recession where some groups have increased fertility."[37]

The enthusiastic childbearing of the women I met at West Point was cultural in the sense that it took place in a culture in which having children was socially expected and rewarded, but it wasn't *only* cultural. It was also structural. A military life carries great risk, of course, but it also offers stability: good pay, housing stipends, free health care, subsidized day care, and—despite frequent geographic dislocations—strong community networks, often run by women, that envelop newcomers with material and emotional support. In spite of the sacrifices it requires of its members, the American military does a very good job of providing conditions under which people can—and do—have large families. In a sense, the West Point ladies' coffee was a trip back to an earlier era for the white middle class, when time, money, and community support gave people good reasons to believe in their present and future stability. Many of the reasons American women cite for not having children didn't apply to the women in that room because of decisions—policies, laws, and structures—made by people outside it.

Most explanations for why women aren't having children focus on individual choices made by individual women. One wants to have children but doesn't think she can afford it. Another was too picky for too long and didn't find a partner until it was too late. Another doesn't want to grow up, get her life together, or take the leap of reproductive faith her parents did. Another chose her career or buying a house or saving for retirement over having children. Another is unwilling to look past our current crises— political, environmental, economic, take your pick—and choose hope. These women, we tell ourselves, are not mothers because they didn't *choose* to be mothers. If they wanted kids, we tell ourselves, they would have chosen differently.

We can be forgiven for thinking this way. In the United States, choice is just another word for freedom. In his concurring opinion in *Roe v. Wade*, conservative Supreme Court justice Potter Stewart wrote that "freedom of personal choice in matters of marriage and family life"—including, he reasoned, the choice to have an abortion—"is one of the liberties" protected by the Fourteenth Amendment. The word "choice" has since become a rallying cry of progressive women's movements, a synonym for abortion access expertly pitched to a society with a soft spot for claims to individual freedoms. The idea of choice "made" second-wave feminism, Susan Brownmiller, a prominent and controversial feminist of the 1970s, famously wrote. The *choice* to have an abortion. The *choice* between career and family. The *choice* to not have children. Choice was concrete, a specific ask that didn't require making any larger, vaguer, harder changes to the world women made choices in—or to the world they would have to raise their children in.[38] Framing feminist demands in terms of "choice" played nicely with the individualist ideals deeply ingrained in the American Dream: that the various paths to life, liberty, and happiness were laid at the feet of each individual American, and that they need only lace up their walking shoes and head off down the one they like best. Today, this apparent freedom to choose makes any individual's motherhood or non-motherhood appear entirely deliberate.

Throughout our history, framing non-motherhood as a deliberate choice was also useful for those who saw not having children as abnormal or deviant. These women could have become mothers but didn't, and so they deserve our scorn. Infertility, of course, threatened to muddy the waters, since it generally involved women who aspired to become mothers—and who presumably accepted motherhood as a desirable social norm—but were unable to. Because of this, prominent American politicians and thinkers worked hard to distinguish between infertile women and the childless by choice; between women who would have chosen motherhood if they could have and women who could have become mothers but didn't. "There are many good people who are denied the supreme blessing of children, and for these we have . . . respect and sympathy," a bespectacled Theodore Roosevelt told the National Congress of Mothers, an organization now known as the Parent-Teacher Association, or PTA, in 1905. But women who opted out of motherhood by choice were "unlovely creatures," as useful to society as "unleavened bread," and "one of the most unpleasant and unwholesome features of modern life."[39] It was not simply a woman's non-motherhood that was the problem, in other words. The problem was her *choice* not to become a mother.

With the introduction of assisted reproductive technologies like in vitro fertilization in the last decades of the twentieth century, such feats of distinction became unnecessary: even though infertility treatment was and is financially out of reach for most Americans, and even though success rates from IVF vary widely, its very existence—and the multibillion-dollar global industry that has been built up around it—makes it seem as though infertility is cured. We live in a society that believes women *can* choose to prevent, terminate, or initiate a pregnancy at will, even if it does not morally condone all those choices. Any woman without a child must have chosen that life.

Empirically, logically, anecdotally, we know this just isn't true. Feminists of color have been pointing out the inadequacy of "choice" since at least 1994, when a group of Black women leaders, scholars, and activists offered "reproductive justice" in its place.[40] The word "choice" implies the agency to choose, an agency that many American women have long been denied. Enslaved women did not legally own their own bodies, much less the right to make their own reproductive decisions. In the twentieth century, states in the Jim Crow South set up publicly funded birth-control clinics specifically to limit Black births.[41] By the 1960s and 1970s, southern doctors were performing involuntary sterilizations on Black women so frequently that the civil rights activist Fannie Lou Hamer termed the procedure a "Mississippi appendectomy."[42] In the 1970s, the Indian Health Service was accused of having sterilized up to one-quarter of Native women without their consent.[43] This is not ancient history: in the fall of 2020, a whistleblower alleged that a for-profit Immigration and Customs Enforcement detention center in Georgia was forcing sterilizations on immigrant women who neither gave their consent nor, in many cases, knew enough English to understand what had been done to them.[44]

Laurie Bertram Roberts, executive director of the Mississippi Reproductive Freedom Fund, recently explained that "reproductive justice" is "the human right to have a child, not have a child, be able to raise your families in safe, secure surroundings with your basic needs met."[45] The point is less about abortion, less about the choice to have a child or not, and more about the conditions in which that choice is made, and the conditions in which any resulting child will be raised. The right question may not be "Why are American women not having children?" but "What other decisions are women having to make that affect their reproductive choices, and what conditions are they making them under?" Or it might be even simpler still: How—*how on earth*—could they? For many young women—even those who have not experienced the violence of forced sterilization—the conditions in which they must make reproductive choices are so constrained that they don't feel like choices at all.

The numbers bear this out. Over the past four decades, studies from the Centers for Disease Control and Prevention have consistently found that very few women are willing to label themselves "voluntarily childless": 6 percent in 2017, up just slightly from 4.9 percent in 1982.[46] Another researcher found that 5 percent or so identify as "involuntarily childless," usually meaning that they wanted children but infertility intervened.[47] For the rest of us, the majority without kids, our non-motherhood was arrived at slowly, indirectly, through a series of decisions that sometimes had nothing, and yet everything, to do with reproduction: to go back to school to get a graduate degree and change careers, to leave a loveless marriage at thirty-five, to take a job far from family networks that could have provided support, to hold out for a partner who makes you happier than you can make yourself, to look hard at the fires and floods and storms that augur climate catastrophe within the next generation's lifetime. In some cases, the choice was made for us, by jobs without paid parental leave or the dizzying cost of day care or our staggering student loan payments or the careful math it takes in twenty-first-century America to own a home or ever hope to retire. Some of us tried fertility drugs or IUI or IVF, decided to stop when it got too expensive or physically grueling, and exist in a gray zone between choosing not to have children and not being able to. We are what one scholar calls "perpetual postponers," women who might have been mothers had our lives broken another way or the society we live in been different— whose biological clocks struck midnight, or taste for sleepless nights ran out, or aging parents began needing care before having a baby made even the least bit of sense.[48]

The explanations for individual and collective childlessness are complicated. It's not just our finances, or the joy of living a selfish and hedonic existence, or the grief of infertility. For some of us, it's all of these, and more: the lack of support in our current society that makes parenting a profoundly individual, isolated project; the financial pressures that make us prioritize careers and income over almost anything else; the fear of raising children on a planet already groaning under the weight of a mass of humanity doing its best to destroy it; the fear of creating another human to aid in that destruction. Some of us want to live lives that don't allow space for children, lives that demand we spend our reserves of time, energy, and love in other ways.

None of these reasons are new. History is full of women who may have wanted kids badly, or been ambivalent about them, or been freed by not having them, but who in any case never did have them. They were not having children long before the highly effective forms of birth control we have today existed, and long before feminist theory began to tease out the space between motherhood and womanhood. In our struggle to build our lives and to figure out whether those lives allow for children, we are products of our historical moment, of the tiny gift of time we have been given on this planet. But history also tells us we are not alone.

I began writing this book in the early days of lockdown, during the coronavirus pandemic. With schools and day cares closed, extended family support systems cut off, friends out of reach, and parents working inside the same four walls as active toddlers, bored elementary schoolers, and sullen teenagers, in some ways the gulf between parents and nonparents was greater than ever. In particular, the experiences of mothers—who took on the lion's share of childcare and virtual school responsibilities under lockdown—and women without children were stretched so far apart that the last threads they held in common threatened to snap.[49] For many mothers, tales of boredom baking and at-home yoga and Netflix binges from their friends without children were as unintelligible as they were infuriating. For those friends, the early months of lockdown may have felt like vindication. "There's a reason I chose not to have kids," one woman wrote on Twitter, "and while being stuck at home for weeks during a pandemic wasn't explicitly [it], it isn't far off."[50]

The crisis of American motherhood is not a product of the virus, of course. COVID-19 exposed what women with children and without both already knew: that despite the expectation we all become mothers, we receive little support once we do. Pediatricians' offices are open Monday to Friday, nine to five. The American school day ends at two or three o'clock, hours before the end of even the most humane twenty-first-century workday. In some parts of the country, paying for day care or preschool can cost nearly one full professional salary. Small humans must be fed every day, it turns out, multiple times per day. Someone must fold the clean laundry, pack everyone's lunches, book after-school programs and summer camps, help with homework, make it to doctor's appointments, and spend precious paid time off to stay home with sick kids. Parenting in our society requires pouring time, money, and energy into holes in systems that never worked—often, systems that were never set up to work in the first place.

In recent years, the so-called Mommy Wars have pitted mother against mother in fierce disagreements over the "right" way to parent. Battle lines have sprung up around unmedicated childbirth versus epidurals, breast versus bottle, staying at home versus day care, co-sleeping versus sleep training, vaccines, and whether your kid should be wearing a coat in the parking lot of Trader Joe's in October. It's worth pointing out that these are all things individual mothers largely *can* control. The Mommy

Wars are not fought over the vast territory outside of that control: the cost of childcare and medical care, or our collective lack of maternity leave and paid time off, or the so-called motherhood penalty that suppresses the salaries of women with children. This makes sense. American mothers are set up to fail on the big things, so it's no wonder they're fighting over the scraps. Even after becoming a mother, fulfilling the role society demands of you, you still can't win.

Not having children, of course, is nothing new. But in other places, and in other times, the hands and hearts that cared for a child didn't necessarily, or solely, belong to the same person as the uterus that incubated them. There and then, the risks, responsibilities, and rewards of raising the next generation would have been shared by communities—communities that included women who had not given birth alongside biological mothers. Today, in the absence of community, societal, institutional, or really *any* support, reproductive life has been reduced to a question of individual willingness to assume the responsibilities and risks that come with reproducing. Parenthood is demanded of us, but we are asked to parent in isolated bubbles, supported—to put it crudely—by our bank accounts and little else. The reward for acquiescing is shouldering the sole responsibility for every aspect of your children's care; the punishment for not doing so is having little recognized role in the lives of children at all.

History shows us that this need not be the case. Women— from eleventh-century nuns, to nineteenth-century suffragists, to twentieth-century environmentalists and Black and Indigenous feminists—have been telling all of us for a long time that supporting mothers and restoring societal value to women without children are two sides of the same coin. Maybe it's time we listened.

When I started writing this book, I thought I'd exclusively focus on the stories of women without children. Their stories haven't been told, I thought, and now's the time. But I slowly realized how little sense it made to tell the stories of childless women in isolation from the stories of the mothers they loved and helped, from the men they slept with and turned to for medical advice, from the broader communities they interacted with every day. In most places on earth, and even in the not-so-deep American past, the distinction between mothers and non-mothers wasn't so stark. From West Africa to the Haude-nosaunee (or Iroquois) Confederacy to the American colonies, there was far more space for motherhood to be a social role, not just a biological one, more space for women who did not birth children to fully participate in loving and raising them. Throughout history, women without children lived their lives in societies that included mothers, men, and structures and policies that others made for them. As the historian Natalie Zemon Davis once pointed out, you can't expect your reader to understand feudalism, the medieval European economic system, if you write only about peasants and never mention that there were also lords.[51] When Davis wrote this in 1976, scholars were just beginning to study the history of women in earnest, and her point was that women's history had to be about women in relationship with men, just as those women lived their lives in relationship with men. If you popped women out of their social context and viewed them as a historical phenomenon unto themselves, you would never understand the full picture. In the book that follows, you'll meet women without children you might not have heard of; women you might have heard of for reasons other than their non-motherhood; men whose decisions, work, and lives had some bearing on the experiences of women who were not mothers; and mothers of every kind: biological, social, step, adoptive, temporary, and part-time. The full picture of women without children is a picture of all of us. We are not as different as we have been led to think.

Among the women I know without children, very few fit cleanly into the categories society wants to slot us into: voluntarily or involuntarily childless, joyfully childfree or devastated by infertility. Our reproductive status has come with griefs large and small: watching our parents mourn the grandchildren they will not have; regretting past choices that may have led us here and anticipating what regret might come; shedding tears over another negative pregnancy test or an abortion that felt like the only way to keep the load-bearing pillars of our lives standing; realizing that the pain of failed infertility treatments has faded into joy at the life that failure allowed us to live—and finding that there is grief in that too. There is sadness in missing out on, or even not wanting, the thing that so many others say gives their life its meaning.[52] Many of us have mourned the passage of what Cheryl Strayed has called "the ghost ship that didn't carry us," the shadowy, silent version of the life we did not choose that glides parallel to us, barely visible through the mist.[53] For everyone I know, even those for whom not having children has made possible lives they love and would not change, the decision (if it could be called a decision) involved some measure of anguish. There is both joy and grief in lives that don't look quite like they're expected to.

It can be tempting to see rising rates of childlessness as a feminist triumph, as the normalization of a lifestyle that breaks, or at least bends, the heteronormative box that has for so long contained the American family, as the collective expression of a generation of women with options and the ability to choose the life they most want to lead. But I hesitate to call it a triumph when so many of those choices were determined by economic pain, lack of support, and fear about the future. The reasons American parents struggled in COVID lockdowns, the reasons American parents struggle even in the best of times, are not so different from the reasons American women give when they say they don't plan to have children at all. This is a depressing thought. I hope it is also a unifying one.

The activist and writer Jenny Brown has argued that we should understand falling births in America as a work slowdown or a strike: the people who do the labor of birthing and raising children are increasingly refusing to do it under the poor conditions they've been provided.[54] On the scale of aggregate social trends, this *is* probably the best way to think about it. But the word "strike" also implies agency and intention—a lot more agency and intention than many women report feeling in regard to their reproductive decisions.[55] The anthropologist Michel-Rolph Trouillot has observed that workers' absence from the workplace is not a sufficient definition of a strike. A large number of employees failing to show up for work on the same day could be the effect of a large snowstorm, perhaps, or of a stomach virus making its way around the office, or simple coincidence. They need reasons, collective ones, and they need to have made a collective decision not to show. "To put it most simply," Trouillot writes, "a strike is only a strike if the workers know they're striking."[56]

I'm not convinced that American women know that we're striking. We aren't having children for reasons that seem more diffuse and individual than they do collective or connected, reasons that often seem to have little to do with children in the first place: lack of money, social support, partners, or flexible work schedules; fear of fires and floods; failures of biology; desire for different lives. These reasons also aren't new, but they're presented to us stripped of their history: Feminism made us prioritize our careers, we're told. Alarmists made us paranoid about the climate, they tell us. Waiting too long made us infertile. Being born in the eighties and nineties and early aughts made us selfish, somehow. Without the history that helps to link them, the reasons women aren't having children look and feel less like a strike than like individual decisions to opt out, less like a shared experience and more like a personal failure to overcome modern-day stresses, real and imagined. If this is a strike, a wise friend observed, we don't even get the solidarity. It is that solidarity, with each other and with history, that this book hopes to offer.

CHAPTER 1

BECAUSE WE'VE ALWAYS MADE CHOICES

ON THE LAST DAY OF ANN LOHMAN'S TRIAL, THE VIEWING GALLERY of the Court of the General Sessions of New York was overflowing, with every seat taken and latecomers crowding in the back. The jury had reached a decision, and people from across the city spilled into the courtroom to hear Lohman's fate. Journalists clutching notepads and concerned citizens filled the gallery, each vying for a glimpse of the defendant: "The wickedest woman in New York," some had called her, a "monster in human shape." Lohman, better known by her alias, Madame Restell, entered around noon, accompanied by her husband and court guards. She stood out conspicuously, as she had throughout the trial: Restell was the only woman in a room packed with men. The white bonnet covering her long, dark hair emphasized that fact, as did the black satin of her dress, which pooled around her feet when she took her seat next to her attorney. The judge called the court to order, and then reminded the room of the charges: performing an abortion on a woman named Maria Purdy, and ultimately causing her death. As one observer put it, it was "one of the most hellish acts ever perpetrated in a Christian land." It was the summer of 1841, and Madame Restell was an abortion provider on trial for murder.[1]

The woman who would become known as the wickedest in New York was born Ann Trow in Painswick, England, in 1812. She grew up in poverty, and left home to work as a serving maid as soon as she was old enough. While she was still in her teens, Ann Trow married a tailor named Henry Sommers. When she was nineteen, the couple joined the throngs of working-class European immigrants who arrived in New York in the first decades of the nineteenth century, looking for better lives and more opportunities than what they'd left behind. Henry caught typhus and died shortly after they arrived, leaving Ann Sommers alone in a new country with an infant daughter. She first found work as a seamstress, a profession flooded with European immigrants, all of them barely scraping by on meager wages. She supplemented her income by working as a midwife on the side, delivering babies for her neighbors with skills she must have learned from the women around her during her rural upbringing. Eventually, Sommers expanded her side business from delivering babies to preventing their birth, compounding herbs into contraceptives and abortifacients and selling them to a virtually limitless market of women who wanted to avoid or end a pregnancy. Mifepristone and misoprostol, the two components of a medical abortion today, were approved by the FDA in 2000, but in the 1830s Sommers knew of plenty of herbs that would work: ergot, calomel, aloe, or black hellebore were powdered and mixed into pills that could cause a miscarriage. Sommers and others referred to such medications with euphemisms like "female monthly regulating pills," promising they would "restore" menstruation.[2]

In 1836, Sommers got remarried to a *New York Herald* executive named Charles Lohman, who eagerly lent his advertising chops to his new bride's side business. Together, the Lohmans concocted a story about her midwifery training in France—though she must have learned her recipes somewhere, the reality was that Ann Sommers, now Ann Lohman, had no formal medical training—and the mysterious Madame Restell was born. Ann Lohman as Madame Restell built a career selling contraception and abortion drugs out of an expanding network of offices around the city to married women and single women, mothers and not, wealthy and working-class. Restell's services were comprehensive: For women too far along in their pregnancies for herbal solutions, she provided referrals to a surgical abortionist and rented out beds in a boardinghouse where inconveniently pregnant women who did not wish to terminate could pay to grow round and give birth in comfort and total discretion. For an additional fee, Restell would also take care of adoption arrangements.[3]

Madame Restell's trial captivated the public's imagination in part because it was lurid—an abortion was the result of a young woman having sex, after all, and then having the audacity to separate sex from motherhood—but also because it was relatively novel. Prior to the 1820s, there were no laws restricting abortion anywhere in the United States. American colonists brought with them centuries of legal and cultural precedent from Europe, which saw little issue with abortion at least up to quickening, the moment at which the pregnant woman first felt the fetus move.[4] Long before sonograms and ultrasounds opened a uterus's contents to public view, such a stance made practical sense: before quickening, who was to know that a woman's missed periods, nausea, and increasing roundness were actually symptoms of pregnancy, and not simply a result of something more mundane—like "flatulence in the bowels," as one expert witness put it at Madame Restell's trial.[5] Connecticut was first to outlaw abortion, in 1821, and by 1880 it was a felony in every state.[6] The early laws, in the 1820s and 1830s, had little to do with the fetus, or even pregnancy at all. Many were poison-control measures, designed to protect pregnant women from buying and taking dangerous substances that might, and sometimes did, kill them. In the 1840s and 1850s, anti-abortion legislation was driven by a growing class of professionally trained medical doctors— joined, in the late 1850s, by the newly formed American Medical Association—as part of a larger effort to establish their professional dominance over medical matters and to drive out competitors like midwives and homeopathic practitioners.[7]

These motivations—concern about women unknowingly buying lethal poisons from unlicensed practitioners like Restell, and a desire to control the medical marketplace—make sense when you consider that efforts to make abortion illegal coincided with a massive increase in demand for the procedure. In the first three decades of the nineteenth century, historians estimate that abortion was relatively rare in the United States: women terminated one out of every twenty-five to thirty pregnancies. By 1860, estimates suggest, one in every five or six pregnancies ended in abortion.[8] "I know three married women, respectable ones," W. M. Smith, a doctor in the small farming town of Atkinson, Illinois, reported in a medical journal in 1874, "who are notorious for giving instructions to their younger sisters as to the modus operandi of 'coming around.'" "One old doctor near here was so obliging," Smith continued, "as to furnish a wire with a handle, to one of his patients, which did the work for her, after which she passed it to one of her neighbors, who succeeded in destroying the foetus and nearly so herself."[9] In 1898, the State of Michigan's Special Committee on Criminal Abortions concluded with no small amount of horror that one-third of pregnancies in the state were aborted.[10]

While modern anti-abortion rhetoric tends to center on the fetus, early anti-abortion activists were at least as concerned about the sexual behavior of women. Abortion, they argued, allowed women to have sex without consequences. Without the threat of pregnancy, what was to stop them from having premarital sex, cheating on their husbands, or even working as prostitutes under cover of night? Newspapers across the country portrayed abortion as "a dangerous, immoral activity," sought out by loose women and performed by doctors-turned-criminals who would help them hide their sins.[11] The eager New Yorkers who crowded into the courtroom on that summer day in 1841 were well aware that the charge Madame Restell was being tried for—aborting a pregnancy after quickening—was not her most grievous crime. Restell was guilty, as the journalist George Washington Dixon wrote in his chronicle of the trial, of "show[ing] your spouse how she may commit as many adulteries as there are hours in the year without the possibility of detection."[12]

In the courtroom, Restell's lawyers mounted a defense for the charges levied against her by the state of New York. But outside it, Restell launched a propaganda campaign in defense of the services she provided. In a series of advertisements, she offered a then-impressive sum of $100 to anyone who could prove that her medicines were unsafe. Even as her case worked its way through the courts, Restell's ads continued to appear in the *Herald*'s classified pages: she remained available for "treatment of all cases of irregularity or suppression of those functions of nature upon which the health of every female depends." One of her advertisements asked, "Is it not wise and virtuous to prevent evils to which we are subject"—like adding a child that would stretch a family's finances to the breaking point, perhaps, or risking another childbirth that could threaten the life of the mother—"by simple and healthy means within our control? This is all," the advertisement concluded, "that Madame Restell recommends or has ever recommended."[13]

The jury in Madame Restell's 1841 trial—all men, of course, as women didn't win the right to sit on juries in New York State until 1937—deliberated for a mere ten minutes. "GUILTY," they pronounced her, "on the 3d and 4th counts, of producing an abortion, and causing the death of [Maria] Purdy!"[14] The Lohmans and their lawyers appealed, and in February 1844 the verdict was reversed. The only evidence against Restell was Purdy's dying claim that she'd received an abortion after she felt her fetus move, and New York State law prohibited deathbed confessions from being used in court. Also in Restell's favor was the fact that Purdy had died of tuberculosis more than a year after she supposedly received an abortion, events that were unlikely to be related. Emboldened by the verdict, Madame Restell went back to work. The Lohmans expanded their practice, moving to a larger office space and opening satellite locations across the city. Then, in 1845, New York made abortion a felony at any stage of pregnancy, doing away with the legal distinction between procedures before quickening and after. Even as her customer base continued to grow, and even as she practiced her trade for three more decades, most of Restell's business moved into the shadows.[15]

When I began writing this book, more than one person asked me how it was possible to tell a "long history" of not having children, since, as they correctly pointed out, hormonal contraception was invented in the 1950s. Contraception of all kinds has been legal for married women in the United States only since 1965, and for all American women to access since 1972. *Roe v. Wade*'s recent fall means that something like two and a half generations of Americans had the right to legal and safe abortions. Was I writing a history of infertility, nuns, and spinsterhood, then? Fortunately for all of us, the answer is no. The history of not having children is far longer than what we think of as the modern age of choice. Present-day conversations around non-motherhood tend to frame today's young women as a historical aberration: liberated—or cursed, depending on your taste—by reproductive options, they are making new, baffling decisions about avoiding motherhood that require explanation. But we know that women without children existed in history. The childlessness of Elizabeth I of England, the daughter of Henry VIII and Anne Boleyn, is so storied that Elizabeth has long been referred to by the nickname the Virgin Queen. After her father burned through wives in a frantic and ultimately failed attempt to produce a male heir, Elizabeth ascended to the throne and ruled for almost half a century. Though her virginity was and remains a topic of great debate—King Henry IV of France reportedly joked that one of the three burning questions of Europe was "whether Queen Elizabeth was a maid or no"—what we know for certain is that she had none of the heirs her father so strenuously pursued.[16] The nineteenth- and early twentieth-century English-language literary canon is basically a who's who of childless women: Jane Austen, George Eliot, all three of the Brontës, Louisa May Alcott, Emily Dickinson, Edith Wharton, Virginia Woolf, Gertrude Stein. Harriet Tubman adopted a baby girl named Gertie in 1874, at the age of fifty-two, after neither of her two marriages produced biological children— and after she was done advising the Union Army on military and political strategy.[17] Susan B. Anthony. Rosa Parks. Julia Child.

Some of these women may have avoided sex with men or been unable to conceive, but—though they lived some or all of their fertile years before the advent of modern birth control—these are not the only possible explanations. They also could have been actively avoiding pregnancy using the tools that were available to them. Medical treatises dating back to the Middle Ages in Europe list dozens of herbal contraceptives and abortifacients, many of which present-day science confirms would have been effective at least some of the time. By analyzing the birth patterns of married couples in medieval and early modern Europe,

historians have shown that women—likely along with their husbands or other male sexual partners—have long been making
explicit choices about having and not having children. For example, in northern Europe for much of the early modern period, the
median age at first birth for a married woman was twenty-seven,
children were spaced suspiciously far apart, and youngest children were often born well before the end of most women's fertile years. Only the most naive of historians would conclude that
early modern Europeans began having sex in their late twenties
and abandoned the practice by their midthirties, after indulging
only infrequently. In the last five centuries or so, it's been the
norm for about 20 percent of women in northwestern Europe to
remain childless their whole lives.[18] Not having children didn't
start with the method of heating rubber with sulfur that made
the first modern condom possible, or with FDA approval of a
medication that would become so common, so ubiquitous, so important that you can refer to it as "the pill" and everyone will
know which one you mean. It also didn't start with a 7–2 decision of the US Supreme Court that made abortion the decision of
a woman and her doctor, not the government—and it's certainly
not going to end with a 6–3 decision that allows the government
to make that decision once again on women's behalf. There have
always been reasons to opt out of motherhood, and there have
always been ways to do it. The historical evidence we have suggests women have not been having children, well, for about as
long as they've been having them.

An Egyptian papyrus from nearly four millennia ago, 1900
BCE, includes a recipe for a spermicide made by mixing hydrated
sodium carbonate with crocodile droppings. Another, from about
1500 BCE, suggests blocking the cervix with a disk made of aca-
cia gum, which modern science has shown to have spermicidal
properties. "Gossip records a miracle," Pliny the Elder wrote in
77 or 78 CE, just before the eruption of Mount Vesuvius in the

year 79 froze both his body and his words in time, "that to rub it"—"it" being crushed juniper berries—"all over the male part before coitus prevents conception." While on campaign, Roman soldiers reportedly made good extracurricular use of the intestines and bladders of the goats the legions brought with them for meat and milk, fashioning them into makeshift condoms. At home, one of the more popular forms of contraception in ancient Rome was simpler, though logistically difficult to imagine: inserting half a lemon into the vagina before having sex. The Talmud, the ancient rabbinic text that serves as the main source of Jewish law, recommends women breastfeed each child for a minimum of twenty-four months and up to four years, a two-birds-one-stone command that, in an era before baby formula filled grocery store shelves, had the dual benefit of ensuring the child's nutrition and suppressing the mother's fertility. Breastfeeding is hardly a guarantee of sterility (a fact I was taught with great emphasis by my high school sex-ed teacher, after she delivered her third child in less than two years), but it can limit the production of hormones that cause ovulation. The Talmud also allows certain categories of women to avoid pregnancy by using a device called a *mokh*, usually made from strips of absorbent muslin or cotton and inserted in front of the cervix.[19]

Early thinkers saw little distinction between preventing pregnancy and ending it, except that the former was easier and safer than the latter. Soranus, a gynecological authority during the reigns of the Roman emperors Trajan and Hadrian, counseled, "It is more advantageous not to conceive than to destroy the embryo." But should the woman become pregnant despite her precautions, Soranus compiled a list of "diuretic decoctions which also have the power to bring on menstruation," as well as laxatives to "empty and purge the abdomen."[20] The Greek physician Hippocrates, the great-grandfather of medicine, famously opposed herbal methods of abortion. "I will not give to a woman an abortive remedy," the Greek text of the Hippocratic oath reads. But Hippocrates saw no issue with physical methods of terminating pregnancy. In his treatise *On the Generating Seed and the Nature of the Child*, Hippocrates recommends a woman perform strenuous exercise until she miscarries.[21]

In Europe, methods of contraception and abortion appear in medical texts going as far back as we have them, ranging from the dubious to the highly effective, like the crushed seeds of a flowering plant called Queen Anne's lace. Queen Anne's lace is reportedly in regular, daily use as a contraceptive and herbal morning-after pill of sorts in the Appalachian Mountains in the United States, and recent studies have confirmed its powerful anti-fertility properties. Ayurvedic medicine, which originated on the Indian subcontinent, uses twenty-eight different plants that are said to be effective at terminating pregnancy. On the central Asian steppe, a particular variety of fennel is commonly used to abort unwanted pregnancies. In Mexico, Indigenous people have used rue to end pregnancy for centuries. Some Indigenous people in the Arctic rely on tree bark lichen for contraception. In the Brazilian Amazon, the Deni swear by a native plant; one dose, modern research has suggested, can produce sterility in men for up to six months.[22]

By the late eighteenth century, recipes for herbal contraceptives and abortifacients were also circulating among women in Europe and the newly formed United States. German medical treatises offer scores of herbal concoctions intended to end pregnancies.[23] Europeans also had a particular fondness for coitus interruptus, as evidenced by the colorful euphemisms for the practice that peppered every European language going back at least to the early modern period. Fortified by biblical precedent (in Genesis, Onan "spilled his semen on the ground" to avoid impregnating his late brother's wife), across Europe people "threshed in the barn and winnowed outside," "emptied the cart at the door of the mill," and "worked the earth and then threw the seed upon stone." Voltaire recommended "watering the lawn without wetting the earth." The French practiced "the Italian method," the Dutch and the Flemish practiced "the French method," and Germans "did business in the suburbs."[24]

Whatever couples were using, it worked. Between the late eighteenth and early twentieth centuries, fertility fell off sharply across the Northern Hemisphere, from France to Britain to Japan to the United States. The drop was dramatic enough that scholars have given the phenomenon a name: the demographic transition. In the aftermath of the Napoleonic Wars, both England and France cut their fertility rates by 30 percent.[25] By the end of the nineteenth century, fertility in England was down by half.[26] Across the pond, at the beginning of the nineteenth century, American women had an average of seven children. By the dawn of the twentieth, Black women were averaging five; white women in the rural South, six; white women in the North, 3.56.[27] As fertility fell in the American nineteenth century, the percentage of American women without children rose. Just over 7 percent of married white women born in 1835 had no children. For the same cohort born in 1870, nearly 16 percent had none. Among Black women born in 1835—who lived most of their childbearing years under slavery, and whose reproductive decisions were largely not their own—just 3 percent were not mothers. Thirteen percent of Black women born after emancipation, in 1870, had no children.[28] For many formerly enslaved women, the legal historian Peggy Cooper Davis has observed, "liberty meant, among other things, the capacity to decline to reproduce."[29]

This phenomenon of falling fertility caught the attention of nineteenth-century moral reformers, who didn't see liberty so much as catastrophe. The end of the Civil War had given way to what historians have termed the second industrial revolution, a societal transformation driven by assembly line production and consumer technology: cars, electricity, and telephones.

Like moths to the bright flame of the future, young, unmarried men and women poured into cities, chasing wages and economic mobility, and—especially for young women—lifestyles and experiences their childhood homes wouldn't have allowed. Black men and women, freed from the official institution of slavery but not the racism and racist policies that thrived in the post-Reconstruction South, sought out freer lives in northern cities, though they often did not find them there.[30] In 1870, the United States was a majority-rural country. By 1920, more than half the population lived in cities. In the intervening half century, millions of people traded country air and horse-drawn plows for urban smog and the assembly line.[31]

For women, swapping rural lives for urban ones also often meant trading certainty about what life would look like—marriage, motherhood, and domestic tasks—for the unknown. A demographic study published in the *New York Times* on Valentine's Day in 1869 observed that there were a quarter million more women than men living in states along the Eastern Seaboard, a surplus that made it seem likely that a large number of women would never marry.[32] Lillie Devereux Blake, a novelist turned impassioned advocate for women's suffrage, testified before Congress in 1883 that "marriage is no longer a career for women, nor a means of support for them."[33] This was a brave new world of young, unmarried women living on their own, and at least some of them were experimenting with sex without any immediate thought of marriage. For some prominent figures in American politics and religion, contraception and abortion started to look like the gateway to a dark future. "The prevention of conception would work the greatest demoralization," a man named Anthony Comstock told a journalist from *Harper's Weekly*. "God has set certain natural barriers," like pregnancy, he continued, to discourage casual sex. "If you turn loose the passions and break down that fear you bring worse disaster than the war. It would debase sacred things, break down the health of women and disseminate a greater curse than the plagues and diseases of Europe."[34]

Anthony Comstock, an elegantly dressed man who paired jaunty bow ties with a horseshoe mustache, was one of the most powerful social reformers of the American nineteenth century. His was the zeal of a convert: as a teenager in the late 1850s and early 1860s, Comstock had reportedly been addicted to masturbation, and confessed in his journals that prayer and hymns were of no use.[35] Comstock apparently cured himself by the time he joined the Union Army in the Civil War, only to be scandalized by the lewdness and obscenity of his fellow soldiers, not to mention their smoking, drinking, and card playing. When the war concluded, Comstock moved to New York City, determined to save his fellow Americans from the many evils of their nature. In 1872, he founded the New York Society for the Suppression of Vice, which sought to eradicate a long list of sins, including prostitution, pornography, gambling, tobacco, alcohol, atheism, premarital sex, and extramarital sex. In particular, he saw danger in contraception and abortion. It was a straight line from separating sex and reproduction, Comstock thought, to the general breakdown of society.

Comstock had chosen his moment well. The temperance movement, long the fringy purview of Calvinists and Latter-day Saints, went mainstream in the decades after the Civil War. The growth of evangelical Protestantism and its belief in the perfectibility of man also helped to fuel the war on our baser natures. Vice was a hot topic, and Comstock's society quickly found widespread support among America's wealthy and powerful and began to influence national policy.[36] In February 1873, An Act for the Suppression of Trade in, and Circulation of, Obscene Literature and Articles of Immoral Use appeared before Congress. Known as the Comstock Act for short, the law proposed prohibiting sending "obscene, lewd or lascivious," "immoral," or "indecent" publications through the mail. This sweeping category of literature included everything from child pornography to information about contraceptive methods to anatomy textbooks used by medical students—until states sought carve-outs for their campuses. The law also barred Americans from mailing "every article or thing designed or intended for the prevention of conception or procuring of abortion," from condoms to powders and tinctures intended to terminate a pregnancy.[37]

The Senate gave Comstock's namesake bill all of ten minutes of deliberation before voting in favor.[38] When it arrived on the floor of the House, Representative Clinton Merriam of New York suggested that the legislation was so important that the body should suspend its normal rules and vote it through immediately, without so much as a floor debate. Michael Kerr, a Democrat from Indiana, briefly protested, warning that there was danger in passing legislation in "hot haste" that could very easily violate the First Amendment's guaranteed right of free expression. But Merriam won out, the rules were suspended, and Comstock got his way.[39] On March 3, President Ulysses S. Grant confirmed with a swipe of his pen that federal authorities could censor anything that "might arouse in young and inexperienced minds, lewd or libidinous thoughts."[40] By the end of 1874, 134,000 pounds of books and 194,000 "bad pictures and photographs" had been seized and destroyed.[41] In 1880 alone, Post Office inspectors confiscated 64,094 "rubber articles for immoral use."[42] Confronting a world saturated by sin, Comstock's law refused to draw distinctions of degree: it painted everything from contraception to child pornography with the same broad brush. "If you open the door to anything," he said, "the filth will all pour in and the degradation of youth will follow."[43]

With the law on his side, a disguised Anthony Comstock rang the bell of Madame Restell's Fifty-Second Street offices in New

York City in 1878, pretending to be a distraught husband. His newly pregnant wife had given him too many children already, Comstock told her, feigning despair, and he feared he could not provide for another. Restell fell for the ruse and sold him a package of pills that, she said, would end the pregnancy. A triumphant Comstock returned the next day with a police officer in tow, and the two took Restell into custody. This time the charges against her were more serious: she was accused not just of violations of New York State law, but of major infractions under Comstock's federal law. Restell knew that the punishment she faced would be severe: with nothing short of civilization at stake, Comstock and his law could justify causing almost limitless immediate harm. Under the Comstock Act, even elderly men had been sentenced to years in prison or hard labor. On the morning of her trial, sixty-six-year-old Madame Restell got into the bathtub and slit her throat with a knife, severing her carotid artery and both jugular veins. The "wickedest women in New York" became one of more than a dozen of Comstock's defendants to die by suicide.[44]

The law also outlived Comstock, who died in 1915. Pressure to repeal or amend it—whether from birth control activists like Margaret Sanger or from the US Army, which came home from the First World War firmly convinced of the strategic value of condoms after recording 415,000 cases of sexually transmitted infections among three million deployed troops—was fruitless.[45] Comstock's unwillingness to separate condoms from child pornography in the original law made it almost impervious to repeal. No one in Congress wanted to be the one arguing in favor of "obscene," "lewd," and "immoral" items, even at the behest of the Army. For decades no one did.[46]

Of course, the fact that something is illegal does not make it disappear. Often, it just moves into the shadows, onto the black market, or into the unwritten subtext of an FDA filing. When the Chicago-based pharmaceutical company G. D. Searle applied for approval for a pill that combined synthetic progestogen and estrogen in 1957, they couldn't call it birth control, even though they'd developed and tested the drug with precisely that purpose in mind. It treated menstrual disorders like heavy bleeding or irregular periods, Searle told the FDA. It was the FDA who gave away what the drug was really for. Regulators required Searle to print a warning on every bottle: "This drug prevents ovulation." As Searle's director of clinical research remembered, this "was like a free ad." By 1965, 6.5 million American women were on the pill—many of them, we have to assume, hoping to achieve the very effect the bottles warned them about.[47]

Comstock's legal legacy stood firm until 1972, just shy of his act's one hundredth birthday. In a 6–1 decision in the case *Eisenstadt v. Baird*, the US Supreme Court gave all Americans the right to access contraception. "If the right of privacy means anything," Justice William J. Brennan wrote, "it is the right of the individual, married or single, to be free from unwarranted governmental intrusion into matters so fundamentally affecting a person as the decision whether to bear or beget a child."[48] Justice Brennan's particular turn of phrase, "bear or beget," would turn out to be prophetic: it laid a foundation for the following year's decision that a Texas law barring women from obtaining abortions was also a violation of their constitutional right to privacy.

Today, American law students are taught that *Roe v. Wade*, the US Supreme Court decision that established the right to abortion, was hardly the legal revolution we have built it up to be. The legal reasoning in *Roe* was based on two birth control cases that preceded it: 1965's *Griswold v. Connecticut*, which allowed married couples legal access to contraception, and *Eisenstadt v. Baird* in 1972. The three cases were bricks in a wall that sought to keep the government's prying eyes out of people's bedrooms, doctor's appointments, and medicine cabinets. These cases—and, more generally, the legality and availability of birth control and abortion—matter, of course. Deaths from sepsis after abortion fell 89 percent after the procedure was legalized because it could be—indeed had to be—performed by a doctor in a clinical setting.[49] After the Affordable Care Act required insurers to cover the full cost of contraception in 2011, birth control usage rose, especially among low-income women.[50] Researchers also credit the ACA's contraception mandate for teen pregnancies hitting a record low in 2018, and then beating that record again in 2019.[51] Without the protection of *Roe*, some experts have expressed concern that America's already high maternal mortality rate could rise, as doctors hesitate or refuse to offer lifesaving care—for example, to patients with ectopic pregnancies or partial miscarriages—out of fear that doing so may violate their state's abortion laws.[52]

But legality and ease of access are only part of the story. *Roe* did not invent the idea of abortion any more than *Dobbs v. Jackson Women's Health*, the case that overturned it, will make it disappear. What Comstock and his fellow nineteenth-century moral reformers missed, what the appellants in *Burwell v. Hobby Lobby Stores, Inc.* (the Supreme Court case that sought to limit insurance coverage for contraception) missed, what state legislatures seeking to criminalize abortion miss, what even advocates of contraception and abortion rights risk missing is that technology and access to it are not the only factors driving trends in childlessness or fertility. They are factors. But at least as important is the person confronted with that technology, and the reasons they have for having or not having children. If there is one thing this history teaches us, it is that women who do not want or cannot care for a child will seek out ways to not have one—even at great legal risk, or at great risk to their lives.

In the nineteenth century, American women limited their fertility, mostly in the absence of legal reproductive options and definitely without modern birth control technology. As the sociologist S. Philip Morgan has put it, American women increasingly "were willing and able to postpone childbearing." Much like women today, as they put off having kids, it became "less likely that women would ever . . . have children."[53] The longer they waited, the more experience they gained: experience with avoiding sex, with having sex but avoiding pregnancy or childbirth, and with the kinds of opportunities—professional, political, economic, social—that having no children allows for. The reasons nineteenth-century women didn't have children likely weren't that different from our own. They didn't have the technology we do, of course. For most, a life without children probably required a combination of abstinence, coitus interruptus, herbs, prayers, and luck to pull off. But otherwise, they weren't so different. Like us, they were postponers. Like us, they made hard choices. Like us, they built the best lives they could in the world and with the tools they were given.

Anthony Comstock took great satisfaction in removing thousands of condoms and people like Madame Restell from American streets, even if it took defendants' suicides to make it happen. He took it for granted that the emergence or availability of technology made it newly possible for women to avoid births without avoiding sex. People who oppose abortion and contraception access today assume the same thing: that technology—be it the synthetic progestogen in the first birth control pill, the copper wires of an IUD, or mifepristone and misoprostol, the components of a modern medical abortion—disrupts what would otherwise be a state of nature, in which sex is always procreative and pregnancies always result in babies. The thing is, as far as we can tell, historically, the "state of nature" theory of sex and reproduction has likely never been true. Birth control technology and legal abortion procedures have allowed us to avoid the worst outcomes of a pregnant woman's desperation, like the Illinois woman who "destroyed the foetus and nearly also herself" with a wire given to her by a doctor in 1874; like the 2,700 American women in 1930 whose death certificates listed "abortion" as the official cause.[54] But fertility was down and childlessness was on the rise well before Charles Goodyear invented vulcanized rubber in 1844, which made condoms possible; well before G. D. Searle patented the pill; well before *Roe* made abortion a right. Long before birth control technology made it easier or twentieth-century feminist movements offered language to explain it, women were making very deliberate choices about when, under what circumstances, and even whether to have children. The legality and availability of modern contraception and, while it lasted, the right to safe and legal abortion certainly make it easier and safer to limit births. But they did not give women the idea that they might want to.

CHAPTER 2

BECAUSE WE'LL BE ON OUR OWN

ELLA BAKER WAS BORN IN 1903 IN NORFOLK, VIRGINIA, INTO AN upwardly mobile Black family that was able to flee after race riots rocked the city in 1910. At the age of seven, Baker moved to her mother's hometown of Littleton, North Carolina, where the family owned a good-sized farm. Littleton sat squarely in North Carolina's second congressional district, one known derisively by southern Democrats as the "Black Second," because it was one of the few districts in the nation with a Black voting majority. In the middle-class East End neighborhood of Littleton, the Baker children grew up insulated from the worst of the poverty and racism many Black southerners faced.[1] In their two-story home, Ella's mother, Anna, read in the drawing room, Ella and her sister played the piano, and the dining room table was set with high-quality silver. Anna Baker had been a teacher in her younger years, one of the only career paths open to educated Black women at the time. She stopped working outside of the home after she married, mostly because her husband, Ella's father,

wanted her to.[2] Blake Baker was a waiter on a steamship that ran
between Norfolk and Washington, DC, a job that paid relatively
well. Like many men of his generation, white and Black, Blake
aspired to that most visible marker of the middle class: a wife and
mother who remained in the home, her lack of wage labor serving as proof that his job could provide for the family.[3]

Despite her family's status, Baker's memory of her childhood
was one of what she called "family socialism": a Black community not divided by class differences but bound together in spite
of them, one in which food, homes, family, tools, and wealth
were shared by those who had more with those who had less.
The community had "but one threshing machine for threshing
the wheat. And so today they might be on Grandpa's place, and
all the people who had wheat who needed the thresher would
be there . . . and then they would move around." The Bakers
mortgaged the family farm twice, apparently to raise money for
Littleton families in need.[4] When the Bakers' garden produced
more black-eyed peas than the family could eat, "you'd give
them to the neighbors who didn't have them," she remembered.
"That's the way you *did*. It was no hassle about it. I don't think it
ever occurred to our immediate family to indoctrinate children
against sharing. Because they had the privilege of growing up
where they raised a lot of food. They were never hungry. They
could share their food with people. And so, you share your *lives*
with people."[5]

They also shared their children. Informal adoption was common in Littleton, and children were passed from those who
birthed them to those who could care for them without anyone
raising an eyebrow.[6] At ten, Baker was regularly enlisted to care
for children in the neighborhood whose biological mother had
passed away, leaving their father overwhelmed. "Mama would
say, 'You must take the clothes to Mr. Powell, and give so-
and-so a bath,'" Baker remembered. "The children were running

wild. . . . We'd chase them down and bring them back, and put 'em in the tub, and wash 'em off, and change clothes, and carry the dirty ones home, and wash them. Those kinds of things were routine." One of Baker's aunts had thirteen biological children and raised three more as her own, including a son she acquired through her work as a midwife. At one birth she attended, she delivered an infant that was covered in sores. "No one was particularly wanting the child, so she took him and raised him. He's one of the best of her brood," Baker remembered. All three informally adopted children "were part of the family."[7]

The kind of family Baker grew up in, a kind that shape-shifted to include whomever needed to be included, would come to define her politics and activism as an adult. As a civil rights leader, Baker would see Littleton as a model for Black communities everywhere, a model of what community can be when everyone is treated like family. But for others, this vision of family beyond blood, of community as family, came to shape a very different kind of politics, one that saw in it a threat to American values, not the hope of restoring them.

In May 1992, President George H. W. Bush and Vice President Dan Quayle's lackluster reelection bid was briefly reanimated by a three-day tear of speeches Quayle gave on what he called "family values"—specifically, on how America was losing them. In the days and weeks that followed, hundreds of articles appeared in the national press with "family values" in their headlines, sparking a nationwide debate about what a family was, and what our values relating to families should be.[8] The candidates in question, Bush and Quayle, and their opponents Bill Clinton and Al Gore, rushed to provide intimate details about their families, in the hope of convincing Americans that they had the answers.

The American public was invited into these politicians' homes as never before. They heard the Quayles disagree publicly over whether abortion would be appropriate if their teenage daughter became pregnant. (Dan Quayle said yes, abortion would be an option. His wife, Marilyn, said no.)[9] The country mourned the Bushes' loss of their three-year-old daughter to leukemia all over again and revisited the Gores' anguish over the car accident that had nearly killed their six-year-old son after an Orioles game in 1989. They hailed the ease and grace with which Barbara Bush adopted the role of grandmother to the nation, and wondered aloud whether Hillary Clinton, a successful lawyer prior to her husband's election campaign, was an attentive enough wife and mother—and whether any woman with a career was an appropriate First Lady.[10]

In the end, the debate was unnecessary. To politicians and voters who would come to support a platform of capital *F*, capital *V* Family Values, the answer was obvious: family was a married mother and father living with their biological offspring. Such a family, Quayle said, was in keeping not only with "Judeo-Christian values," but with American ones. Unfortunately, he mused to a roomful of Republican donors in San Francisco, a wide swath of Americans—Quayle's speech named everyone from Hollywood actors to television viewers, professional women, single mothers, Black Americans, liberals, Democrats, and the "cultural elite"—"seem to think the family is an arbitrary arrangement of people who decide to live under one roof."[11]

Quayle may have been dismayed to learn that, for a lot of American history, "an arbitrary arrangement of people who decide to live under one roof" would have seemed as good a definition of family as any. The historian Helena Wall has observed that American colonists of the seventeenth and eighteenth centuries "conceived of the family almost entirely within the context of the community." For them, raising children was a communal act.[12] Children were regularly passed between homes, off-loaded onto relatives without children of their own, and collected in households of the wealthy, who had the means to feed, care, and educate or train them. For Black Americans, enslaved and free, rebuilding and refashioning family and kinship networks based on proximity rather than blood had been integral to survival since the first European ships tore individuals away from their communities and relatives.[13] Many Indigenous societies were traditionally "sustained by strong kin relationships in which women had significant authority," writes Kim Anderson, a Cree/Métis scholar. "Native women and their children lived and worked in extended kin networks."[14]

The story of how American families came to be on their own is a long one. In western Europe, marriage patterns began to shift in the second half of the eighteenth century, as couples increasingly struck out on their own after they wed rather than joining an extended family home, which had previously been the norm. As they did, people started controlling their fertility: having fewer kids, spacing them out in longer intervals, and stopping well before nature would otherwise have forced them to. Americans made a decisive move toward what would later be called the nuclear family around the dawn of the nineteenth century, when the individualist rhetoric of the revolution found its way into their dining rooms and hearths, and Americans pulled back from their neighbors as never before. At the same time, the nineteenth century saw a dramatic reduction in the American fertility rate. The move toward the isolated nuclear family accelerated after the Second World War, as many women left wartime jobs to marry and have children in the suburbs, where community connections tended to be more tenuous. Despite the legendary fertility of American women in the twenty years after the end of World War II, when it was time for the girls born and raised in those suburban homes to have children, many of them didn't, and few matched the fertility of their mothers. American fertility fell below replacement rate in 1971 and has continued on a downward trend ever since.

That the isolation of the American family would correspond to its shrinking makes sense. We know from historical data that social support doesn't just help parents. It also helps people *become* parents. A team of evolutionary biologists recently examined seventeenth- and eighteenth-century birth records from 149 parishes along the Saint Lawrence River, which flows northeast for about 1,900 miles, from the Great Lakes basin to the Atlantic Ocean. Today, the river forms the border between the province of Ontario and New York State, but then it was a French colonial project, with settlements dotting the river valley. French Catholic priests started keeping birth, marriage, and death records as soon as the first colonists arrived in 1608 and continued as the colonial population ballooned over the next two centuries. Fertility was high throughout this period: women had an average of 10.2 children, and grandmothers could easily have more than fifty grandchildren. But that number of grandchildren ranged widely: in this sample, from just one to an astonishing 195. The researchers were surprised to discover that much of this variation could be explained by the distance a woman lived from her mother—and, therefore, the distance she lived from the community and extended family she was born into. For example, a woman who lived two hundred miles from her mom could be expected to have 1.75 fewer children than a woman who lived in the same parish as her. "After all," the anthropologist Kristen Hawkes has explained, "if you're in Quebec but your grandma's in Cleveland, she may not be much help." Women who lived near their mothers were more likely to have children in the first place, more likely to start having them young, and therefore more likely to have more of them. The support of their mothers, families, and communities also meant that the children they did have fared better overall. Researchers found that the presence of grandmothers was also "protective," making it significantly more likely that children would survive to the age of fifteen, compared to children whose grandmothers had died or lived far away.[15]

In Europe, the growing trend of adult children moving away from their parents began raising alarms in the nineteenth century. In the 1850s, the French sociologist Frédéric Le Play observed that the modern family shattered as children reached adulthood: they moved out of the family home and formed families of their own, sometimes far from their parents or siblings. Each resulting family was so far from home and financially precarious that no one was particularly well equipped to care for their parents or their wider community. Even more concerning was the fact that each family was so inwardly focused that the members felt little responsibility to offer that care in the first place. Le Play called this new model the "unstable family."[16] In the first decades of the twentieth century, the Polish-born anthropologist Bronisław Malinowski would give it a more familiar name: the nuclear family. Just as the nucleus forms the core of a cell, a nuclear family includes only the core family unit: a mother and father and their biological children.[17]

What became the nuclear family unit had long existed in a dense network of neighbors, grandparents, sisters-in-law, childless aunts, and friends whose doors you didn't need to knock on before you let yourself in. This wasn't just nice; it was necessary, especially for the ability of those families to have kids. When these networks fell apart, it was in part because American families pulled back from those communities and shifted their focus to their own family units. They also cracked for more practical reasons, because people started moving to the West, to cities, to the North, to faraway places where they believed they could build better lives. More women found themselves in Quebec, figuratively speaking—tenement apartments in Chicago, farms and mining boomtowns in the Great Plains and the West, and later suburbs and subdivisions everywhere—while their moms and the support they represented stayed in Cleveland. The isolation of families from the support of their communities resulted in higher rates of childlessness and fewer babies overall. Ironically but not illogically, the shift toward Quayle's preferred definition of family made it less likely people would—or could—create those families at all.

In 1745, an eight-year-old child named John arrived on the front doorstep of a wealthy Boston merchant, in the leafy, fashionable neighborhood of Beacon Hill. The two-story Georgian-style home stood on the hill's south slope, facing Boston Common and surrounded by expansive gardens and fruit orchards. A rail fence ringed the property, a probably vain attempt to prevent the cows that then grazed on the common from trampling the landscaping. Standing on the elegant stoop with all his worldly possessions, John must have been awed. The child hailed from far humbler roots: he spent his early years in then-rural Braintree, Massachusetts, where his father was a minister. When his father died suddenly at the age of forty-two, John's idyllic country childhood was turned upside down. The family lived in a parsonage provided by the church, and John and his mother, Mary, had to pack up quickly to make room for the town's new first family. Overwhelmed and grief-stricken, Mary sent John to Boston to live with his uncle, the merchant.[18]

The merchant and his wife, Thomas and Lydia, were members of Boston's intellectual and social elite, on the vanguard of the brewing discontent with British rule that would ultimately spark the American Revolution. They were wealthy, successful, and extremely well housed. They were also, despite thirteen apparently happy years of marriage, without children of their own. We can't know what Thomas and Lydia felt about John's arrival, whether they greeted it as an answer to their prayers or simply a duty they were obligated to take on, whether they welcomed John as their long-awaited child or whether they'd been content without children and their parental feelings took time to grow. What we do know is what they did: Thomas and Lydia raised John as their own, saw him through the Boston Latin School and Harvard College, and set him to work alongside his uncle as his business partner, successor, and heir.[19] When Thomas died in 1764, John inherited his warehouses, shops, ships, inventory, and real estate, a fortune estimated at more than £100,000, nearly $20 million today.[20] Lydia inherited the house on Boston Common but quickly signed that over to her nephew as well, on the condition that she be allowed to live there for the rest of her life. John also inherited his adoptive parents' frustrations with the British-imposed Navigation Acts. At twenty-seven years old, he found himself firmly at the helm of his uncle's firm, the House of Hancock, and one of the American colonies' wealthiest and most influential men.[21]

It is barely a footnote in the grand sweep of American history, but John Hancock, the most flamboyant signatory of the Declaration of Independence, was raised by his childless aunt. Even more to the point, John Hancock's success, the very fact we know his name at all, was the product of people outside his immediate, nuclear family—a product of his broader family and community. Mary and Lydia Hancock lived in a world where children were traded from one home to another with some regularity, where women without children would have filled in as mothers at least some of the time, where networks of women tied families to their communities. When she found herself in an emotional and financial crisis, Mary Hancock could rely on another woman to step in and mother her child.

The early American family may have looked more or less as it does today: adult children usually moved to their own homes when they married, and they raised their children in those homes. But the doors that shut between them were rarely locked, literally or figuratively.[22] Mary Sollas, in seventeenth-century Massachusetts, once walked into the house next door "without knocking, the door being open, she being a neighbour," and found the occupants occupied in "lascivious carriages." In Maryland, Brigid Johnson got an even bigger surprise when she let herself into her neighbor's home, unconcerned that it was "Shutt and made fast with the Pestle": Johnson found her own fiancé in bed with the lady of the house.[23] As one historian has poetically observed, the house a family lived in was neither "a castle nor a womb."[24] For women, this meant they spent their days passing in and out of each other's homes, sometimes interrupting the process of baby making but more often helping with the work baby making created: sewing, baking, cleaning, and shopping, passing babies from arm to arm, exchanging breast milk, disciplining and loving each other's children. The foundation of these networks was extended family: sisters, aunts, cousins, and sisters-in-law—it was common for women to spend at least as much time with their husband's sisters as they did their husband himself—but they spiraled out into relationships with people who weren't related at all, friendships that often formed the most intense emotional bonds in women's lives. Women gave birth, became mothers, and raised their children in a dense network of other women, not all of whom had biological children of their own, but most of whom served, at some point or other, as someone's mother.[25]

Children like the young John Hancock, who made two living women mothers before his eighth birthday, were a shared resource and duty. Parents loved their children, of course, but few would have conceived of those children as "theirs," in the way modern parents often articulate the relationship: as sole possession, even ownership.[26] In many cases this was literal. In 1776, one in five American children was enslaved, meaning they were legally owned by a person who was not their parent. In some southern states, there were more enslaved children than free.[27] White fathers did have legal claims over their children, but across the colonies and across the economic spectrum white families regularly sent at least one preteen child to another household to work for pay or to learn a trade. The practice of "putting out" meant placing a child in another family's home for both labor *and* care. The child would work as a servant or farmhand or apprentice in a trade, and in exchange received housing and meals as well as guidance, education, and, sometimes, love.[28] In Quaker families in New York, New Jersey, Pennsylvania, and Delaware, just over one-third of parents had eight or more biological children, but more than 60 percent of children lived in homes with at least seven other children.[29] In other words, these large households were often formed by collecting kids who were not biological siblings. As children passed from home to home, neighbors, friends, assorted family members, the church, and whatever household took a child in were expected to play at least as large a role in teaching, disciplining, and caring for them as their parents were.

This definition of a family was malleable, permeable, and constantly changing, allowing people related by blood or not at all to participate to varying degrees in the family's intimate life. On the whole, early Americans were willing to trade privacy and insularity for support and community, to trade sole possession of their children for communal ways of child-rearing that spread the burden more evenly across the adults who had bandwidth and the homes that had space.[30] Sometimes, this looked like Lydia Hancock, a woman with plenty of resources to take on a child's care. Other times, it looked like Ella Baker's hometown of

Littleton, where times could be hard but the community pitched in to help, taking turns substituting as mothers and raising each other's children.

Ella Baker graduated first in her class from North Carolina's Shaw University, the second-oldest historically Black university in the country, and was "gung ho," as she put it, on one life path: to become a medical missionary. She planned to start graduate work at the University of Chicago in sociology or medicine, training that would set her up for a future of both science- and God-guided service to the poor. The problem was money: her family was comfortable in the rural South but couldn't afford city rent, and they had no family in Chicago to help. So instead of to the Midwest, Baker went northeast to Manhattan, where a cousin could offer shelter and a safety net while she found her feet.[31]

Baker landed in Harlem in the fall of 1927, at the height of the Harlem Renaissance, a revival of Black art, music, and intellectual life that electrified the northern tip of Manhattan for much of the 1920s. The energy intoxicated her. "Boy it was *good*," she'd say later.[32] The community ethos Baker brought with her from the rural South found both home and fertile ground in evening meetings in church basements and packed living rooms, the site of lively debates about whether communism and socialism or something else entirely would lay the path toward Black equality. Drawing on her childhood memories of community, Baker joined the Young Negroes Cooperative League in 1931, a mutual-aid organization that bulk bought food and other essentials to lower their cost. The Cooperative League offered a model of how Baker's "family socialism" could scale, by helping communities care for their own. Baker quickly became the organization's national director, and she spent most of the decade crisscrossing the country to give lectures and workshops on how Black communities could see themselves through the Depression by collecting and redistributing money, food, and other material goods.[33]

As the 1940s dawned, Baker moved on to the big leagues of civil rights work, the NAACP. She got a job as a field secretary and spent much of 1941 in and around Birmingham, Alabama, spearheading a membership drive in what Martin Luther King Jr. would call "the most thoroughly segregated city in the United States."[34] She usually traveled alone with a briefcase stuffed with NAACP promotional material and pamphlets about civil rights, facts that put a target on her back. Civil rights activists were regularly beaten up or killed in Alabama, and the police were, at best, of little help.[35] In spite of the dangers, Baker loved working there. Her comfortable upbringing, college education, and New York City address could have made her stand out, but instead she leaned on the lessons her childhood in Littleton had taught her. Back in New York, Baker clashed with the NAACP's leadership over the organization's platform—which she found "stale and uninteresting" by 1941—and what she saw as its limited ambition: gaining Black Americans access to the white middle class.[36] Baker thought the NAACP spent too much time in the halls of power and not enough in church basements and living rooms, too much time caring about membership numbers and too little time involving those members in meaningful ways. Her vision was to rebuild the kind of community ethos that she remembered from her childhood and the sense of mutual aid and support that she had seen in Harlem during the Depression.[37]

Baker committed her life to her community, and, as she put it, she "wasn't interested, really, in having children, per se," in part because she'd seen how motherhood had frustrated her own mother's professional ambitions. But at forty-two, motherhood was what her community asked of her. A letter arrived at Baker's Harlem apartment from her brother, Curtis, carrying news that Jackie, Baker's young niece, "had been asking about relatives up north." Curtis Baker's letter made a request Ella had been expecting for years. Jackie's mother, Maggie, Ella and Curtis's sister, had gotten pregnant young and had long been unable to care for her child. Anna, Ella Baker's mother, had cared for Jackie through her younger years. By 1945, Anna was getting older, frailer, and less able to mother another generation. Baker had been trained since childhood to expect and accept the responsibility of mothering a child who was not her own. She agreed to take over, and Jackie headed to New York.[38]

When Jackie came into her life, Baker was the NAACP's national director of branches and president of the New York City office. As a grade-schooler, Jackie remembered she "had to move fast to keep up" with her aunt. "I would sit in the back of meetings and do my homework many a night." Baker's husband, Bob, took an active role in caring for Jackie. But Bob traveled too, as a salesman and mechanic in the refrigerator business.[39] Baker depended on her neighbors and friends to fill in the gaps. Their next-door neighbor, Miss Lena, was only distantly related by marriage, but she became the glue that made their family function. "We could depend on Miss Lena being there to look out the window at the right time," Baker told an interviewer in 1977. "And then [Jackie] would go upstairs to her place and be fed." When Jackie walked the two blocks home from elementary school and found neither Bob nor Ella there, she knew to knock on Miss Lena's door for a snack, company, and help with her homework. "Did that change your lifestyle drastically then," an interviewer asked Baker later in life, "to have an eight-year-old?" "Not to the point of not having meetings," Baker laughed.[40] Caring for Jackie never superseded the care Baker expended on the wider Black community, and the community, in turn, helped her care for Jackie.

Jackie got married in the fall of 1960 in the Audubon Theatre and Ballroom, an art nouveau jewel box of a building in New York's Washington Heights neighborhood that is now best known as the site of Malcolm X's assassination in 1965. But on

September 7, 1960, the Audubon Ballroom was a place full of
joy, where Ella Baker, Jackie's biological mother Maggie, and the
rest of their family and close friends gathered to celebrate. In a
photograph, Baker beams as Jackie pins a corsage to her suit. She
may not have been *the* mother of the bride, but she was one of
them. Jackie's wedding—and her lifelong close relationship with
Jackie more generally—was, as one biographer has put it, "a high
point in Ella Baker's personal life."[41]

When the American anthropologist Niara Sudarkasa arrived
in Nigeria in the early 1960s to study kinship patterns among
Yoruba women, she found a kind of community ethos and care
that shared much in common with Baker's childhood in Littleton *and* Baker's adulthood as one of Jackie's mothers. "I was an
oddity in the small town where I lived," Sudarkasa writes. She
was unmarried, in her late twenties, and had no children, facts
that put her well within the norm among highly educated American women, then and now.[42] But it struck her Yoruba hosts as
strange. "Various people wanted to 'give' me a child," Sudarkasa remembers, "for whom I would take on the assigned role of
mother." To the women who made it, the offer made perfect sense:
the anthropologist was an adult woman whose capable hands
were seemingly empty, and the compound where she was staying was full of children and women who had more than enough
to handle. To spread the burden of raising a community's next
generation, Sudarkasa explains, Yoruba women were regularly
assigned children who were not "'theirs' in an exclusive sense,
but to whom they relate 'as a mother.'" Her hosts were inviting
her to participate in a community where the joy of children was
shared beyond the biological parents, along with the work of
raising them.[43]

Sudarkasa wrapped up her field research in Nigeria in 1964
and returned to Columbia University to complete her PhD. That
same year, another young anthropologist, named Carol Stack,

was just beginning her own project on kinship and Black families. Stack's research site was far closer to home: she studied "the Flats," a poor Black neighborhood in a midwestern city she rendered anonymous with the nickname "Jackson Harbor," but which was probably Urbana-Champaign, Illinois. Just as Sudarkasa had been in northeastern Nigeria, Stack was an oddity in the Flats: she was white—her informants took to fondly calling her "white Caroline," to distinguish her from someone's niece of the same name—and from a middle-class background, where biological ties and the nuclear family reigned.[44] In the Flats, family was broadly defined, and actions were thicker than blood. "Friends are classified as kinsmen," Stack wrote, simply when they begin to act like family. Kin, bonded by blood or action, formed "mutual aid domestic networks which are not bounded by genealogical distance or genealogical criteria." No one offered Stack their child, but she watched as children were regularly transferred between households, family, and friends. Sometimes, such a transfer would be permanent: for example, a very young mother might "give the child" to a childless couple, with no intention of playing any further role in the baby's care. But more common was what Stack called "child keeping," the practice of assuming responsibility for someone else's child for a temporary, though often indefinite, period.[45] In each of these cases, parental rights, responsibility, and care would be transferred from the biological parent to other adults in the community.

One sunny summer afternoon, Stack sat on a porch in the Flats with a woman named Georgia. Georgia winced in disapproval as her Aunt Ethel tried to pull a loose tooth out of a child named Alice's mouth—too early, Georgia's silent glare implied. Alice was Georgia's biological child, but mother and daughter lived with Ethel, and Ethel had cared for Alice alone for six months some time earlier, while Georgia temporarily moved to another city. In the white, middle-class world Stack hailed from, she wrote, "few persons, not even kin, would be authorized or would feel free to participate in health care or disciplinary behavior with regard to children without specific permission, or except in the case of an emergency." But in the Flats, Ethel's parental authority over the child—in this case, her right to determine when and whether a loose tooth should be forcibly evicted from its spot in Alice's gums—equaled or even superseded Georgia's biological claim.[46]

The kinds of kinship Stack observed in the Flats had some similarities to Yoruba kinship—a system flexible enough that an anthropologist from halfway around the world might participate fully—and to the "family socialism" Baker grew up with in Littleton. Kin was flexible and fluid. Children of kin were potentially children of yours, and from a child's perspective, any one of a number of adults might act as their mother, whether or not she had given birth to them. These similarities aren't a coincidence. The traditions that informed Black parenting in Littleton, in the Flats of Jackson Harbor, and in the United States more generally had roots in West African values of communal support and interdependence. Enslaved Africans brought these traditions to American shores, where recreating "African notions of family as extended kin units" became a form of survival and resistance. Mothering in West Africa, the sociologist Patricia Hill Collins has observed, "was not a privatized nurturing 'occupation' reserved for biological mothers." In many West African cultures, a biological mother was understood to have a *special* relationship with her children, but she was hardly the only woman with the right or responsibility to mother them. Childcare and child-rearing were done by the community, collectively, in the context of what Collins calls "cooperative, age-stratified, woman-centered 'mothering' networks," which survived the end of slavery and found new homes in the fertile soil of Baker's rural southern upbringing and in the northern urban Black communities where she lived as an adult.[47]

Grandmothers like Anna Baker long served as a primary and consistent source of parenting support within these Black networks, and not just financially or in times of crisis, as they often are in white communities. Grandmothers provided day care when facilities were too expensive or didn't exist, gave exhausted biological parents some childfree hours, and taught children to expect their needs to be met by a community, not just by one person.[48] In other words, grandmothers were critical to the project of raising the next generation—a role human evolution may have prepared them for. In 1957, a biologist named George C. Williams theorized that human females live for decades after they can no longer reproduce—unlike most other mammals, which die shortly after their last birth—because the care they provide for their children and grandchildren is essential to their survival and thriving.[49] In recent years, scientists have nicknamed this the "grandmother hypothesis": the idea that older women might stop reproducing because they can do more good by caring for their communities and extended families than by having additional children of their own.

The kind of families where grandmothers and other extended kin would have played central roles in raising and caring for children was the norm for much of history. But something weird happened in the second half of the eighteenth century in western Europe, something that left Europeans—and, eventually, Americans—without their grandmothers, and out of step with virtually everywhere else in the world. Sifting through historical marriage records from across Europe, an economist named John Hajnal noticed that marriage patterns, which had been pretty consistent across the continent, started to diverge between east and west around the middle of the eighteenth century. Hajnal took a ruler and drew a diagonal line across his map, from Saint Petersburg on the Gulf of Finland in the northeast to Trieste, Italy, in the southwest. East of the line, people carried on more or less as they had for centuries, and households resembled those in many other parts of the world: women were married young, often to much older men; they lived in multigenerational, extended-family households after the wedding; and only a small fraction of the female population was unmarried, most of whom were widows or nuns. West of the line, things looked increasingly strange: people started marrying later, in their mid- or even late twenties, with little age difference between spouses; couples moved into individual, financially independent households upon marriage; and a large proportion of the adult population was unmarried at any given time, including *half* of all women. "There is no known example of a population of non-European civilization which has a similar pattern," Hajnal remarked.[50] He called it the "European marriage pattern."

The emergence of the European marriage pattern upended the math around marriage and kids. If, after the wedding, you were going to move into your husband's family home and join in on whatever economic activity already kept it afloat, there would be little reason to delay marriage. Once you were married, why not start having children quickly, and why not have more than a few? There were aunts, sisters-in-law, and grandmothers around who could help house, feed, clothe, and care for any babies you might produce. If, on the other hand, you were expected to move out on your own and start your own household after the wedding, you'd need to get a career, a trade, land, or crops going first, and you'd have to be economically stable enough to feed, house, and clothe yourself and your family. This meant people married older. It meant that those who failed to reach this level of stability may have never married at all. And it meant fewer kids. Much of the sharp decline in fertility in the European nineteenth century happened west of Hajnal's line, while births in the east carried on more or less as they always had.[51] One part of the explanation is obvious: women who married at twenty-five or twenty-seven would naturally have fewer fertile, married years than brides of seventeen or eighteen. But demographers have also found evidence that couples in western and northern Europe were deliberately limiting their reproduction by spacing their children out—the average number of months between siblings steadily rose in this region from the sixteenth century to the nineteenth—and "stopping": having their last child before the end of a woman's fertile years. In sixteenth-century Zurich, for example, the average age at last birth was 41.4 years old. In 1819, it was just over thirty-four.[52]

The European marriage pattern washed ashore in the American colonies in the heady days after the revolution, even as newly minted republicans were trying to cast off most other things European. Perhaps inspired by Revolutionary political ideals of independence and self-sufficiency, Americans began to distinguish between family and community as never before.[53] The community, which had long been almost seamlessly merged with the family, came to seem like a threat. "We go forth into the world," wrote one contributor to *Ladies' Magazine* in 1830, "amidst the scenes of business and of pleasure . . . [and] behold every principle of justice and of honor, and even the dictates of common honesty disregarded, and the delicacy of our moral sense is wounded." As protection from the dangers outside their door, "we look to the *sanctuary of home*; there sympathy, honor, virtue are assembled."[54] This moral distinction between public and private, the family home and the community, would have made little sense in colonial America, but in the early republic, the family became a form of protection from the very society Americans had fought a revolution to create. The modern nuclear family was not just a biological unit, but also, in the public imagination, a social unit bonded by a kind of love and loyalty that was both natural and unique.[55]

"Every family is a little state, or empire within itself," Heman Humphrey wrote in 1840, "bound together with endearing attractions and governed by its patriarchal head, with whose prerogatives no power on earth has a right to interfere." Humphrey was the longtime president of Amherst College, and his book *Domestic Education* might be considered the original family values treatise. By then, the nuclear family had become the American ideal. It had also been naturalized into a self-evident fact about the world, like a law of physics. "Nations may change their forms of government at pleasure. . . . But in the family there is but one model for all times and all places. It is just the same now, as it was in the beginning, and it is impossible to alter it, without marring its beauty, and directly contravening the wisdom and benevolence of the creator."[56]

As Manifest Destiny drew nineteenth-century American settlers west, they encountered Native family structures that challenged the idea that there was one eternal, natural family model. Lewis Henry Morgan, an anthropologist and railroad lawyer, spent some Smithsonian-funded years in the late 1850s documenting the kinship networks of Native Americans from Kansas, up the Missouri River, and into today's Montana. By 1862, Morgan had recorded fifty-one distinct kinship patterns. All of them, he concluded, were inferior to the unit bound by blood and marriage that had so recently become the American middle-class norm. In adopting the nuclear family, man had "raised himself from promiscuous intercourse," from a "barbarous" past, as Morgan puts it, "to final civilization."[57]

More than a few of the fifty-one kinship patterns Morgan recorded featured women cooperatively raising the community's children across generations and across bloodlines. The Dakota word for extended family is *tiospaye*, a term that encompasses non-blood kin, cross-generational ties, co-mothers, and even plural marriages.[58] As the guardians of future generations, women often occupied positions of considerable authority and controlled family or community property. The "promiscuous intercourse" or "barbarity" implied in such a system made the Indigenous family one of the primary targets of American colonialism.[59] As the gospel of private property replaced collective land stewardship, laws in western territories tied the right to own land to the act of marriage, effectively requiring Native people to start individual family units away from their kin, on individual plots of land, if they wanted any hope of land access or economic survival.[60] "Assimilation" to white American culture and society demanded nothing less than the destruction of communal support networks and the isolation of nuclear families from each other. By choice or by force, by the middle of the nineteenth century Americans had largely come around to the sort of family Dan Quayle would have admired: a father, the breadwinner, providing for the family; a mother, keeper of all things domestic and the family's moral compass; and their biological children.

Heman Humphrey's claim about the naturalness of the nuclear family wasn't true, of course. It falls apart if you look elsewhere in the world or two centuries in our past. But the widespread belief that it was true had consequences: it made the ways in which community and family have long overlapped and sustained each other seem *un*natural. Surviving as "a little state" requires material resources to cover the kind of shared domestic labor that neighbors and friends might once have helped with, to make up for the bumper crop of black-eyed peas the Baker family might once have shared, to care for children that might once have been raised by the others in the community. A society that believes such support should not be necessary—indeed, that to be dependent on others is against the laws of nature—does not readily offer it. And at times, it even seeks to punish families for needing it.

In the 1990s, more than thirty years after Carol Stack sat on front porches and at kitchen tables in Jackson Harbor and observed the community networks and communal parenting practices that made surviving and thriving possible in the Flats, another anthropologist began her own study of Black family and kinship. Like Stack, Leith Mullings was a bit of an outsider: she was born in Jamaica and trained as a nurse at Cornell University before pivoting to an anthropology PhD program at the University of Chicago. It was Mullings's job as a professor at the City University of New York that brought her to the place she would ultimately study. And like Stack, Mullings went door-to-door in an urban Black neighborhood as part of her work. This time it was Harlem, the place that had so captivated Ella Baker with its vibrance when she arrived in the late 1920s and that had inspired her with its spirit of community support and resilience in the hard economic times that followed. Mullings's work was funded by a grant from the reproductive health division at the CDC, part of what Mullings called "a bold initiative to examine the social context in which reproductive behaviors are practiced." There was growing alarm in the medical and public health world about a widening disparity in infant mortality and health outcomes for white and Black children, a disparity that could not be accounted for by risk factors associated with individual mothers. Mullings's study was qualitative—that is, not focused on crunching numbers but on talking to people and documenting the economic, environmental, and social conditions that stress a community's members in ways that only sometimes show up in their medical charts. Mullings called it the Harlem Birth Right Project.

The Harlem Mullings found was no less vibrant than the one that Baker encountered in the 1920s. It was "the mecca of urban African American culture," Mullings wrote, and often the first stop for Black Americans moving to the city from out of state and for immigrants from other countries. The mix of backgrounds made for a unique food, art, and music scene, and in many ways having people move there from everywhere reinforced community bonds. For example, Sandra Bourne, a Harlem Birth Right Project participant in her early thirties, had some biological family members scattered across the Eastern Seaboard from Long Island to Virginia, but no one lived nearby. When she became pregnant, it was her Harlem community, not her blood relatives, that pulled together to offer support: her coworkers at a fast-food restaurant held a baby shower for her and went in together to buy a car seat, stroller, and baby clothes; the restaurant's owners, who were also Black women, bought her a crib and outfitted the baby's nursery.[61]

In other ways, though, the years had been unkind to Harlem. The global economic crisis of the mid-1970s ushered in steep budget cuts in New York City, as well as the rollback of social services. The loss of manufacturing jobs in the same period meant there was less high-paying union work to go around. By 1990, more than half of the employed adults in Harlem worked in clerical or service jobs, which generally offered low wages and limited benefits. The economic recovery of the 1980s did little to help. In the twelve years between 1975 and 1987, the national poverty rate climbed from 15 percent to 23 percent. In the decade between 1988 and 1998, the gross income of New York's poorest families fell almost 20 percent. To make matters worse, in the mid-1990s, the city cut funding to schools and education by $1 billion and moved to privatize public hospitals and housing, gutting the support systems that less affluent communities like Harlem had long relied on. Meanwhile, crack cocaine flooded into cities across the United States, bringing addiction and violence along with it. The project of mass incarceration that followed frayed the fabric of many Black urban neighborhoods still further. Today, as many as one in seven Black children in the United States has a parent behind bars.[62]

Over and over, participants in the Harlem Birth Right Project told Mullings and her team that raising children under the conditions of poverty, violence, incarceration, and addiction was a cause of constant stress. "The depth of worry about children growing up in these conditions," Mullings observed, "is difficult to convey."[63] In the absence—often the deliberate absence—of institutional support systems, grandmothers still stepped in to offer care, but Mullings found that that care was less about maintaining a tradition of woman-centered support networks or community bonds than it was about survival, the sheer necessity to mother their grandchildren as their daughters battled addiction or worked multiple jobs.[64] On the other side of the economic spectrum, Black families that joined the middle and upper-middle classes often adopted the values and lifestyles of their white counterparts, moving to suburbs or cities far from extended family or other kin. "The erosion of such networks in the face of the changing institutional fabric of Black civil society points to the need either to refashion these networks or develop some other way of supporting Black children," Patricia Hill Collins observed. "For far too many African-American children, assuming that a grandmother or 'fictive kin' will care for them is no longer a reality."[65]

Littleton "wasn't a town," Ella Baker has explained. "It was people." But a community of people needs roots to thrive, roots sent deep into the soil and tended by time, trust, and mutual support. The middle decades of the twentieth century tore those roots from the earth repeatedly, replanting their delicate strands in more anemic soil amid a harsher climate. People moved into towns and cities and encountered people they had no ties to, who lived differently and who had different expectations of their neighbors. "They lost their roots," Baker said. "And when you lose that, what do you do? You *hope* that you begin to think in terms of the wider brotherhood."[66] But under the triple pressures of racism, poverty, and dislocation, not to mention the expectation that nuclear families should be able to care for themselves without any external support, community was, and still is, hard to sustain. As economic conditions in Harlem deteriorated, Black grandmothers struggled to provide the care that working mothers in the suburbs or farther downtown would have paid nannies or day care workers to do. Over the past two centuries, as our homes became castles, as our families became wombs, we jettisoned expansive ideas of kinship, isolated parents, disinvested from communities, and replaced community care with a kind of care that individuals have to pay for.

That's not to say we couldn't rebuild systems of community support if we wanted to, or that we lack examples of how we might do it. In December 1865, the Thirteenth Amendment outlawed slavery and freed more than one hundred thousand people, including a woman named Carrie Steele Logan. Logan, along with thousands of others, left the only life she'd ever known and headed to Atlanta. There, she found a job as a maid at Union Station in the city's downtown, where she spent her days sweeping floors, wiping down train cars, and collecting trash. To her surprise, Logan also found children huddling in corners and infants tucked out of the wind, carefully wrapped in blankets, all of them hungry, abandoned, and homeless. "Tossed hither and thither by the rude winds of adversity," one of Logan's biographers explained, they were "waifs drifting down the stream of destruction!"[67]

Logan had been an orphan herself. She was born into slavery around the year 1829 on a plantation in rural Georgia. Her mother died when she was very young, leaving her reliant on other adults for protection, guidance, and love. This kind of community parenting was common under slavery. Older enslaved women would often serve as "social mothers," caring for children while their parents worked and informally adopting orphaned children.[68] We know that Logan benefitted from this kind of care when she was a child: someone taught her to read and write, possibly at great risk to themselves. Remembering the women who went out of their way to care for her, Logan found she couldn't ignore the children's dire situation. She started stashing the children she found in empty boxcars during the day and taking them home with her at night. But the number of abandoned children quickly overwhelmed her meager wages and stretched the capacity of her small two-bedroom home to the breaking point.[69]

Logan was unwilling to give up. She put her literary skills to good use and wrote a short book that was one part autobiography—the inspiring story of the life of an enslaved, orphaned, and then freed woman—and one part fundraising pitch for her work with Atlanta's orphans. "It is appointed to me in my old age what I believe to be a great and glorious work," she wrote, "and one that shall live long after my poor frail body has dropped into the dust whence it came." That work was building the Carrie Steele Orphan Home, the first orphanage for Black children in the United States. Using revenue from her book and donations from supporters across the country, Logan bought a three-story brick building on four acres of land in the outskirts of Atlanta. By the end of the nineteenth century, the campus included a school and a medical clinic, and had provided a home, education, and vocational training for more than 225 children.[70] The Carrie Steele-Pitts Home, as it is now known, has provided housing and reconstructed kin for thousands of orphaned children, some of whom, like the organization's second director, Ollivette Allison, returned as adults to devote their professional lives to the home's younger generations. Allison "never had children of her own," read the first line of her obituary when she died in 2010, "but she cared for thousands of babies" over her six-decade career.[71] The Carrie Steele-Pitts Home, its website says, is "a legacy of love," a community bonded by necessity that has made itself into a family.[72]

Our more recent efforts to do what Carrie Steel Logan did in Atlanta, to relink community and family, to build public support systems that would be accessible to all on a national scale, have had far less success. In 1971, Walter Mondale, a Democratic senator from Minnesota, announced bipartisan legislation that would radically expand government-funded early childhood care and support for families with young kids. While Democrats and Republicans had different ideas of how it would work, the general concept was to create a network of publicly funded day care centers available to all parents. At the time, universal day care had a remarkably broad base of support. Feminists and women's groups believed the bill would expand women's ability to work outside the home. Labor groups thought it would offer a solution to childcare problems during the workday. Civil rights groups hoped it would expand the Head Start programs that many Black families relied on in the American South. And to some conservative groups, funding programs and care for young children seemed appealingly pro-family. In its final form, the Comprehensive Child Development Act proposed a system of childcare centers that charged on a sliding scale for day care and after-school care, and which incorporated educational, nutritional, health, and developmental support for families. "The only non-negotiable criterion," Mondale said, as the bill was debated, "is that these early childhood programs enhance the child's development rather than simply enabling the mother to work." In other words, these programs would not just provide a safe place to deposit your kid during the day, but also participate in real ways in raising them. The Comprehensive Child Development Act passed the Senate by a nearly two-thirds margin, and a sister bill cleared the House.[73]

The act made its way to the White House in December. Its supporters hoped the bipartisan law would serve as a Christmas gift to the pre-Watergate but already embattled president Richard Nixon, the public face of the increasingly divisive war in Vietnam. But Nixon didn't see it that way. To him, the bill was a Trojan horse: generous and attractive on the outside but concealing something inside that could bring the republic to its knees. The president vetoed the bill, and then took the unusual step of writing a searing rebuke to his colleagues in Congress. The Comprehensive Child Development Act, Nixon wrote, was "a long leap into the dark," one that would "commit the vast moral authority of the national government to the side of communal approaches to child rearing over against the family-centered approach." The very concept of day care—that children would be cared for and at least partially raised by someone other than their mother, while she went to work—was a direct challenge to the American ideal of the nuclear family. "This President, this Government," Nixon wrote, "is unwilling to take that step."[74]

Critics of the act worried that encouraging women to work rather than stay home with their children would cause birth rates to fall, just as women's workplace participation had accompanied lower fertility in the nineteenth century. The irony, of course, is that *not* having an infrastructure of support for young children and families—or, more correctly, having that infrastructure available only to those who can afford it—seems to have gotten us there anyway. We've spent a century and a half valorizing the nuclear family that could take care of itself, building walls between ourselves and our communities, and expecting parents to shoulder the burden of raising their children alone—or to pay for any help they need. Today, it's safe to say we need each other more than ever: childcare is staggeringly expensive, we work more hours than ever before, and, in most two-parent households, both adults must work outside the home to make ends meet. But rebuilding the kind of community that would give us back time and energy *takes* time and energy—and, without external support networks, who has enough of either?

Women without children of their own who acted as mothers to the children of others, like Lydia Hancock and Ella and Anna Baker, or women who acted as mothers to their community, like Carrie Steele Logan and Ollivette Allison, are examples of what Stanlie M. James calls mother*ing*: a kind of caring for children and community that is not dependent on biological reproduction. The word "mother," used as a noun and as a strictly defined identity, can isolate women, a fact that's become all the clearer in recent years. Mothering, as a verb, as something anyone can do— whether they've birthed children, whether they've birthed the particular child they are called to mother, whether they have the anatomy to birth children—has helped communities from Boston to Littleton to Nigeria spread the burden and the joy of raising children. Women from communities far more familiar with crisis than the white middle class have known for generations, for centuries, that community support and a community's ability to survive, to reproduce itself, are linked. Mothering, the activist Bernice Johnson Reagon has written, is best understood as cultural work, "the entire way a community organizes to nurture itself and future generations."[75]

In the boxcars, in her small Atlanta apartment, and finally in a well-funded organization that has thrived for nearly a century and a half, Carrie Steele Logan rebuilt community and family out of a more total societal upheaval than many of our twenty-first-century selves can imagine. Family, community, kin group, *tiospaye*: they don't have to be organic, and expecting them to be is one reason we've lost them. Communities that support biological parents by sharing the work of loving and raising children—like Littleton, like the Flats, like an early New England town—can be *made*. Sometimes, as Carrie Steele Logan knew, they need to be.

CHAPTER 3

BECAUSE WE CAN'T HAVE IT ALL

THE 1950S AND 1960S WERE NOT A GOOD TIME TO BE SINGLE AND childless in America, a fact Helen Gurley knew intimately. "If you were female and not married by age 30, you might as well go to the Grand Canyon and throw yourself in," she explained, only half joking. She married and became Helen Gurley Brown at thirty-seven, well after her expiration date. Maybe because of that, she remained a lifelong advocate of single women doing, well, whatever they wanted, and not feeling shame about it. "Being smart about money is sexy," she wrote. Sex was good too. "You inherited your proclivity for it," she reassured women in her 1962 book, *Sex and the Single Girl*. "It isn't some random piece of mischief you dreamed up because you're a bad, wicked girl."[1]

Brown was born in a tiny town in the Ozark mountains, tucked in the northwest corner of Arkansas. She grew up in a family of "hillbillies," in her words: the backwoods-raised daughter of a Fish and Game Commission official who died when she was ten.[2] As a teenager, Brown moved with her mother and sister to Los

Angeles, where she enrolled in Woodbury Business College. Her
family eventually moved back to Arkansas, but Brown stayed in
LA and hustled, taking secretarial work at some seventeen different advertising agencies, working her way up the ladder until she was the highest-paid female copywriter in California. In
1965, at the age of forty-three, Brown was named editor in chief
of *Cosmopolitan* magazine. She spent the next three decades offering up career pointers, beauty tips, and increasingly explicit sex
advice in the magazine's pages. She also clashed with the feminist titans of her day. Reportedly, Gloria Steinem once led an in-
vasion of *Cosmo*'s New York offices. Betty Friedan famously said
that Brown's magazine sold nothing but an "immature teenage-
level sexual fantasy." The kind of liberation Brown offered
women was sexy, feminine, and best experienced in power heels,
a far cry from Friedan's middle-class respectability or Steinem's
hippie-inflected, politically radical feminism.[3] When Brown died
in 2012, National Public Radio's Audie Cornish called her "a pioneer in Prada, a revolutionary in stilettos."[4] She was the inventor
of *Sex and the City*–style feminism, the OG Carrie Bradshaw.[5]

Brown spent the first years of the 1980s in her office in New
York City's Hearst Tower, fending off criticism from feminists
on the left and Reagan-inspired traditionalists on the right, all
of whom found plenty of reasons to hate *Cosmopolitan*. In her
spare time, she drafted a book she planned to call *The Mouseburger Plan*, a manual for people she called "mouseburgers":
women, like her, who had been born without particularly good
looks or genius IQ scores or privileged backgrounds but who
were scrappy, ambitious, and driven to succeed. Brown's publisher vetoed the *Mouseburger* title, and instead she became the
author of a bestseller called *Having It All*. The book's pages were
bursting with tried-and-true tips for how to "mouseburger your
way to the top," ranging from the highly questionable but not
entirely surprising for a *Cosmopolitan* editor ("dieting really *is*

moral, sexy, and healthy") to the practical if explicit ("don't grab too hard" and "keep your teeth *behind* your lips") to the actually helpful ("don't surrender your soul"). Have sex with whomever you want, Brown advised her mouseburgers—even your boss— but don't confuse sexual prowess with professional success. "You can't sleep your way to the top or even to the middle," Brown cautioned. "You have to do it yourself, so you might as well get started."[6]

On the book's original cover, Brown smiles, sixty years old and impeccably dressed in burgundy silk and pearls, her brown hair poofed into a helmet-shaped, immovable coif. The book's subtitle floats above her head, offering her definition of "it all": *Love, Success, Sex, Money.* This may have accurately described the book's contents, but Brown hated the title. "I've always visualized this as a book for the downtrodden," she lamented, "a book by a near loser who got to be a winner, instead of somebody who sounds—based on the title—like a smartass all-the-time winner from the beginning." Besides, she told her editors, *Having It All* "sounds so fucking cliché to me."[7]

Unfortunately for Brown, the cliché she heard in "having it all" was almost immediately replaced with another, one she liked even less. "Do you think it's possible," Harriet, a character in Wendy Wasserstein's 1981 play, *Isn't It Romantic,* asked her mother, "to be married, or living with a man, have a good relationship and children that you share equal responsibility for, and a career, and still read novels, play the piano, have women friends and swim twice a week?" "You mean what the women's magazines call 'having it all'?" her mother replies, sarcastically. "That's just your generation's fantasy."[8] From a women's liberation–inflected vision of love, success, sex, and money, having it all quickly morphed into a fantasy of a far more traditional kind. "It all" came to mean the "three big component parts for women," Brown recalled later: having a job, a man, and children.[9]

Considering how central they have become to the idea of having it all, it's more than a little ironic that children were never part of Brown's vision. Her extremely unpopular opinion among feminists and anti-feminists alike was that motherhood, not bras or beauty standards, stood in the way of women's liberation. "Getting us to be beautiful ain't the problem," a nearly seventy-year-old Brown insisted in 1991, when she was invited to debate Naomi Wolf on a television program hosted by Ron Reagan, the former president's son. In her now-classic book *The Beauty Myth*, Wolf argued that unrealistic beauty standards were intended to preoccupy women, sapping their professional and intellectual talents and holding them back in society. Brown argued that beauty standards were hardly the biggest obstacle women faced. "We are encouraged to be mothers, to be pregnant," she retorted. The primary goal of the pro-life movement, Brown argued, was to keep women "encumbered with children" so they would be less likely to succeed in the traditionally male corners of the professional world that had recently opened to them.[10] In her book, Brown acknowledged that it was possible to be a mother and a mouseburger: "If you're so *inclined*, and you're willing to pay your dues, you *can* have both—job success and well raised children."[11] But why would you want to? Combining motherhood and a career, Brown writes: "Isn't that a hard sell if you ever heard one?"[12] In Brown's early iteration, having it all had nothing to do with marriage or motherhood—it was about women's sexual and professional liberation.

Today, all ends of the political spectrum have soured on having it all, at least in the aspirational job-husband-kids sense that Brown never intended. Anne-Marie Slaughter, who served as director of policy planning at the State Department under President Barack Obama, made waves when she admitted in *The Atlantic* in 2012 that even she—a mother of two, a tenured Princeton professor, and a presidential appointee—was failing to "have it all."[13] Michelle Obama told a sold-out crowd at Brooklyn's Barclays Center in 2018 "that whole 'you can have it all' [idea], nope, not at the same time, that's a lie. It's not always enough to lean in," she continued, to loud applause, "because that shit doesn't work."[14] On the political right, having it all has long been laughed off as a con, a liberal conspiracy to convince women that they should feel free to pursue careers because they can "work full time and become leaders of industries," said Carrie L. Lukas, president of the conservative Independent Women's Forum, "without sacrificing time with families."[15] "Sure, you can have it all," former vice president Mike Pence wrote in an op-ed in 1997, "but your day-care kids get the short end of the emotional stick."[16]

Having it all has survived the changing tides of opinion in some places, like Silicon Valley, which continues to insist that we could have it all if we were willing to just lean in.[17] In March 2022, the politically uncategorizable Kim Kardashian gave women, many of whom were struggling after two years with unreliable school and childcare and the total collapse of work and life into each other during the COVID-19 pandemic, similar advice: "Get your fucking ass up and work."[18] But the idea has been most enthusiastically revived on the political right, adopted and transformed by a conservative women's movement that holds that having it all is not just possible in today's world; it is *so* possible that it renders things like abortion and feminism unnecessary, silly, obsolete. The avatar of this thinking is Supreme Court justice Amy Coney Barrett, who has seven children, does CrossFit every morning, and has strongly implied that her rise to the highest court in the land is proof that the material and economic consequences of having children—consequences the justices in *Roe v. Wade* reasoned were too burdensome for the government to require women to bear against their will—no longer exist.[19] The Amy Coney Barretts of the world, this movement reasons, prove we already do have it all, or at least we could, if we just got up earlier to do push-ups and stopped being so lazy.

To be fair, liberals are hardly immune from fetishizing women who appear to have it all. When President Barack Obama nominated Elena Kagan to the Supreme Court in 2010, her reproductive record came under scrutiny alongside her judicial one. Kagan was the second female justice Obama appointed to the court and, along with Sonia Sotomayor, the second of his appointees to have no children. For many, even on the left, this was a mistake. In the *New York Times*, writer Lisa Belkin recounted the complaint of a "feminist friend": "I wish she"—Kagan—"were a mother. This sends the wrong message."[20] In opting out of having children, some thought, Kagan and Sotomayor cut corners on the road to the Supreme Court. Wouldn't it be better, this argument implied, to elevate women who had done it all?

The funny thing about our fixation on having it all is that "it all," in the sense of having a husband and children and working at the same time, isn't particularly new or innovative. Most women, for most of history, would have been expected to have children and contribute economically to their families. American women of color, immigrant women, and working-class and impoverished women have rarely had the option of devoting their full attention and full labor resources to their children. The experience of Black women in the United States has long been one of working outside their homes, forced by violence under slavery and often by economic necessity after its end. In agricultural regions of Europe, women, no less than the children they gave birth to, would have been valuable sets of hands, backs, and knees in the ongoing struggle to coax enough calories from the ground to ensure a family's survival. Indigenous women lived, worked, and mothered on the North American continent long before Europeans showed up on their shores. And when those ships came, they carried working women too: economic productivity was a prized characteristic of a colonial "goodwife."[21]

The nineteenth century brought major changes to how and where people labored: work, in the sense of labor in exchange for pay, for the most part moved out of the home. When it did, the decision to keep mothers at home was sometimes a rational one—someone, after all, had to care for young children and keep everyone fed and clothed—but it also became aspirational, a marker of the family's socioeconomic status, the way you punched your membership card in the emerging industrial middle class.[22] What one historian has dubbed the "breadwinner-homemaker household"—the *Leave It to Beaver* model, in which a father worked for wages and a mother cared for children and the home—was the norm for only a century and a half or so, little more than a blip in historical terms, and even then it really existed only for people who were middle class or close enough that they could pretend they were.[23] Even in 1959, with the Cleavers on TV and the baby boom at its height, even among families where both parents were white and born in the United States, one-third of households could not survive on the income of one breadwinner alone. "Contrary to popular opinion," the historian Stephanie Coontz writes, "*Leave It to Beaver* was not a documentary."[24]

Today, as in the past, the vast majority of mothers *do* work: more than 70 percent of American women with children under eighteen are employed outside the home, according to the Bureau of Labor Statistics, about 80 percent of them full-time.[25] The always contingent reality of the breadwinner-homemaker household may have faded, but the myths it's left us with—that a woman's role is to be a mother, that to be a mother is to be home, and that to be home is to not work—have come to seem as eternal as they do natural. In a 2002 survey, just 11 percent of Americans said it was appropriate for mothers of young children to work full-time. In 2003, nearly three-quarters agreed with the statement, "Too many children are being raised in child-care centers these days."[26] With numbers like these, it's not terribly surprising that many American women feel a tension between their professional ambitions or financial needs and their ability to have and raise children.

When people talk about women not having children because of their jobs, the stereotype is usually overeducated feminists sporting pantsuits in offices and boardrooms and then going home to nice houses filled with cats. But not having children because of work or for economic reasons has also looked like the one in five women in preindustrial Europe who remained unmarried and childless to offset population growth and help support their families. It looked like the years of the Great Depression, when economic pain gripped the United States and a greater percentage of women remained childless than at any other point in American history. It looked like the one in three Black women in the first decades of the twentieth century who had no children because, scholars have argued, they saw economic mobility and reproduction as mutually exclusive, and chose the former. It looked like Appalachian coal country, where births rose and fell with fossil fuel prices in the 1970s and 1980s.[27]

In the nineteenth century, American women collectively decided to have fewer children just as their economic lives were radically transformed. The American population shifted from majority rural to majority urban within a single generation. In the second half of the century, unmarried women moved to cities by the millions to find work, including formerly enslaved Black women who sought to support freer lives with wage-earning labor. With emancipation and the early successes of the suffragist movement, education and professional jobs started to crack open to some. Work, in the sense of wage labor, largely moved out of the home. As the world split into two spheres, home and work, the idea that most women would have children and contribute economically to their families came to seem less like an inevitability and more like an either-or: you can have children, or you can make money, but not both. Most women continued to try, doing their best to shoehorn work around child-rearing. But not having children, or at least delaying motherhood and restricting the number of children they had overall, became an increasingly viable and appealing option. For the last century and a half, across the income spectrum, women have been asked to reproduce in the face of increasing economic pressures that pitted motherhood against their professional ambitions, intellectual endeavors, and/or economic survival. And they have responded rationally: by doing it less.

Some, like the philosopher Simone de Beauvoir, didn't do it at all. Simone Lucie Ernestine Marie Bertrand de Beauvoir was born in Paris in 1908. She was the first child of Françoise and Georges Bertrand de Beauvoir, a couple that was, at the time, bourgeois enough to justify four first names for their child. Françoise was the deeply Catholic daughter of a wealthy banker, and Georges was a legal secretary with aristocratic aspirations and subpar business skills. He lost the family's fortune shortly before World War I, leaving them unable to provide dowries for Beauvoir and her sister, Hélène. For Beauvoir, this was, if anything, a relief: she would later say that she never wanted to be a mother or a wife. Freed from that possibility, Beauvoir threw herself into her studies, hoping to become a writer and a teacher. "Simone," her father once said approvingly, "thinks like a man!"[28]

Thinking "like a man" got Beauvoir far. In 1929, at the age of twenty-one, she became the youngest person ever to pass a highly competitive annual academic exam, a distinction that won her the privilege of teaching philosophy at the École Normale, one of the most selective and prestigious graduate schools in Paris. And Beauvoir didn't just pass. She recorded the second-highest score that year, barely edged out for first prize by a mind no less sharp than Jean-Paul Sartre. First and second place quickly became inseparable. Sartre proposed to Beauvoir two years later, though he knew better than to ask for her hand on a permanent basis. "Let's sign a two-year lease," he suggested, as the couple sat on a bench outside the Sorbonne in the crisp autumn air. Beauvoir asked if he was joking. Later, he tried again, offering an open relationship as only a philosopher could: "What we have is an *essential* love," he told her. "But it is also good for us to experience *contingent* love affairs."[29] Their existential love forged one of the most wondered-about partnerships in modern history: Beauvoir and Sartre never lived together and never had children, but they remained each other's primary romantic partner for half a century, until Sartre's death in 1980.[30]

Beauvoir's most famous work, the 1949 book *The Second Sex*, deployed the existentialist philosophy that was in vogue at the time to feminist ends: "One is not born, but rather becomes a woman," she argued, through a lifetime of exposure to cultural norms and societal expectations. Judith Butler, the great philosopher of gender in the late twentieth and early twenty-first centuries, would later point to Beauvoir's work as one of the earliest to draw a distinction between biological sex and gender roles.[31] "No biological, psychological or economic fate determines the figure that the human female presents in society," Beauvoir argued; instead, "it is civilization" that delineates what women must be.[32] And what they must be is made clear to girls at a very young age: mothers.

In general, *The Second Sex* has very little good to say about the institution of motherhood, which Beauvoir describes as "a strange mixture of narcissism, altruism, idle daydreaming, sincerity, bad faith, devotion and cynicism." It was a "dangerous misconception," she writes, to believe that "motherhood in all cases is enough to fulfill a woman." Even readers bold enough to pick up a work of philosophy whose politics were clearly advertised in the title might have been scandalized to find that Beauvoir spends the first dozen or so pages of her chapter titled "The Mother" on abortion and contraception, and then the next ten on the terror many women feel at the idea of motherhood: of losing autonomy over their bodies in pregnancy, of being torn apart in childbirth, and of sacrificing their identity, ambition, and marriage for the tiny person whose needs will take priority over their own.[33] (Beauvoir cites Hegel: "The birth of children is the death of the parents." Ejaculation, she adds, gravely, "is the promise of death.")[34] Such opinions may have made her controversial, but they also sold books. *The Second Sex* was published in France in 1949 and flew off the shelves more like a spy thriller than the work of an academic philosopher. The book sold twenty-two thousand copies in its first week on the market, and well north of a million in the decades since.[35]

In her memoirs, Beauvoir remembers that she and Sartre ruled out parenthood very early on in their relationship. "I never felt as though I was holding out against motherhood: it simply was not my natural lot in life, and by remaining childless I was fulfilling my proper function."[36] It never occurred to her that she could do both. "I thought I couldn't have children because I wanted to write," Beauvoir told Betty Friedan in an early 1960s interview that appeared in Friedan's second book, *"It Changed My Life": Writings on the Women's Movement.*[37] Beauvoir believed it would be impossible to pursue her intellectual career—which meant thinking like a man—and become a mother, which would require her to live like a woman. She had to choose, and she chose her work.

———————

When she got to the University of Virginia in the fall of 1974, it never occurred to my mom that she would have to choose. My mom was a long-haired, hippie-adjacent kid straight out of a Quaker boarding school in rural Pennsylvania, facts that made her a fish out of water on the Charlottesville campus: her assigned roommate was a cheerleader with a wardrobe at least four times bigger than the one my mom unpacked from her suitcases. But my mom's expectations about the possible futures that lay ahead also set her apart. Her mother, my grandmother, proudly says she was "born a feminist" in 1928, just eight years after the Nineteenth Amendment gave women the right to vote. My grandmother put herself through college and was completing a graduate degree in anatomy and physiology when she went on a blind date with a handsome young PhD student in sociology— "the soft sciences," she'll still sniff dismissively, teasing me, her historian granddaughter. They were engaged six weeks later. My mom and her sisters were raised by a woman who had a career as a professor and mentor, four children, and a reasonably balanced marriage, and who expected them to have the same. But at UVA, my mom remembers, most of her peers understood there were two paths ahead of them: you could have a career, or you could find a man who would have a career while you had the kids. There was no third option. When the sociologist Carolyn Morell surveyed women without children in the 1990s, more than four decades after Beauvoir published *The Second Sex* and almost twenty years after my mom graduated from college, many of her subjects still didn't see a path toward children and a career. "These women," Morell wrote, "equated having children with leaving paid employment and staying at home, a sexual division of labor, economic dependence, and the erosion of their power within marriage."[38] As recently as 2014, a Harvard Business School survey of couples made up of a man and a woman who each had an MBA found that the vast majority of men and more than half of women expected that the woman would be the primary parent.[39]

There's this classic story that some historians tell about how women got pushed out of the labor force just as the labor force was becoming a thing it was important to be in.[40] That story often begins in a premodern, preindustrial, somewhere-in-Europe past, where farmer families worked land they owned for food and supplemented their income with part-time artisanship. Happy families spent evenings and long winter days weaving or jam making or rug braiding together by candlelight, wives working alongside their husbands and contributing equally to the family's economic footing.[41] In the hands of a particular sort of historian, these half-mythic before times come to represent a "golden age" of female labor. As long as work remained in the home, it was more or less genderless; and as long as work remained genderless, women maintained a partial hold on equal household power. Then, catastrophe struck: the machines that powered the Industrial Revolution wrested workers from kitchen tables to factory floors. Just as surely as mechanized spinning jennies smoothly transformed wool into yarn, the quickly multiplying rows of the devices on factory floors in the decades on either side of 1800 transformed England's agricultural peasants into what Friedrich Engels called the proletariat, the working class. People flocked to urban centers, trading farm and artisan labor for wage labor and small, family-owned household farms for rented units in urban tenements, where home life was strictly separated from work. The historian E. P. Thompson puts it dramatically. The family, he writes, "was roughly torn apart each morning by the factory bell."[42] Dad went to work, leaving Mom behind to oversee a family whose importance had been hollowed out. No longer the site of economic productivity or industrious familial labor, the family was reduced to just two functions: raising children and creating a soft, loving, comfortable environment to do it in, a "haven in a heartless world."[43] Along the way, women lost the ability to contribute economically to their families, and the household power that comes with that contribution.[44]

The part about the mythical, genderless preindustrial history of work is contested, to say the least, as are accounts of precisely how and why changing labor conditions affected women and families. But the Industrial Revolution was undoubtedly a revolution in women's lives and roles. The historians Leonore Davidoff and Catherine Hall have shown that the variety of jobs British women held declined sharply between the late decades of the eighteenth century and the early nineteenth, roughly the same years the Industrial Revolution took to transform England. In the 1790s, women were listed in local directories as jailers, plumbers, butchers, farmers, tailors, and saddlers; by the 1850s, their options had been whittled down to teaching, dressmaking, and millinery—the art of making women's hats.[45]

At the same time, keeping women at home, away from wage labor, took on a kind of social importance. Many families in the working class could not afford to separate the feminized, private home from the masculine, public workplace. But families in the emerging middle class, neither aristocracy nor simply surviving, *could* make this distinction—or at least pull off pretending that they could. The labor of a household's wife and mother thus became the most visible line separating the new middle class from the working masses. More precisely, it was her *lack* of labor that separated them. "Gentlemen may employ their hours of business in almost any degrading occupation, and, if they but have the means of supporting a respectable establishment at home, may be gentlemen still," Sarah Stickney Ellis, one of Britain's primary authorities on domesticity, wrote in 1839. "While, if a lady but touch any article, no matter how delicate, in the way of trade, she loses caste, and ceases to be a lady." Whatever kind of work the man of the house did, however dirty or manual, the fact that his wife remained in the home meant, to them and others, that they were middle class.[46]

Across the pond and on the other end of the nineteenth century, it was this same desire to appear middle class—to *be* middle class, insofar as those are different things—that would end Ella Baker's mother's teaching career in favor of full-time motherhood. Writers described men "working" and "laboring," but women had "occupations," "culinary mysteries," and "duties." The only time a woman really "labored," if we want to get pedantic about it, was when she was physically pushing a new American into the world. After that, she labored no more. If a woman's highest calling was to be a mother, then carrying out motherhood's attendant duties should be anything but work.[47]

Women themselves, of course, were under no such illusions. Susan B. Anthony—the women's rights and suffrage activist who would later appear, with her angular features shown in profile and a coiled bun at the nape of her neck, as the first woman featured on US currency—famously never married and had no children. Anthony saw clearly that her lack of domestic workload was directly responsible for her political influence, allowing her to crisscross the United States to give speeches about women's voting rights to crowds of thousands. Elizabeth Cady Stanton, Anthony's close friend and political collaborator, was homebound with seven children and unable to take her place at the forefront of the suffrage movement—even as she remained one of its most luminous thinkers. "You see," Stanton wrote to Anthony in 1853, "while I am about the house, surrounded by my children, washing dishes, baking, sewing, etc., I can think up many points, but I cannot search books, for my hands as well as my brains would be necessary for that work."[48] Anthony regretted her friend's constraints, not least because Stanton, she said, was the pair's intellectual force. "She forged the thunderbolts," Anthony told a journalist after Stanton's death, "and I fired them."[49] Nineteenth-century feminists like Anthony saw clearly that the duty to perform domestic work, including motherhood, and the ability to perform intellectual, political, or professional work were more or less mutually exclusive. This, they suspected, was not an accident.[50]

Beginning in the 1880s, employers in the United States began instituting "marriage bars," policies that mandated women leave their jobs as soon as they married. A 1931 survey of companies in Kansas City and Philadelphia found that 61 percent of insurance businesses, 37 percent of publishing houses, and 35 percent of banking firms had strict policies against hiring married women. Forty-six percent of insurance companies, 34 percent of publishers, and 21 percent of banks would fire female employees after they walked down the aisle.[51] The liberal lawyer and future Supreme Court justice Louis D. Brandeis filed an amicus brief in support of these kinds of laws at the US Supreme Court in 1908. Because all women were "potential mothers," Brandeis wrote, they "cannot be allowed to unfit themselves for motherhood by excessive hours of work."[52] The Supreme Court agreed later that year, upholding an Oregon law that limited the number of hours women in commercial laundries could work in a day. "As healthy mothers are essential to vigorous offspring," the court reasoned, "the physical wellbeing of women becomes an object of public interest and care in order to preserve the strength and rigor of the race."[53]

With this SCOTUS stamp of approval, a cascade of laws limiting married women and mothers' workforce participation followed. In 1932, a federal policy mandated that if two government employees got married, one of them must leave their job. Two government incomes flowing to one household during the Great Depression, when so many were out of work, seemed unconscionable.[54] But there was more than economic fairness at stake. In Wisconsin, the state senate passed a resolution in 1935 raising "a serious moral question" about dual-income households. In such families, the senators worried, "the practice of birth control is encouraged and the selfishness that arises from the income of employment of husband and wife bids fair to break down civilization and a healthy atmosphere, disrupts the idea of making a home, and is the calling card for disintegration of family life."[55] In Massachusetts, laws allowed employers to strictly control the schedules of working women, and in many states women were barred from working night shifts entirely, limiting their ability to take jobs in twenty-four-hour workplaces like hospitals. Until the early 1970s, teachers were routinely fired from their jobs when they conceived their first child, and airline policies let pregnant flight attendants go and barred the hiring of mothers. The people passing marriage bars and protective laws in the nineteenth and twentieth centuries thought they were offering women an obvious choice: childless spinsterhood, they thought, was self-evidently worse than giving up a teaching job or leaving work as a typist, nurse, or government employee. But they miscalculated. Instead of forcing women out of the workforce to be mothers, they may have succeeded in doing exactly the opposite: forcing some women out of motherhood in order to work.[56]

Even after the Civil Rights Act of 1964 did away with many of these laws, after it became *legally* possible to have children and a career, combining work and motherhood still wasn't easy. In the early 1980s, one anthropologist argued that professional women existed in a limbo so strange they should be considered a "third sex": not men, because they had the potential to carry and birth children, but not women either, because they had careers. That anthropologist, Patricia McBroom, spent years observing these strange creatures in the high-rises, coffee shops, and bistros on New York's Wall Street and in San Francisco's Financial District. McBroom took notes on their dress ("navy blue suit, white blouse tied into a bow below the chin, low heeled shoes"), mannerisms ("aggressive rationality and clear work focus"), vocalizations ("ultra-low, powerful voice[s] pushing aggressively" whatever point they were trying to make), emotional state ("no matter the pain, [she] does not cry, does not show anger"), and, perhaps most of all, the alarming condition

of their reproductive capacities. "Nothing identifies a pattern
as maladaptive more quickly than a substantial decline in the
rate of reproduction," McBroom wrote. "When women can't
have children, something is wrong." The professional woman
was so ill-suited to the environment where she spent her days,
McBroom concluded, that she had all but lost her ability to reproduce. Sixty-one percent of female corporate executives in
Fortune 1000 companies in 1981 were childless, McBroom reported, compared to just 3 percent of their male counterparts.
The needle had moved little since 1913, when a survey of 880
prominent professional women found that three-quarters of
them had no children.[57]

The 1970s and 1980s ushered in tectonic shifts in American
society and culture, upending gender and workplace norms.
One of the most visible changes was the large-scale entrance of
American women into wage labor. By 1990, close to 60 percent
of women worked outside the home, a number that included both
women who needed to work for their family's economic survival
and women who wanted to work out of professional ambition or
intellectual interest.[58] According to the Bureau of Labor Statistics, in 2019 nearly two-thirds of "married-couple families with
children" both had jobs, at least in part because it is no longer
possible in much of the country to live a comfortable life on one
salary.[59] The breadwinner-homemaker model is a blip, remember. In the context of a history that features mothers making
economic contributions to their families far more often than it
does not, the problem isn't that motherhood is incompatible with
work. The problem is that the way we work today is increasingly
incompatible with motherhood. In the crunch between work and
family, income and children, everyone loses. Births in America
have been declining for decades, *and* the percentage of women in
the American workforce was 5 percent lower in 2014 than it was
in 1999.[60]

Across the world and throughout history, drought, inflation, economic decline, disease, and famine have been accompanied by declining births. It is tempting to chalk this correlation up to physiological factors. A malnourished woman is far less likely to conceive. Extreme stress can cause miscarriage, impotence, loss of libido. But we shouldn't be so quick to reduce humans to deprived versions of Pavlov's dogs: no bell, no drool; no food, money, or security, no babies. As much as a stressed body is less likely to be able to reproduce, a stressed person is also less likely to want to. Fertility doesn't just happen *to* people. Condom usage, abortions, and rates of childlessness exploded in the 1930s. The microgeneration of American women born between 1900 and 1910—who met Black Tuesday, the stock market crash that touched off the Great Depression, in the prime of their childbearing years—had the highest overall national rate of childlessness so far in American history: 20 percent.[61] One in three Black women born in those years would never become a mother.[62] The percentage of non-mothers peaked in the Great Depression. Given the financial implications of having children, there is an obvious explanation for why women remained childless during the Depression: they chose, or they had to choose, money and the ability to make it over having kids. Two decades later, fertility exploded during the baby boom, which also happened to coincide with the most generous social welfare programs in American history.[63]

The unkindest stereotype of a woman without children— shoulder padded and career obsessed, with diplomas hanging where family photos should be on her wall, with stacks of cash in the extra room where the crib should be—is, in its barest outlines, not wrong. Overall, American women without children are wealthier, more educated, and more professionally successful than mothers.[64] But this neat picture is a fun-house mirror version of the truth: to say that non-mothers are more educated and wealthier is to comment only on their *current* economic status. In one study of women without children, three-quarters said they came from poor or working-class backgrounds. Childlessness, they said, was responsible for their elevated economic status, not the other way around.[65] Like Ella Baker or Simone de Beauvoir, they chose demanding intellectual and political work over children. Like Helen Gurley Brown, they chose man-size salaries over the motherhood penalty. Like countless other women whose names we do and do not know, they chose economic survival or the promise of social mobility over becoming mothers. Not having children, writes the sociologist S. Philip Morgan, "is not a new strategy adopted only by educated women interested in careers" but a "time honored, normatively approved response to harsh economic conditions."[66] The demographer Dowell Myers is blunter. "The birth rate," he writes, "is a barometer of despair."[67]

The fact that it was hard for Patricia McBroom or Helen Gurley Brown to imagine someone as both mother and worker—the fact that it is hard to *be* both mother and worker—is one part biology: until science fiction becomes reality, every person walking this earth will have been incubated in a uterus and birthed in a way that requires considerable physical recovery. But it's another part historical: a two-century-old belief that women and motherhood belong at home and that work takes place elsewhere. And when children are pitted against income, many of us have no choice—or feel that we have no choice—but to make the economically rational call: to have fewer, or none at all.

Young women in America today have already seen two history-making recessions. Some are working multiple jobs to make ends meet; others are seeing their professional salaries swallowed nearly whole by city rents and student loan payments. The average cost of day care in the United States for one child

is roughly equivalent to the pretax income of someone working full-time at the federal minimum wage.[68] Across the income
spectrum, women take a larger wage penalty for having children
than men.[69] The distinction between women who needed to work
for economic survival and those who wanted to work out of professional ambition may have been clear in the past, but as college
graduates struggle financially and the middle class erodes, it's
collapsing. "The perceived price of having children has really increased since I first talked to women in the mid-1990s," Kathryn
Edin, a sociologist at Princeton University, has noted. Regardless of income level, Edin observes, "there's a recognition that a
career is part of a life course."[70]

It's been a century and a half since the first batch of laws designed to keep women out of the workforce to boost their fertility, and it's clear that they backfired. In western Europe today,
fertility is *higher* in countries with a higher percentage of women
in the labor force. "In the 1960s–70s advocates of traditional
family values claimed that the birthrate would be the first thing
to suffer from [efforts to achieve gender equality]," Anne Chemin, a journalist for the French newspaper *Le Monde*, observed.
"Fifty years on it seems they were mistaken: fertility in Europe
is higher in countries where women go out to work, lower in
those where they generally stay at home."

In European countries where women are expected to stay
home with their children—countries with more rigid family and
gender norms like Spain, Portugal, and Italy—they have fewer
of them, 1.3 or 1.4 on average. The higher fertility, higher labor
force participation countries—such as France and the Scandina-
vian countries, where women average around 1.8 children—tend
to have generous maternity leave policies, prenatal and postpartum support, free day care, and shorter workdays for nursing
mothers. "In France," demographer Laurent Toulemon has observed, where in recent years the state has poured resources into

nanny and nurse visits after birth, where there is high-quality and low-cost childcare, and where each parent can take up to three years of parental leave, "the package is more flexible."[71] In countries without such policies—in countries like ours—women see a starker choice between work and motherhood. Steffen Kröhnert, a researcher at the Institute for Population and Development in Berlin, puts things simply: "The question today is not if women will work. The question is if they will have children."[72]

CHAPTER 4

BECAUSE OF THE PLANET

"I AM TERRIBLY SADDENED BY THE FACT THAT THE MOST HUMANE thing for me to do is have no children at all." Stephanie Mills peered over the podium at the members of the Mills College class of 1969, newly minted graduates of a small women's college tucked into the green hillsides of Oakland, California. "But the piper is finally demanding payment." Mills's long dark hair was parted down the middle and thrown back over her shoulders as she leaned forward to deliver what has to be one of the least optimistic commencement addresses ever given. "As an ex-potential parent, I have asked myself what kind of world my children would grow up in. And the answer was, 'not very pretty, not very clean. Sad, in fact.' Because, you see, if the population continues to grow, the facilities to accommodate that population must grow, too. Thus we have more highways and fewer trees, more electricity and fewer undammed rivers, more cities and less clean air."[1] The speech got her headlines nationwide, and Mills became an overnight celebrity. The *New York Times* called it "perhaps the most anguished . . . of the year's crop of valedictory speeches."[2]

Stephanie Mills grew up in Phoenix, Arizona, a city whose population and geographic reach exploded during her lifetime, from just over one hundred thousand residents in seventeen square miles when she was born to more than half a million people in 250 square miles when she graduated from college.[3] People poured in from across the country, lured by the promise of the Sunbelt: three hundred sunny days each year, no snow to shovel, plenty of space, and dry, clean air. They came prepared to enjoy that weather, sinking in-ground pools in their backyards and planting green golf fairways, seemingly unconcerned with one basic geographic fact: Phoenix sits squarely in the Sonoran Desert, a forbidding landscape that covers a large swath of the American Southwest, northern Mexico, and Baja California. The city receives less than ten inches of rainfall per year, roughly a quarter of the national average. Some years, it's much less.[4] In July, temperatures regularly soar well above one hundred degrees Fahrenheit.

When she arrived at Mills College, Mills must have been awed by the sheer verdancy of the western face of the Oakland hills: ancient redwoods, lush forests, flowers so obscenely fragrant that the air itself smells sweet. Each summer day, the Golden Gate Bridge's reddish arches seem to hold back the foggy mixture of warm air and cold Pacific water gathering on its western side. By late afternoon the fog breaks free, tendrils and then giant puffs of it slipping under the bridge and across the bay and then creeping up the ripple of hills in Oakland and Berkeley, soaking everything—plants, people, the inside walls of poorly insulated midcentury homes—with a cold, muggy sheen. The coastal wetness of the East Bay masks one of the Bay Area's other climates: had Mills left her college dorm and driven east on Route 24 through the Caldecott Tunnel, she would have emerged on the

hills' eastern side to find a landscape that, in the summers anyway, is nearly as dry as the one she left in Phoenix. During the
rainy winter, plants thrive. Then they wither in the arid summer,
leaving by September a toasted landscape of dry shrubs ranging
from buttery yellow to dusty brown. Contra Costa County, on
the east side of the Caldecott, doubled in population in Mills's
lifetime, and by the 1960s houses dotted the forested hills in
what we now call the WUI, the wildland-urban interface.[5] Today
in the American West, the term WUI is used in one context:
fire. In 1991, a catastrophic blaze swept through the Oakland
hills, killing twenty-five people and destroying 2,800 homes.[6] In
the three decades since, thousands of homes in Northern California have been destroyed by fire, and a combination of drought,
climate change, and soaring real estate prices, which have con-
spired to encourage the construction of homes farther into the
WUI, augurs many more to come.

Oakland wasn't burning yet, but, standing on stage in 1969,
Mills saw a future when it would—and she worried that more
people would only make things worse. She wasn't alone. One year
earlier, a Stanford University biologist named Paul Ehrlich had
published *The Population Bomb*, a two-hundred-page treatise on
the dangers of overpopulation. Humans had already outstripped
the earth's carrying capacity, Ehrlich wrote, and if we did not
immediately check our numbers, famines, wars, mass death, and
the collapse of civilization loomed in the immediate future. A
yellow-highlighted, all-caps warning slashed across the first edition's cover: "WHILE YOU ARE READING THESE WORDS FOUR PEOPLE
WILL HAVE DIED FROM STARVATION, MOST OF THEM CHILDREN." "The
battle to feed all of humanity," reads the book's ominous opening line, "is over."[7] Despite its apocalyptic pessimism, *The Population Bomb* was one of the best-selling environmental books of the
1960s, bringing the threat of overpopulation—which only those
on the fringe edges of environmental movements had previously

dared to whisper about—to the masses. By 1971, after buying out twenty print runs of the paperback version, nearly half of Americans believed that population control would be necessary to maintain their current standard of living in the decades to come.[8]

Stephanie Mills was every bit what you'd expect a women's college graduate to be on the eve of the summer of love. She was known around campus for wearing a pair of earrings she'd fashioned out of IUDs.[9] She declared her future childlessness out of love for the planet and her fellow humans. But she was also a member of an unlikely cohort of feminists and environmentalists and economists and Republican and Democratic politicians who, for a brief moment in the late 1960s and early 1970s, all agreed on the unignorable urgency of one basic truth: we needed to make fewer babies. Humans have a long history of worrying about whether the earth's resources could support its population, and in this moment, those anxieties briefly aligned themselves with a wide range of other political goals, from ensuring continued economic prosperity and national security to protecting our air and water and increasing access to birth control and abortions for those who wanted them.

This alliance of strange bedfellows broke down quickly. Ronald Reagan's ideology of optimism about the American future and the rise of the religious Right made both apocalyptic thinking and birth control political nonstarters by the early 1980s. On the left, ethical conflicts arose with other liberal priorities like immigration (if the American population was a concern, did that mean immigration should be sharply restricted?), anti-imperialism (if global population was a concern, should the United States impose policies to limit births in the developing world, where fertility was often higher than at home?), and reproductive rights. Population control measures some environmentalists thought were necessary, like involuntary sterilization of women after their second child, sat uncomfortably alongside feminist demands that the government be less involved in their bedrooms and uteruses, not more. But in 1969, Stephanie Mills's IUD earrings and environmental concerns put her on the same page as President Richard Nixon, who told Congress later that summer that the "dramatically increasing rate of population growth" was among "the most serious challenges to human destiny in the last third of this century." Controlling population "is a must," Nixon told his advisors. "A top priority national policy."[10] The way to serve your country was not, as it long had been, to create more Americans. For this brief moment in time, it was restraint in having kids, for everyone's sake.

In contemplating "the kind of world [her] children would grow up in," Mills represented a new era of environmentally inspired reproductive angst. For centuries, thinkers and economists and activists had worried about the impact any given child would have on the planet, though their precise concerns shifted over time. In the eighteenth and nineteenth centuries, people were concerned about stretching the supply of natural resources; in the twentieth century, about contributing to pollution. Today, in the twenty-first, people cite the "carbon footprint" of babies and its contribution to human-caused climate change. Mills represented another, subtler shift in thinking about reproduction and the environment. She worried, as people had in the decades and centuries before her, about the impact her child would have on the planet, about the resources they would consume and the pollution they would create. But her graduation address focused less on the child's contribution to environmental damage and more on their experience of it, on the impact the planet—and the warming, burning, flooding, and loss of biodiversity that Mills already saw coming—would have on her child.

With the reality of climate change looming, the ethics of reproduction have gotten only more complicated in the last half century. The concern remains that having a child may make our environmental situation just that little bit worse. But we are also faced with the inescapable fact that the situation is already very, very bad—and bad in ways that will make our children's lives harder, quite possibly worse than our own. "The life of every child born today," a 2019 report published in the medical journal *The Lancet* concluded, "will be profoundly affected by climate change."[11] For two centuries, women have chosen, or felt they had to choose, not to have children for environmental reasons. Today, for many of us, that choice feels starker than ever.

Thomas Malthus was the sixth child of Henrietta and Daniel Malthus, raised in their middle-class household in Surrey, in the southeast corner of England. Daniel Malthus was a "gentleman," as one historian has described him, and a scholar: he went to Oxford and kept regular company with the intellectual luminaries of the day, men like David Hume and Jean-Jacques Rousseau.[12] Shortly after his eighteenth birthday in 1784, Thomas Malthus arrived at Jesus College at Cambridge University, where he planned to study math. Cambridge of the eighteenth century was still living in the shadow of its great alumnus of the seventeenth, Isaac Newton, and this meant that pure math, speculative math, was the most reliable route to academic success and prestige. But Malthus had spent too many childhood evenings overhearing Enlightenment ideas debated at the dinner table. Math was only worth doing, he thought, if it was done to better the condition of mankind. So, Malthus became known as a bit of an outlier in his cohort, "rather remark'd in College," as he wrote to his father, "for talking of what actually exists in nature, or may be put to real practical use."[13]

Malthus graduated from Cambridge and was ordained in the Church of England in 1789, the same year as the French

Revolution, which he vehemently opposed. He took a job as a curate, a sort of assistant priest, at the Okewood Chapel back home in Surrey. A university-educated priest of Malthus's day could easily retreat into obscurity in his home church, delivering indifferent, often recycled sermons on Sunday mornings to indifferent, often hungover parishioners. But his training in philosophy and mathematics set Malthus apart, as did his desire to be fully financially independent from his parents, who at that point still housed and fed him. Malthus labored on the writing project that would make his name for two years, working nights and weekends to figure out how math might help him understand the slow-moving catastrophe he saw happening before his eyes in Surrey.

The blast furnaces that fired the Industrial Revolution in London demanded lumber from somewhere, and the forests in Surrey had been all but clear-cut during Malthus's lifetime. Meanwhile, most of the region's residents—those who hadn't pulled up stakes and headed for factory jobs in the cities—were still subsistence farmers, growing crops to feed their families and barely keeping their heads above water.[14] Malthus looked nervously across the channel at a France that had been transformed—for the significantly worse, he believed—by a similar kind of desperation. A popular belief among political economists of his day was that the more people a nation had, the greater its economic output could be, and, in turn, the higher its standard of living.[15] But sitting in a Surrey made poorer by the Industrial Revolution, not richer, Malthus couldn't square these economic theories with "what actually exists in nature."

The problem, Malthus wrote in his 1798 book, *An Essay on the Principle of Population*, was, in so many words, that people really liked sex. If they *could* have more children—either because their bodies were nourished enough to be fertile, or because they were reasonably confident that their economic circumstances could support more—they would. In times of plenty, the number of new humans would increase faster than resources could support them, and demand for basics like food would outstrip supply until one of any number of crises knocked the population back to sustainable levels: war over resources, famine, or disease. Then another time of plenty and rising population, another crisis and population crash. This cycle would repeat again and again, Malthus argued, unless people took matters into their own hands, reducing births to a level their environment could comfortably sustain.

It was this ability to be rational about reproduction that Malthus believed set humans apart from other forms of life. "Plants and irrational animals . . . are impelled by a powerful instinct to the increase of their species; and this instinct is interrupted by no doubts about providing for their offspring." Even something as benign as fennel would take over the "face of the earth" if it were "vacant of other plants." Humans alone had the ability to counter their instincts with reason. Before having children, Malthus writes, a person can and therefore must look hard at the consequences. "Does he even feel secure that, should he have a large family, his utmost exertions can save them from rags, squalid poverty, and their consequent degradation in the community?" Should the answer be in the negative, Malthus, good clergyman that he was, prescribed celibacy and delayed marriage. He believed humans must rely on self-control—a rational mastering of bodily desires to serve the greater good—so there was no place in his thinking for contraception or abortion. Where self-control failed, government policy could step in, adding things like a minimum age requirement for marriage or asking a couple to prove their financial stability before issuing a license to wed. Denying themselves sex would make people miserable, Malthus allowed, but it was a lot less miserable than starving to death.[16]

Insofar as the goal of his *Essay* was financial independence from his parents, Malthus succeeded: the 1798 edition sold briskly enough that he expanded it for a second edition, which was reissued at least five times in the next quarter century. As for the goal of convincing people to have fewer babies, the score was less clear. Malthus's ideas didn't win him many friends. The Romantics, a movement of poets, artists, and thinkers who valued emotion over the cold rationality of the Enlightenment, directed a fair bit of that emotion into a passionate hatred of Malthus. The poet Samuel Taylor Coleridge, one of the founders of Britain's Romantic movement, was left spluttering. "I declare solemnly," Coleridge wrote, "that I do not believe all the heresies and sects and factions which the ignorance and the weakness and the wickedness of man have ever given birth to, were altogether so disgraceful to man as a Christian, a philosopher, a statesman, or citizen as this abominable tenet."[17] The "abominable tenet," of course, was the idea that people should have fewer children. The great Romantic poet Percy Shelley was more succinct. Malthus, he wrote, was "a eunuch and a tyrant."[18]

Malthus died in 1834, but that didn't stop mid-nineteenth-century Marxists from hating him too. Friedrich Engels called Malthusianism a "vile, infamous theory, [a] revolting blasphemy against nature and mankind," "a system of despair which struck down all those beautiful phrases about love thy neighbour and world citizenship."[19] Marx himself was less sentimental: Malthus was "an author of nonsense," "a miserable sinner against science," "the agent of the landed aristocracy," the "principle enemy of the people," and, perhaps worst of all, "superficial."[20] The Marxists had a point: even as he argued in scientific terms that a too-large population posed a threat to everyone, Malthus was primarily concerned with the number of children poor families were having. Supported in relative comfort by selling the argument that people should have fewer children, Malthus and his wife Harriet felt free to have three.

When Annie Besant founded the British Malthusian League in 1877, half a century after its namesake's death, she probably sent the good reverend rolling in his grave. At the time, Besant was at the center of a salacious courtroom battle that captivated the city of London and catapulted her from her previous role as a respected member of the public lecture circuit to a full-fledged celebrity and household name.[21] Earlier that year, Besant had arranged for the British publication of *The Fruits of Philosophy, or the Private Companion of Young Married People*, a wryly titled volume by the American doctor Charles Knowlton. In the book, Knowlton explained the mechanics of conception in frank terms, something many couples likely had to figure out from scratch on their wedding night, and illustrated his instructions with diagrams graphic enough to make even the most open-minded Victorian sweat. Knowlton also offered his reader various, if ill-advised, methods of birth control, like advising women to douche with caustic chemicals after intercourse. The final nail in the coffin—his, and Besant's, for having invited such blasphemy onto British shores—was his belief in the benefits of small families. Knowlton insisted that a couple could be truly happy only if they could limit their family size, or even choose to have no children at all.[22]

Besant and Knowlton were neo-Malthusians, members of a movement in the late nineteenth century that adopted some of Malthus's ideas and then expanded on them. Neo-Malthusians agreed with their namesake that everyone's quality of life depended on individuals limiting their reproduction. They agreed that demand for natural resources was rapidly outstripping supply. And they agreed that a less populated world would be a happier, wealthier, better-fed one. But neo-Malthusian beliefs differed from the original sort in a couple of critical ways. For one, they took issue with Malthus's diagnosis that poor people having too many children was the cause of their poverty or pressure on natural resources. Besant, Knowlton, and their political kindred lived after Marx. Poverty was caused by inequality at the level of society, they argued, not individual choices. But they pointed out that making contraception illegal for individuals to access, or even to talk about, wasn't exactly helping matters.[23] Neo-Malthusians had no patience with the reverend's self-denial: population, they believed, would be limited through contraception, not abstinence. They encouraged the use of birth control and the separation of lovemaking from baby making—and even from marriage altogether. Neo-Malthusians advocated "sexual freedom and parental prudence," a combination, they believed, that would not only improve people's lives but also result in fewer babies and lessen the demand for limited natural resources.[24]

Annie Besant had been born into an upper-middle-class family in London in 1847. Her mother was Irish Catholic and her father, an Englishman, had been educated in Dublin, and Besant and her siblings were raised on passionate dinner table arguments in favor of Irish home rule. At twenty, she married a clergyman named Frank Besant. Though they quickly had two children, Arthur and Mabel, she and Frank were "an ill-matched pair," Besant would later write. They fought over money: because married women couldn't own property or assets, Frank controlled the royalties from Besant's flourishing writing and speaking career. They fought over politics: Besant was increasingly concerned about the rights and lives of the urban poor, while Frank was far more worried about their souls and deaths. And they fought over religion: the church's role in abetting Britain's imperial conquests had shaken Besant's faith to the core. In 1873, Besant left Frank, took the children, and moved to London, where she became an in-demand public lecturer on everything from women's rights to poverty, imperialism, secularism, and the benefits of birth control.[25]

Just as it was under Comstock's law in the United States, contraception of all kinds, and talking about it, was illegal in Britain. Shortly after *The Fruits of Philosophy* appeared in print in Britain, Besant was arrested by the English Society for the Suppression of Vice—a quasi–law enforcement agency made up of religious leaders—and charged with obscenity. Unfortunately for British authorities, Besant's trial gave neo-Malthusianism the most powerful propaganda boost it had ever received: Britons eagerly swapped details about the case, discussing birth control on street corners, around dinner tables, and in pubs. Besant and her codefendant Charles Bradlaugh, an activist who would later become the first avowed atheist to serve in Parliament, each gave speeches in open court on what they called the "population question," making impassioned arguments about the benefits of contraception for women, urban dwellers, and members of the working class before their biggest audience yet. When the trial concluded, the genie was out of the bottle. Suppressing knowledge of vice in the first place is a lot easier than getting people to forget what they already know.[26]

Besant ultimately escaped jail time on a legal technicality, but the judge ruled that her atheism and advocacy for contraception access made her an unfit mother. He granted Frank full and permanent custody of their children.[27] Politically neutered by the courts and formally stripped of her role as a mother, Besant eventually found her way back to the cause that had so animated her parents: British imperial rule. She applied their arguments about Irish home rule to the British colonial project in India, and became a vocal and tireless advocate for Indian independence. Besant then became a theosophist in the 1890s, distancing herself from Marxist and feminist causes to join an esoteric religion founded in the United States but based on ideas drawn from Asian religions such as Hinduism and Buddhism. By the early years of the twentieth century, Besant was the leader of the global theosophist movement, president of the Indian Home Rule League, and—despite being a British national—an elected member of the Indian National Congress. When she died in 1933, her body was wrapped in silk and placed on a pyre at the mouth of the river Adyar in Madras, India. Hundreds of mourners knelt on the river's banks and prayed, chanting verses from the Bhagavad Gita, a Hindu scripture, as the smoke from her pyre drifted out to sea.[28]

By the time of her death, Besant had been reunited with her daughter, Mabel, who, after a brief stint as a Roman Catholic, became a theosophist herself. But Besant had missed more than a decade of her life. Today, a picture of Mabel hangs in Britain's National Portrait Gallery. In the photo, she is about eight years old and dressed in an elaborate pleated dress with two rows of military-style buttons. She stares straight into the camera. "Mabel Emily Besant," the inscription at the bottom of the photograph reads. "Deprived of her mother May 23, 1878 . . . on account of that mother's heresy."[29]

Credit for starting the modern environmentalist movement is usually given to another heretic of sorts: a marine biologist and National Book Award–winning author named Rachel Carson, who warned that Americans' unquestioned reverence for technology and progress was causing environmental harm. In her 1962 bestseller, *Silent Spring*, Carson presented such a compelling case about the dangers of the widely used pesticide DDT that it caught the attention of American politicians and the public alike. *Silent Spring* was the book that launched a thousand laws: after its publication, the use of DDT was banned in the United States, President Nixon created the Environmental Protection Agency in 1970, and the Clean Air Act, the Wilderness Act, the National Environmental Policy Act, the Clean Water Act, and the Endangered Species Act were signed, all within the decade.

In his office at Stanford University, Paul Ehrlich watched the success of *Silent Spring* closely. Ehrlich and others, like the

University of Chicago sociologist Donald Bogue, had spent the early 1960s warning about the impact of people on the environment in academic conference papers and journals. Bogue was the president of the Population Association of America, a nonprofit devoted to rigorous social science research on population and demography. The baby boom, Bogue would say, had already set catastrophic future events in motion. "When the demographic facts for the United States are assembled, they suggest that instead of smugly patting ourselves on the back for escaping the impact of the population explosion, we must realize that we are participants." If drastic action was not taken, the growing population in the United States threatened to send the country "crash[ing] on the Malthusian reefs."[30] Ehrlich agreed that people weren't freaking out like they should be. "I'm scared," he told *Look* magazine. "My world is being destroyed. I'm 37, and I'd kind of like to live to be 67 in a reasonably pleasant world, not to die in some kind of holocaust in the next decade."[31] The problem was, no one was listening.

Carson had a hard enough time convincing people of her argument that human-developed technologies like DDT could be harmful, that their reckless use was harming the environment. Ehrlich and Bogue's warnings were an even harder sell: people, they argued, didn't need a weapon like DDT to cause immense harm—*people themselves* were an existential threat to the natural world. Even Ehrlich admitted that he had been reluctant to see population as a problem, or limiting births as the solution. "I didn't stand up one day and say, 'My God, I'm going to get everybody to stop fucking.' It's sort of one thing led to another."[32] But once he got there, Ehrlich couldn't shake the belief that the growing population in the United States and around the world was the single most important issue facing both humans and nature.

The success of *Silent Spring* gave him an idea: Carson had demonstrated the power of a well-written book to convince people that unpopular policy changes were necessary. Maybe another well-written book could convince them to have fewer children.[33] Speaking to a gathering of Stanford faculty and alumni in 1965, Ehrlich encouraged his colleagues to "follow Rachel Carson's lead." Scientists, he said, urgently needed to "come out of our ivory towers" and figure out how to get the public to listen.[34] To make sure his book would appeal to nonacademic audiences, Ehrlich paid his twelve-year-old daughter $10 to read a draft of *The Population Bomb*, and then rewrote anything she didn't understand or thought was boring.[35] His unconventional editing method apparently worked: brought to press by an alliance of the Sierra Club and Ballantine Books, Ehrlich's middle-schooler-approved book sold out printing after printing, reportedly more than two million copies in all.[36]

On the cover of the first edition of *The Population Bomb*, a bright blue font above the title presents a stark choice: "Population control or race to oblivion?" In the bottom left, a cartoonish rendering of a bomb threatens to explode. "The population bomb," a caption reads, "keeps ticking." Once they made it past the warning-strewn cover, Ehrlich's readers were greeted with a barrage of bleak-sounding statistics: from the 1930s to the 1960s, the global population doubled, from two billion to four billion, and was likely to do so again in the generation to follow. Agricultural technology had improved, allowing us to produce more food than ever before, but did we really think we could increase our agricultural output indefinitely? Each year in the decade to come, Ehrlich predicted, ten million people would starve to death, most of them children and most of them in what he called "underdeveloped countries" in the global south. In developed nations of the global north, the symptoms of overpopulation wouldn't present as food shortages or mass starvation. There, they would manifest as environmental damage, often caused by our frantic attempts to meet ever-increasing resource needs.[37] In the long run, Ehrlich argued, no matter how small or slow, no matter the technology or resources a nation has to increase food production or limit damage to the environment, no rate of population increase is sustainable forever.

The strong-stomached readers who made it all the way to the back cover would find a tear-out coupon inviting them to join a newly formed organization called Zero Population Growth—a group whose name doesn't leave much mystery about its goals. Known as ZPG for short, the organization was founded by Charles Remington, an entomologist from Yale, and an attorney from New Haven named Richard Bowers. Remington and Bowers shared Ehrlich's belief that population growth was an existential threat and came up with bumper sticker–ready slogans—"Stop at Two," "Make Love, Not Babies," "Stop Heir Pollution"—to convince others of their position. They opened a Washington, DC, office so they'd have ready access to politicians, and quickly established themselves as a lobbying force to be reckoned with, throwing money and enthusiasm into opposing policies like child tax credits, which they saw as direct government sponsorship of population growth. In 1969, Zero Population Growth had all of one hundred members. But after *The Population Bomb* became a bestseller; after a massive oil spill off the coast of Santa Barbara spewed nearly one hundred thousand barrels onto Southern California beaches and killed birds, dolphins, sea lions, and other marine life; after Stephanie Mills's public vow of childlessness; and after the first official Earth Day in 1970, new members joined in a steady trickle, then in a flood. By the end of 1970, there were 150 chapters across the country with some twenty thousand members. At the organization's peak, there were four hundred chapters and thirty-five thousand members.[38]

Even as it grew, ZPG roiled with internal strife. They had to contend with people "who hopped on the ZPG bandwagon" for reasons that had nothing to do with the environment: "Some of them were racist—there's no doubt about it," the group's former national director remembered, and "some of them were restrictionist," hoping that growing concern about population would result in limits being placed on immigration. In the preceding half century, Malthusian ideas had gone through a bit of a rough patch, to say the least. The birth control pioneer Margaret Sanger, who had leaned on neo-Malthusian ideas early in her career—namely, the idea that allowing individuals to limit births through the use of contraception would improve the quality of life and the quantity of resources for all—went full eugenicist by the late 1920s. Sanger and others in the American eugenics movement believed that the problem was not the total number of births, but the number of *undesirable* births. Sanger argued that legalizing contraception and abortion would prevent "unfit" women from becoming mothers and believed that under some circumstances the government would be justified in mandating birth control for certain women, such as those who were poor or disabled. Sanger's birth control campaign was endorsed by the American Eugenics Society in 1933.

The Malthusian talking point that people needed more space and more resources to live their best lives also hadn't aged particularly well. One of the Nazis' primary justifications for invading territories to Germany's east and then ethnically cleansing those territories—removing and killing Jews and Roma, among others—was their supposed need for Lebensraum, or living space. Ethnic Germans, they claimed, needed more space to thrive.[39] The civil rights leader Julian Bond warned, "Without the proper perspective, *The Population Bomb* becomes a theoretical hammer in the hands of angry, frightened and powerful racists, as well as over the heads of black people, as the ultimate justification for genocide."[40]

At the national level, ZPG attempted to "keep the ghost of eugenics locked in the attic," as one scholar has put it.[41] The organization's national leaders recoiled when local offices took "crazy positions," like opposing all immigration, and issued guidelines that required chapters to make clear that such suggestions did not represent official ZPG policy.[42] Though he did not explicitly deal with the history of eugenics in *The Population Bomb*, by the end of 1970, Ehrlich was regularly acknowledging that the kind of population control ZPG advocated for—the kind they thought was necessary for everyone's well-being—had also been popular among supporters of Nazism, racism, and imperialism. Prior efforts to plan and control population, Ehrlich said in speeches and in articles, had often been part of a "white racist plot." At least a third of people who support population control, he estimated, "actually mean control [of] Blacks, or the poor, not the white or the affluent." Ehrlich stopped saying, as he had earlier in his career, that birth control was "color blind."[43]

ZPG leadership also leaned on the work of leading demographers of the day, who demonstrated that American population growth was driven not by lax immigration policies, urban poverty, or the fertility of women of color, but by the individual decisions of white, well-off, suburban families—the group that also happened to produce the most resource-intensive babies.[44] Despite being a "disarming little thing," a 1967 study found, a white, middle-class American child used an immense quantity of resources: in her lifetime, she would consume 26 million tons of water, 21,000 gallons of gasoline, 10,150 pounds of meat, 28,000 pounds of milk and cream, and 9,000 pounds of wheat.[45] It was white births and the consumerism of well-off white parents that drove population growth, ZPG's national leaders maintained—and it was those parents who were most responsible for the environmental harm that followed.

ZPG's critiques of the American family structure and its relationship to consumption made the organization a natural ally of those *other* great critics of the baby boom: feminists, especially the sort who believed that the ability to limit births or avoid them completely was key to women's liberation. For Ehrlich, it was his wife Anne who pushed him make this connection. Paul met Anne during his first year of graduate school at the University of Kansas, where Anne was an undergraduate French major. The two immediately bonded over their common interests: Anne shared Paul's concerns about population and how it stressed the natural environment. But Anne also brought her own feminist perspective to the relationship. Her grandmother had marched in suffragist protests, and both her mother and her aunt had professional careers, a rarity in 1940s and 1950s Des Moines, where she grew up. Anne had every intention to get a college degree and pursue a career of her own. She and Paul married in December 1954 and two months later Anne was pregnant, an outcome they'd neither planned nor particularly desired. Their daughter Lisa was born in November, and Anne dropped out of college to care for her, taking on a role she'd always hoped to avoid, that of a stay-at-home wife and mother. Anne never finished her degree, but over the years she slowly rebuilt her career: first illustrating Paul's biology PhD dissertation, then producing hundreds of scientifically correct drawings of insects for a 1961 book on butterflies, and finally as Paul's coauthor of numerous essays, books, and speeches about the dangers of population. The Ehrlichs never had another child. For a while, their finances wouldn't allow it, and then at some point, between their work on population and Anne's desire for an intellectually rewarding career, it stopped making sense.[46]

The Ehrlichs' accidental pregnancy and the impact it had on Anne's life may help explain why *The Population Bomb* is peppered with calls for increasing women's access to birth control. When they got married in 1954, *Griswold v. Connecticut*, the US Supreme Court case that allowed married couples access to birth control, was more than a decade in the future. When *The*

Population Bomb was published in 1968, you could still get arrested in states like Massachusetts for simply educating unmarried people about contraception. Abortion was illegal with no exceptions in more than half the country. These laws not only limited women's options, as the Ehrlichs knew from personal experience. They also contributed to a growing population. ZPG's leadership vocally advocated for reproductive rights, protesting laws in various states that prohibited women from choosing to be sterilized until they'd had a certain number of children. They sponsored buses to pack state capitols with supporters of abortion access. In 1970, the group's executive director, Shirley Radl, testified before the California legislature in Sacramento. "One of our major goals," she said, "is to provide the means for all members of society to voluntarily limit the size of their families. This means making all forms of birth control, including abortion, readily available." Radl paused, before adding a version of the argument that would ultimately prevail in *Roe v. Wade*: "The uterus should be the concern of the owner and not of the State."[47] It was an environmental activist named Garrett Hardin, not a feminist— and a man, not a woman—who came up with one of the most oft-repeated slogans of the pro-choice movement: "Abortion on demand."[48]

ZPG's focus was on lowering population numbers, not reordering gender roles or remaking the American family. But they were in full agreement with the women's movement that making motherhood synonymous with womanhood wasn't good for anyone: for women, who were taught their value came from their status as mothers; for the environment, which carried the weight of the children women had because they were supposed to; and for all of humanity, which has but one earth to share. "There is one movement on which I am a radical," said Roger Revelle, the founder of Harvard's Center for Population and Development Studies and one of the first scientists to warn that human actions were actively changing the climate, "the Women's Liberation movement."[49]

Just a month before the first Earth Day, in March 1970, the Sierra Club published an essay collection that featured a piece by Stephanie Mills, the newly famous spokesperson for environmental childlessness. In a society that held motherhood to be women's greatest possible accomplishment, Mills knew you could hand out birth control pills all day and the population would continue to grow. Women didn't just need contraception. They also needed other options. "Women's roles must be expanded to encompass much, much more," she wrote, "than the production of children."[50] In *The Population Bomb*, Ehrlich had made a similar argument, stressing the need to offer alternatives for the "satisfaction which many women derive from childbearing."[51] In 1970, he clarified that those alternatives meant "greater equality with men and [a] greater choice of life-styles. . . . A wide variety of professions should be thrown open to women immediately."[52] Anne Ehrlich put it less diplomatically in a letter to a colleague in 1969: "An amazing number of women have another baby because they have nothing else to do."[53]

"Whatever happened to environmental reasons for not having children?" my aunt asked me as we stood side by side along the railing of a restaurant deck at a family wedding in Colorado several years ago. As we talked, both of us gazed up at the Rocky Mountains, two midwesterners unable to tear our eyes away from their jagged outlines etched into the night sky. "That was the big thing with my feminist friends when I was younger." My aunt never had children of her own, though she is a stepmother to two of my cousins and a grandmother. I didn't ask her if her reasons had anything to do with rising population, rising pollution levels, rising temperatures, or rising seas, or if she just wanted to do other things. The latter is entirely possible: she is a talented gardener and cook, a skilled furniture restorer and interior decorator, and enjoys music, art, and life in a way I aspire to. At the time, I didn't know why the allegiance between environmentalists and feminists over the ethics of having children broke down. It's a testament to how completely it had fallen apart that I didn't even know there had been one in the first place.

The answer to my aunt's question, it turns out, is that the forces that brought together feminists, environmentalists, economists, and politicians on the left and right started pulling them in separate directions as the 1970s unfolded. For one thing, the urgency of overpopulation was a much harder sell by 1973, when the number of births per American woman dipped below two for the first time and continued to fall. "Stop at Two" bumper stickers started to seem kind of unnecessary, since pretty much everyone already did.[54] More alarmingly, though, prominent experiments with population control around the world had taken on a distinctly authoritarian flavor. In 1965, President Lyndon Johnson refused to send food aid to India— then teetering on the edge of a major famine—until the government agreed to offer incentives for women to be sterilized. Under pressure from Western countries, and with a check from the World Bank for $66 million, Indira Gandhi's India carried out the largest sterilization campaign the world has ever seen. The government used both carrots and sticks: everything from cash payments to denial of medical care, electricity, government documents, and pay raises until communities met their sterilization quotas. In 1977 alone, more than eight million Indian women were sterilized—most of them rural, poor, and lower caste.[55] In 1980, China instituted its one-child rule and used sterilization, mandatory contraception and abortion, and fines to ensure compliance.[56]

After spending more than a decade demanding privacy, autonomy, and control over their bedrooms and reproductive organs, many feminists bristled when environmentalists started flirting with—and in some cases, wholeheartedly endorsing—coercive measures to bring down population. ZPG activists suggested everything from licensing childbirth, to requiring women to abort any pregnancy after their second, to adding sterility-causing drugs to the public water supply.[57] "No longer can we consider procreation as an individual and private matter," declared Walter E. Howard, a prominent ecologist and environmentalist from the University of California, Davis. "Intercourse, yes, but not unregulated numbers of conceptions, since they affect the welfare of all other individuals living at that time plus those to be born in the future."[58] By the mid-1970s, feminists were loudly pointing out that "population control," even for environmentally sound reasons, was starting to look like a fancy rebranding of good old-fashioned government control over women's bodies.[59]

Finally, environmental movements for population control never did fully succeed in keeping the ghosts of eugenics chained in the attic. Garrett Hardin, the environmental activist who coined the term "abortion on demand," was a white nationalist: the dozens of books and articles Hardin wrote about population control for environmental reasons are explicitly and proudly racist and ethno-nationalist, concerned not just about the number of Americans but also about their skin color, cultural background, and what language they speak.[60] For many on the political left, framing environmental concerns in terms of population became increasingly untenable. Even Stephanie Mills ultimately backed away from environmental reasons to not have children. When she was asked to give a speech on the dangers of overpopulation in 1974, Mills refused. Her decision not to have children was, she said, "a personal matter, not a population or ecology thing."[61]

Between the 1970s and our present, the driving concerns of the environmental movement have shifted decisively, away from pollution and starvation and toward melting ice caps, rising seas, and burning forests; away from Malthusian-adjacent concerns about population and resource scarcity and toward modern climate science, which shows that human actions—specifically, our carbon emissions—are making our planet less habitable for human life. Scientific proof that humans are damaging the environment is hardly new. In 1965, Roger Revelle—the scientist who considered himself a "radical" in the women's liberation movement—was asked by President Lyndon Johnson's administration to study the potential of human-caused carbon dioxide emissions to warm the planet. "By the year 2000 there will be about 25% more CO_2 in our atmosphere than at present," Revelle concluded, and "this will modify the heat balance of the atmosphere to such an extent that marked changes in climate . . . could occur."[62] The facts were even clearer by the late 1980s, when James Hansen, then the director of NASA's Goddard Institute for Space Studies, testified before Congress that global warming "is already happening now." At the end of the hearing, Senator Timothy E. Wirth, a Democrat from Colorado, observed that Hansen's testimony was a moral challenge for lawmakers. "The Congress must begin to consider how we are going to slow or halt that warming trend," Wirth said, "and how we are going to cope with the changes that may already be inevitable."[63] George H. W. Bush campaigned on climate policy and, as president, made the United States a signatory to the 1992 United Nations Framework Convention on Climate Change.

Even so, climate change still seemed like a problem for the future, one that perhaps needed to be dealt with, but much later. In 1997, when the Clinton administration needed congressional support for binding emissions targets in the Kyoto Protocol—an expansion of the UN Framework Convention that President

Bush's administration had signed—lawmakers balked.[64] Did science about what might happen in the future, they wondered, really warrant action that would definitely hurt business interests today? Meanwhile, oil companies funded a massive, decades-long public relations campaign of climate denial, which sought to make climate concerns sound stupid, paranoid, and wrong.[65]

Despite their best efforts, by the 2010s, the realities of climate change had become nearly impossible to ignore. In the face of record-breaking droughts, heat waves, wildfires, and floods, environmental activism exploded once again. In 2013, tens of thousands of protestors marched in Washington, DC, demanding the Obama administration shut down the Keystone XL pipeline, an oil pipeline system that would have run Canadian crude across the Great Plains, from Alberta to refineries in Illinois and Texas. Bill McKibben, founder of the environmental organization 350.org, described it as "the biggest climate rally by far, by far, by far, in U.S. history."[66] But in spite of, or perhaps because of, this renewed energy for environmental causes, many young people have been left wondering if it is already too late—in particular, if it is too late to have children. A recent global survey of ten thousand young people between the ages of sixteen and twenty-five found that four in ten fear having children because of climate change.[67] For many, Malthus's points about resource scarcity and the environmental damage caused by large populations remain valid, but the driving concerns have shifted in the two centuries since he published his *Essay*. For women from Stephanie Mills in 1969 to my aunt's feminist friends in the 1980s to many young people today, the point was and is less about the environmental impact of any individual child, and more about the collective experience children will have of living and surviving in the world they'll be given. Even if we could figure out how to have "carbon neutral babies," as the writer Meehan Crist put it recently, they would have to live in a carbon-choked world.[68]

The need for potential parents to consider the ability of their child to survive in the world they must live in is not new, of course, nor is it unique to our particular moment or our particular crisis. The lives of the Ayoreo, an Indigenous people from the Gran Chaco, a region on the border between Paraguay and Bolivia, were torn apart when those two nations went to war in 1932. More than a hundred thousand soldiers streamed into the region, bringing weapons and disease. A team of ethnographers interviewed women in one village and found that nearly every Ayoreo mother admitted to infanticide during the war and its aftermath; ultimately, the researchers estimated that nearly 40 percent of births in those years ended in the mother killing her newborn. Ayoreo people value and love children and consider infanticide to be a grave crime. But in an emergency, the survival of the community had to take priority, and more people directly threatened their ability to survive.[69] When Mormon settlers moved into Southern Paiute territory in Utah in the 1850s, bringing diseases that killed more than 90 percent of people in some Paiute settlements, births also plummeted. "My people have been unhappy for so long," a Paiute woman wrote in 1883, after decades of war, death, and loss, "they wish to *disincrease*, rather than multiply."[70] While climate change may feel novel—and while it is unique in its specifics—people from marginalized communities have grappled with these questions before. "In the face of slavery, Jim Crow, lynchings and racism, Black people of the not too distant past trembled for every baby born into that world," Mary Annaïse Heglar wrote recently. "Sound familiar?"[71]

Reproduction is what economists call "pro-cyclical," which means that humans don't breed well in crisis.[72] The anthropologist Sarah Blaffer Hrdy has observed that mothers of all kinds, human and otherwise, make choices about how many children they will raise and when, based on the ecological and historical circumstances they find themselves in. Primates have been seen to abandon babies born in moments of food shortages or environmental distress, the pressure to survive in their given habitat overriding any reproductive instinct or maternal bond.[73] The assumption that your children will be okay, the ability to trust in the future that awaits them, is an innovation of the modern world, and even here it has only ever been the domain of the privileged. "If you're running for your life," Richard Evans, an economist who has studied how perceived danger affects reproduction, told the *New York Times*, "you're not making babies."[74]

In recent years, figures on both ends of the American political spectrum have brushed off the idea of childlessness for environmental reasons as absurd, defeatist, even dangerous. When New York representative Alexandra Ocasio Cortez mused in a 2019 Instagram video that the dire predictions of climate science were leading young people "to have a legitimate question: Is it okay to still have children?" Fox News hosts accused her of advocating for a "no-child policy" or even "civilizational suicide."[75] The *New York Times* has sponsored a cottage industry of think pieces and opinion columns by liberal-leaning writers, which generally acknowledge the reality of climate change and then dismiss concerns about the future of the environment in favor of the "hope" children offer. "The world might well be a terrible place," the British philosopher Tom Whyman wrote in the *Times* in the spring of 2021. "But by having a child, you are introducing something new into it." Perhaps by doing so, he continued, "things really could, conceivably, get better."[76] Weighing legitimate concerns about the future against the joy and wonder new lives can bring into the present is one of the most ethically complicated calculations we as potential parents—we as humans—could ever be asked to do. But delaying or avoiding childbearing out of environmental concerns—whether they are framed in terms of natural resources, pollution, or the climate—is neither absurd, historically speaking, nor particularly novel. We're not the first to be faced with a future that scares us, and we would be far from the first to respond by making fewer people to live in it. For more than two centuries, from Thomas Malthus to Paul Ehrlich and Stephanie Mills to four in ten young adults today, people have been thinking about the environmental impact their children will have *and* the impact a degraded environment will have on their children—and for more than two centuries they have been making perhaps the hardest call of all: to not have them.

CHAPTER 5

BECAUSE WE CAN'T

IN APRIL 2014, A WOMAN NAMED BRIGITTE ADAMS APPEARED ON the cover of *Bloomberg Businessweek*. Her blond, shoulder-length hair was parted neatly on the side, and her long-sleeved black sheath dress and sensible-but-designer heels unmistakably labeled her a businesswoman, and probably a good one. Adams went to Vassar College, an elite institution in New York's Hudson Valley. She spoke Italian fluently. She had more than a decade of experience in marketing for high-profile technology companies. And she'd spent $19,000 out of pocket to freeze her eggs. "Freeze Your Eggs, Free Your Career," read the headline on the magazine's cover. "A new fertility procedure gives women more choices in the quest to have it all." In addition to Adams, the article featured a Manhattan doctor, a Los Angeles lawyer, a Wall Street investment banker, and an author, all of them frustrated about having to worry about fertility on top of their demanding jobs. "I just wanted to take the pressure off," said Suzanne LaJoie, the doctor. "Men don't have a biological clock, and

I felt like it leveled the playing field a bit." Emily, the investment banker, told *Bloomberg* that she had spent "more than a car but less than a house" to freeze her eggs, and that she found the experience "empowering." Her mom was less impressed. "She told me," Emily said, "only half-jokingly, 'I'm glad you went to business school and work 100 hours a week—and don't have time to meet anyone—so you can afford to freeze your eggs.' Thanks, Mom." But for the members of the "egg freezing generation," as the *Bloomberg* writer calls them, the cost-benefit analysis made sense. "By freezing [your eggs]," one of the women featured in the article said, "you're walking taller; your head is held higher. And that can pay off both in your work and your romantic lives."

Adams made the decision to freeze her eggs after getting a divorce in her late thirties. Turning thirty-nine was "desperation level," she remembered: it felt like now or never to do something about having kids. Egg freezing, she thought, would buy her valuable time. Adams remembered later that the procedure gave her a wonderful sense of freedom: suddenly unchained from the biological clock, she could focus on her career for a few more years, find the right guy to marry, and still end up with the big family she'd always wanted. "It's not a sure thing," Adams acknowledged, "but it's a gamble I'm willing to take."[1] As one journalist put it later, Adams's cover photo on *Bloomberg* made her "the poster child for freezing your eggs."[2]

When it emerged in the late 1970s, in vitro fertilization, IVF for short, was nothing short of a revolution for women struggling with infertility. *In vitro* is Latin for "in glass," a reference to the still kind of mind-boggling fact that scientists have figured out how to make conception take place in a glass petri dish on a laboratory table. Before the first IVF baby was born in the United Kingdom in 1978, every human ever born was conceived *in vivo*, in a living human body. Once it was proved possible to do it in glass, the IVF industry exploded. "IVF is big business," a headline in the journal of the American Academy of Pediatrics observed, a little ominously, in 1994. The article warned that in any area of medicine that becomes profitable, "entrepreneurs enter the field and find that to finance expansion and satisfy investors, they must fight for more patients and make more money on each one."[3]

These words have turned out to be prophetic. Since the early aughts, egg freezing has spurred precisely that kind of entrepreneurship, attracting investors, venture capital, and clinics, 97 percent of which offered cryopreservation by 2018. Egg freezing turns someone who wouldn't be a fertility clinic client in the present (because they are not ready to have children) or the future (because they may be able to conceive without assistance when they are ready, or may choose not to have children after all) into both. As Adams learned, the initial retrieval is expensive, and storing frozen eggs can run more than $1,000 each year. And of course, the existence of frozen eggs opens the possibility of paying for even more expensive procedures to use them. One group of economists has called this the fertility industry's "speculative turn": clinics can not only offer expensive solutions to infertility in the present, but they also allow women to purchase solutions to infertility in the future.[4] Globally, fertility treatments—from IVF to egg freezing, egg and sperm donation, and surrogacy—have become a multibillion-dollar industry, in part because the pull of the nuclear, biological family is so strong, as is the history that tells us what is normal, natural, and what makes a family.

Adams's status as the egg-freezing poster child was short-lived. Just shy of her forty-fifth birthday, Adams decided to use her eggs. She hadn't found a partner yet, but she was confident enough in her career to pursue motherhood on her own with a sperm donor. That's where things started to go wrong: of the eleven eggs she'd frozen, two didn't survive the thawing process, three more failed to fertilize, and five, the clinic told her, had yielded embryos that were genetically "abnormal." The final one, a normal, fertilized embryo, was transferred to her uterus but failed to implant. Adams told a journalist that she screamed "like a wild animal" when she got the news that she wasn't pregnant and that she would likely never carry a biological child. She threw her laptop at the wall and collapsed on the ground. "It was one of the worst days of my life. There were so many emotions. I was sad. I was angry. I was ashamed," she said. "I questioned, 'Why me?' 'What did I do wrong?'"[5]

In the midst of her pain and grief, Adams's first thought—as it is for so many women who have found themselves in her shoes—was to blame herself. Infertility is often framed by the media and in popular imagination as a "yuppie disease," an illness unleashed by women's own choices or by women's liberation more generally. Its sufferer is imagined as a woman who spent her twenties and thirties chasing other priorities, all of them misguided—education, professional success, savings account and 401(k) balances—and/or having too much fun to settle down and find a man to make babies with. Then, when she finally realizes that she'd like children after all, she finds, to her dismay, that her biological clock has struck its last hour. The fact that the average in vitro fertilization patient *is* actually the stereotypical yuppie—white (85.5 percent), wealthier than average (two-thirds have a household income of more than $100,000 per year), highly educated (72 percent have a college degree, almost twice the proportion of the population that has one), and well into her thirties—doesn't do much to counter the belief that women who can't conceive are the cause of their own grief.[6] Even observers sympathetic to the anguish infertility causes have drawn a direct line between workforce participation, delayed motherhood, and unintentional childlessness. "Infertility," writes the sociologist Margarete J. Sandelowski, "was the unexpected fallout of the women's revolution."[7]

The truth, of course, is that infertility is far older than the feminist movements of the late twentieth century. Three of the four matriarchs in the book of Genesis—Sarah, Rebekah, and Rachel—struggled for years to conceive. The first words we hear Rachel speak are a demand to her husband, Jacob: "Give me children, or I shall die."[8] The first thing we are told about Sarah, immediately upon meeting her, is that she is unable to have children.[9] Hannah, in 1 Samuel, is tormented by her inability to bear children with her husband, Elkanah. "Hannah, why do you weep?" Elkanah asks his inconsolable wife. "Why do you not eat? Why is your heart sad? Am I not more to you than ten sons?" Desperate, Hannah goes with Elkanah on his annual pilgrimage to the holy site of Shiloh, where she prays fervently for children. A priest sees her talking to herself and accuses her of drunkenness. "How long will you make a drunken spectacle of yourself?" the priest demands. "Put away your wine." "No, my lord," Hannah replies. "I am a woman deeply troubled; I have drunk neither wine nor strong drink, but I have been pouring out my soul before the Lord."[10] Fortunately, God can see that Hannah isn't drunk. She and Elkanah return to their guestroom, where they know each other in the biblical sense. This time, she conceives a son, whom she names Samuel because, she says, "I have asked him of the Lord." As soon as the child is weaned, Hannah carries Samuel back to Shiloh, pulling a three-year-old bull laden with flour and wine behind her. There, she slaughters the bull, hands her son to a priest, and turns toward home. "For this child I prayed; and the Lord has granted me the petition that I made to him," Hannah says. "Then," the biblical narrator tells us, "she left him there for the Lord."[11]

"*That* experiment in parenthood went well," a present-day reader might quip sarcastically. "Return to sender." But when the Puritan minister Benjamin Wadsworth recounted this story to the women of Boston in 1712, he had a different lesson: God decides whether to open your womb. Fertility or infertility was, simply, God's will.[12] For some, the knowledge that God thought them unworthy of motherhood brought them unimaginable anguish. Sally Bliss, a nineteenth-century woman in Worcester, Massachusetts, was racked with despair after eight married but childless years. After attending the funeral of a man who slit his own throat, she wrote in her diary, "I do not know how soon I may be left to do the same."[13] But for others, this explanation may have offered some sense of peace: there was nothing they could do, after all, if God had already made the call.

Infertility is a strange thing, medically and historically. The CDC defines infertility as an opposite-sex couple's failure to conceive after a year of regular unprotected sex.[14] For some, this is an existential crisis, a genuine tragedy and medical condition worthy of aggressive, often expensive, invasive, and painful treatment. For others, avoiding pregnancy after a year of unprotected heterosexual sex is extraordinarily good luck. Infertility, then, may be the only medical condition that is a medical condition only if the person who has it thinks it is. It is also a medical condition whose diagnosis has long been contingent on the specific context of a person's life. The sociologist Sally Macintyre has pointed out that there are "two visions of reality" for women. For unmarried women, "pregnancy and childbearing are abnormal and undesirable and conversely the desire to have a baby is aberrant, selfish, and in need of explanation." For married women, the opposite has long been true: "Pregnancy and childbearing are normal and desirable, and conversely a desire not to have children"—and, I would add, the simple fact of not having them—"is aberrant and in need of explanation."[15] For much of American history, a married woman and an unmarried woman could have had precisely the same physiological issue—be it blocked fallopian tubes, or low egg count, or anovulation—but only one of them would have been considered infertile or in need of medical—or, at some points in history, divine—intervention.

And, for much of American history, the intervention that was available, whether from God or from science, wasn't particularly effective. An American woman in the eighteenth or early nineteenth century who was unable to conceive would have been called barren, like a field where nothing would grow. She may have prayed; she may have fasted; she may have sought penance through good works, trying to convince God, as Hannah had done at the temple in Shiloh, that she was worthy of motherhood. Quietly, because suspicions of witchcraft survived well into the eighteenth century, a woman who had not conceived children may have consulted a midwife or other women in her community for herbal cures to supplement the divine ones. She might have been counseled by a doctor on diet or exercise, or have been advised to have less, and better, sex with her husband. Quality, doctors of this era believed, was to be preferred over quantity. "Women," the popular sex and pregnancy manual *Aristotle's Masterpiece* instructed husbands, "rather choose to have a thing done well, than have it often. And in this Case, to do it well and often too is inconsistent." The earliest doctors working on barrenness, as they would have called it, in Europe and the American colonies almost universally believed that sexual pleasure of both parties was necessary for conception. It was obvious enough to everyone that a man needed to orgasm to produce semen, so—before anyone understood the mechanics of ovulation terribly well—it seemed only logical that an orgasm was also required for women to produce seed of their own. In order to conceive, the British doctor John Marten wrote in 1708, "the womb must be in a state of delight."[16]

In 1781, a questionably credentialed Scotsman named James Graham took this line of thinking about as far as anyone possibly could. Graham was a Scottish doctor, or at least he claimed to be. He studied medicine at the University of Edinburgh in the mid-eighteenth century, though historians can find no evidence that he actually graduated.[17] He practiced medicine and dabbled in the occult in the American colonies before the revolution, where he also became fascinated by Benjamin Franklin's work with electricity.[18] He returned to London as the revolution heated up and set up a thriving infertility practice on London's fashionable Pall Mall, just down the block from Trafalgar Square. He called his clinic the Temple of Prolific Hymen. For the exorbitant price of £50, wealthy London couples who longed for children could overnight in the temple and experience Graham's pièce de résistance, the "medico, magnetico, musico, electrical" wonder that he called the "Celestial Bed." Graham invited his clients into a luxurious room, sumptuously but tastefully decorated with art, busts of Hippocrates and Cupid, shimmering glass mirrors, and colorful lamps. The finest perfume wafted on the air, and a huge silver and crystal chandelier glittered from the ceiling, burning beeswax candles of the highest quality. In the center of the room, the vibrating bed was surrounded by 1,500 pounds of magnets, which were thought to increase sexual attraction. Conception was guaranteed, he told his clients.[19] The "superior ecstasy which the parties enjoy in the Celestial Bed [is] really astonishing," Graham promised. "The barren certainly must become fruitful when they are so powerfully agitated in the delights of love."[20] "I am . . . not only a doctor of medicine," Graham liked to say, "but a physician of the soul."[21]

In the 1840s, an actual doctor of medicine tried a different cure: information. Dr. Frederick Hollick became famous for carting around anatomically correct, French-made papier-mâché dolls on his wildly popular lecture tours around the United States. Hollick and his dolls gave twenty-six speeches in Philadelphia in five years in the 1840s, in addition to talks in Baltimore, Washington, DC, Saint Louis, Cincinnati, Louisville, Pittsburgh, Hartford, and various places in Massachusetts. He even gave an impromptu talk on a steamboat bound for New Orleans, at the request of the passengers. Hollick's talks covered topics well outside the Victorian comfort zone, like female orgasms, menstrual cycles, the process of conception, and the basics of female anatomy. For the women who packed into each of his lectures, this was a new experience. "Many," one newspaper reported, "have fainted away at first view of Hollick's manikins."[22] In 1860, the doctor published *The Marriage Guide, or Natural History of Generation*, which described in frank, nonmedical terms what goes where, so to speak. Hollick thought couples could radically increase their chances of conception if they simply understood how it worked. But even he acknowledged that the information cure could go only so far. When couples were putting everything in the right places and still not conceiving, Hollick didn't have much more to tell them. "Physicians, generally speaking," he conceded, "know little to nothing about such matters."[23] Until the late nineteenth century, aside from prayer, vibrating beds, and reviewing basic mechanics, doctors couldn't offer much to women who struggled to conceive. "It is a mistaken idea that nature has intended that all women should be mothers," one medical textbook explained. "Some may have original imperfections in the uterine system, which cannot be remedied by any operation of art, and which remain often concealed till after death."[24]

Treatments for infertility took a small, though ethically dubious, step forward in 1885, when a wealthy merchant walked into Philadelphia's Sansom Street Hospital for an appointment with Dr. William Pancoast, then one of the city's most respected and prominent physicians. Pancoast belonged to a new generation of medical men, doctors who were beginning to toy with the tantalizing notion that they might have the tools to fix women's bodies after all. The merchant had a simple question: "Why," he asked the doctor, "is my home childless?" From the merchant's perspective, there was no obvious explanation. His wife was ten years younger than him, "a product of one of the old Quaker families of wealth and distinction" in Pennsylvania, and "the perfect picture of health," a woman whom men of both God and medicine might have deemed worthy of motherhood. Intrigued, Pancoast invited the merchant's wife into his examination room, where she lay down on a table at its center, surrounded by the doctor's senior medical students. Victorian prudishness was cast aside in the name of scientific inquiry, and the men performed a thorough examination of her reproductive system. They found she was free of any physical maladies that nineteenth-century doctors thought might cause sterility: her cervix was neither scarred nor inflamed nor too tight or too loose, her ovaries free of lesions, her uterus rightly positioned and of normal size.

Flummoxed, Pancoast took a relatively unusual step: he turned his attention to the merchant. Most American doctors of the mid-nineteenth century believed that as long as a man was not impotent, he could not be the cause of a couple's conception woes. The merchant was also in good health, the doctor found, from a good family, and had never been seriously ill in his life. The only exception was "a slight attack of gonorrhea" in the merchant's youth, an unfortunate result of his time "sowing the proverbial 'wild oats.'" A light bulb went off, and Pancoast took another unconventional step: asking for a semen sample. Pancoast slid a sample of the merchant's semen under the microscope, looking for the tiny, wriggling tadpoles that are the male contribution to the act of conception. He found none—sterility, we now know, can be a consequence of untreated gonorrhea. The merchant, he concluded, was entirely "void of spermatozoons."

The problem now clear, Pancoast and his medical students puzzled over how to help. Finally, one made a bawdy joke: "The only solution to this problem is to call in the hired man!" As his students laughed, the outlines of a miracle cure formed in

Pancoast's head. He called the merchant's wife in again and told her he needed an additional, and more invasive, examination. He chloroformed her, and then grabbed a rubber syringe and his most attractive medical student. Nine months later, the merchant's wife delivered a healthy baby boy. The couple was delighted, but Pancoast, I suppose to his credit, was racked with guilt over the deception. Shortly after the child's birth, the doctor sought out the new father and confessed to the whole thing. The merchant—far from being upset to learn of his son's questionable parentage—broke out into amused laughter. He would keep Pancoast's secret, he said, provided the doctor never breathed a word to his wife. Pancoast agreed and swore his six medical students to absolute secrecy. For a while, all was well: the merchant and his wife were happy, and the child grew up to be a successful New York businessman.

"Three people can keep a secret," Benjamin Franklin famously wrote, "if two of them are dead." William Pancoast died in 1897, but his six medical students and the secret—a major ethical breach, or a major medical breakthrough, depending on whom you asked—lived on. Dr. A. D. Hard broke first. In 1909, Hard penned a two-page letter to the editor of the journal the *Medical World*, with the eye-popping headline "Artificial Impregnation." He dropped his bombshell in the first line: "It has been twenty-five years since Professor Pancoast performed the first artificial impregnation of a woman." The article described the case in detail: the physical examination, the "slight attack" of gonorrhea, the chloroform, the plot with "the hired man."[25]

Hard's article sent the medical community into uproar, and *not* because it represented a medical breakthrough. "The first artificial insemination," the bioethicist Elizabeth Yuko has written, "was an ethical nightmare."[26] "It would have been a thousand-fold more honorable had your professor seduced that woman while conscious," stormed a Dr. C. L. Egbert in a letter published in the June 1909 issue of the *Medical World*. "Or, if you please, just as honorable had he had intercourse with her while unconscious." Egbert suggested Dr. Hard read "the laws of God Almighty, my dear brother; in that you will find good and sufficient on the subject of false intercourse."[27] Others were more concerned with the broader implications of the procedure than they were with the procedure itself. Artificial insemination broke the sacred bonds of marriage, some letter writers worried. A doctor, others warned, should take care not to confuse himself with God.[28]

In a follow-up letter published in the *Medical World*, Hard conceded that future procedures should, ideally, be conducted with the woman's written consent. But what a woman wanted came second, he argued, to the real stakeholder: society. The merchant and his wife—who were, in Hard's mind, racially and economically the sort of Americans it was desirable to have more of—did not have children, and after the procedure they had a professionally successful, upstanding son. "I have shaken hands with him within the past year," Hard added, in case anyone doubted him. Society, Hard believed, could only benefit from more married, well-off white women like the merchant's wife becoming mothers. Surely such an outcome was worth keeping some unsavory secrets and putting a few dings on the sanctity of marriage. Once Americans got over their squeamishness and sentimentality, Hard argued, "artificial insemination by carefully selected seed will become recognized as a race-uplifting procedure."[29]

By the first decades of the twentieth century, there were plenty of people who thought "the race" desperately needed uplifting. It was more or less taken for granted that white, US-born, Protestant women were significantly less healthy than their grandmothers had been.[30] The falling birth rate was powerful evidence in favor of this theory. The cacophony of city life, worried some, was making women sterile! It was the fault of fashion, offered others: in addition to requiring fashionable ladies to keep fainting couches scattered around their homes, the severely restricting corsets that were in vogue at the time threatened "uterine derangement."[31] Or it was newspaper reading, a source of excessive excitement for women. Or exhaustion from long migrations to cities far from their place of birth, or anxiety over the risks their husbands took in business, or the damaging, lifelong stress even a brief stint working outside the home could cause.[32] Education seemed worst of all. George Engelmann, the president of the American Gynecological Society, observed that fertility rates were lowest among female college graduates—clear evidence, he said, that college-level work caused "nerve exhaustion," rendering educated women sterile.[33] Thinking and reproducing, he said, in the keynote address at the society's annual meeting in 1900, had shown themselves to be mutually exclusive.[34] "It is probably not an exaggeration," agreed a 1909 editorial in *The Independent*, a New York City weekly, "to say that to the average cost of each girl's education thru the high school must be added one unborn child."[35] The very things that drove the engine of America's nineteenth-century economic expansion—urbanization, mobility, industry, education, and capitalism—seemed to have screwed up the delicate constitutions and mysterious reproductive systems of American-born white women.

For white, middle-class, Protestant Americans who wanted to see the country continue itself in their image, such declines in "maternal performance" posed an existential threat.[36] A race that only had two children per family, President Theodore Roosevelt warned the National Congress of Mothers in 1905, defying all mathematical logic, "would decrease in population so rapidly that in two or three generations it would very deservedly be on the point of extinction." And that would be a good thing, Roosevelt added, darkly, "for a race that practiced such doctrine—that is, a race that practiced race suicide—would thereby conclusively show that it was unfit to exist."[37]

"Population shortage is the very last thing we Americans have to fear," the social scientist and eugenicist Edward Alsworth Ross wrote in *Century Magazine* in 1924. "We fill two cradles for every one coffin, and the cradle margin is growing."[38] American births were falling in the nineteenth century, but population numbers were exploding anyway: in the first national census in 1790, there were just under four million Americans. In 1900, census takers counted more than seventy-six million.[39] Though fertility had fallen considerably, American women still had an average of three or four children, more than enough to keep population climbing. The problem wasn't quantity. "What we have to worry about," Ross continued, "is *quality*."[40]

The word "eugenics" comes from the Greek, a combination of "good" and "origin" or "birth." Fascination with "good birth" began in England in the late nineteenth century, thanks to an 1869 study by Francis Galton, a British polymath who also happened to be Charles Darwin's half cousin. Galton observed what he saw as the superior qualities of the British upper classes—things like intelligence, hygiene, and lawfulness—and decided they must be hereditary. If the upper classes simply had more babies, he reasoned, then there would be more high-quality Britons, and more high-quality Britons would be great for Britain.[41] When the idea of the "good birth" crossed the pond, it landed in an America where Jim Crow laws had drawn bright lines between who counted as white and Black, and alongside a decades-long immigration boom. There was widespread concern that non-white Americans and immigrants would determine the future racial composition of the country, and perhaps unsurprisingly, Galton's ideas about the desirability of some births over others found fertile ground. Theodore Gaillard Thomas, a gynecologist from South Carolina, warned in an 1891 treatise that the "depreciating habits of civilized life" that caused sterility in the "civilized" woman had no effect on the "North American squaw" or on the "Southern Negress."[42] Indiana passed the nation's first compulsory sterilization law in 1907 and thirty other states followed, kicking off government-funded sterilization and birth control campaigns in Black, Indigenous, and immigrant communities, as well as among poor white people and the mentally ill. Adolf Hitler would later point to these programs as justification and precedent for some of the Nazis' eugenic policies.[43]

Restricting births considered "undesirable" is negative eugenics. The other side of the coin is positive eugenics: policies and actions intended to increase the number of "desirable" births. Some, like Hard, focused on how advances in medicine could help counteract the forces of modernity that seemed to be rendering women sterile. But as the twentieth century dawned, some American men of science began to contemplate an even more chilling scenario: The nation's white women's constitutions and uteruses were perfectly healthy after all. They just weren't using them. "Our educated, restless, esthetic American women," an obstetrician wrote in a 1909 essay in the *Medical Times*, "have developed among the masses an ethical, almost a constitutional reluctance to pregnancy."[44] The doctor C. G. Child was crasser: "Fat" women, "academicians," "public women," and "detached women" were "ultimately responsible" for a population crisis that many believed to be very real.[45] Too distracted by their efforts to win voting rights, legal rights, and access to education and professional employment, women were neglecting to fill their wombs and were directly responsible for what one doctor called a "backward lapse of national progress."[46] Nineteenth-century opinion was ultimately split on whether women were willfully avoiding pregnancy or whether they were simply engaging in behaviors—like education, reading, or fashion—that made it less likely. But either way, then as today, there was general agreement on one point: it was their fault.

There are medical reasons for infertility's persistence in the face of twenty-first-century technology, not the least of which is that reproduction, conceiving and growing a new human, is arguably the most complicated thing any human body ever does. But there are historical reasons too. The people trying to solve infertility have always had other motives. The American nineteenth century saw barrenness, a pitiable state willed by God or exacted by nature, slowly become sterility, a condition brought about by the stresses of modern life and one urgently requiring the attention of skilled medical men. But the nineteenth-century doctors who tried to turn childless women into mothers weren't just seeking to understand and repair ovarian or uterine function. They were also trying to fix what they saw as social ills: the negative effects modernity and education had on white women's fragile constitutions and the lower fertility of white women compared to women of color and immigrants. The goal of fertility treatment, Dr. Hard wanted his profession to understand, was not simply to cure a medical condition, but to create "a race-uplifting procedure."

Today, all of these historical threads—race and reproduction, but also economics and class—collide at the Barbados Fertility Center. The clinic is housed in a grand, white-pillared historic mansion called the Seaston House in the town of Christ Church, just outside Bridgetown, Barbados' largest city. Swaying palm trees and lush tropical plants surround the clinic, and tall, curved windows frame the front door, giving visitors a panoramic view of the sparkling Caribbean Sea and soft white sand right across the street.[47] Today, people come from around the world to visit the Seaston House for "the best IVF treatment in paradise," as the clinic's website advertises. It is, to put it mildly, a strange location for a fertility clinic. The Seaston House is a restored colonial home, the heart of a former sugarcane plantation. Barbados was Britain's first true slave colony, the place where the

British Empire first conceived of and tested the limits of chattel slavery. Slavery in various forms is likely as old as humanity itself, but the scale and totality of chattel slavery was a particularly cruel European invention. Enslaved Africans brought to the Caribbean in chains were legally stripped of their humanity and classified as chattel, or property, for life, along with any children they produced. The 1661 Slave Code clarified that enslaved Africans in British Barbados were "real estate," assets that could be bought and sold at the deed holder's whim. The first enslaved Africans arrived in Bridgetown in the 1630s and hundreds of thousands followed, laboring and dying in brutal conditions in sugarcane fields, hacking at the plant's tough stalks under the blazing Caribbean sun to feed Europeans' insatiable desire for sugar and rum.[48]

Today, the bright and welcoming waiting room on the Seaston House's first floor greets infertile couples, many of whom have traveled from overseas, including the United States and Europe. "Barbados Fertility Center offers excellent IVF success rates, low prices, and stress free treatment in a Tropical Paradise," the website's homepage reads. Cosmetic surgeons abroad have long relied on Americans' willingness to travel for procedures, luring them to the Caribbean, Mexico, India, and eastern Europe with glossy promotional materials and the promise of greatly reduced cost. In recent years, traveling for fertility treatments abroad has also risen in popularity. "Fertility tourism," as it's often known, can offer access to patients who would otherwise be shut out of the process. For example, because Italy doesn't recognize same-sex marriage and requires a patient be married to receive fertility treatment, lesbian couples from Italy regularly travel to Spain for procedures. The Barbados Fertility Center caters to a "predominantly white European or American clientele," as one anthropologist observed, who are shut out for another reason: cost.[49] In addition to the beautiful setting, the website's primary emphasis is on how much couples can save: in Barbados, IVF costs between one-third and one-half of what it would in the United States.

In the United States, one IVF cycle runs, on average, $12,000 to $17,000, and, unless you're in one of the fourteen states where insurance companies are required to cover some portion of treatments, procedures like egg freezing and IVF are pay to play.[50] Because of the expense, one study found that only one-third of women who have difficulty conceiving even raise the issue with their doctor, let alone pursue treatment.[51] Unsurprisingly, the people who do tend to be wealthier, better educated, and whiter than the general population.[52] Black women are significantly more likely to experience infertility than white women, but even so, according to one recent study, more than 85 percent of IVF patients in the United States are white.[53]

Globally, assisted reproductive technology is least available to the people who need it most. Women in southern and central Africa suffer from infertility at dramatically higher rates than women on the continent's north, not to mention those in the global north. There are a host of reasons for this, including untreated bacterial infections and parasites, as well as complications from previous childbirths that can cause sterility. In one study in Zimbabwe, for example, secondary infertility—infertility in women who have had one child—was found to affect 62 percent of women, suggesting that something about labor itself might be preventing them from having more. Researchers have nicknamed this region "the infertility belt," and anthropologists have documented the daily suffering of the women within it. "Women who are unable to bear children are rejected by their husbands and ostracized by society, often living as outcasts and perceived as inferior and useless," one report concluded.[54] Another group of researchers observed that infertility in this region is often experienced as a kind of "social death."[55] Despite need and demand, the infertility belt is almost devoid of fertility clinics or treatment. For some international aid organizations, infertility is simply a "low priority" issue when compared to the triple threat of HIV/AIDS, malaria, and maternal mortality. But for others, infertility offers a convenient solution to overpopulation. "Because high infertility has a dampening effect on overall fertility and the rate of population growth, improvements in the ability to bear children may impede efforts to lower the fertility rate," a 2004 World Health Organization report noted. "For example, it has been estimated that a reduction in infertility in sub-Saharan Africa to 'normal' levels would increase fertility in that region by 15 percent."[56] The implication: In a region with such high fertility, is it really a problem if some women can't have babies?

The answer, for any individual woman experiencing infertility—in the United States or in Africa—is, of course, yes. Research has shown that women who are diagnosed with infertility have levels of stress, anxiety, and depression similar to people diagnosed with cancer.[57] Numerous studies have even shown that women who successfully conceive through fertility treatments or ultimately adopt children say they still do not feel normal—that the social fact of their motherhood does not fully erase the anguish and trauma they experienced over their body's failure to make them a mother on its own.[58] I have friends who were willing to do almost anything—years of monitoring everything they ate and totally rearranging their sex lives, endless self-administered shots and hormone medications that caused wild mood swings and physical changes, tens of thousands of dollars in credit card debt—to have a baby through biological means. I have seen firsthand the intensity of their pain and their desire, and because of that I understand why they would sacrifice so much.

It also makes me feel like an alien. I spent most of my childhood in a big, shaggy household where the ties that made us family had nothing to do with biology. We had four last names among us. Six adults were involved in the biological production of us kids, and all those adults were involved in raising us. I still confuse people when they do the math and realize that the woman I call my sister is only four months older than me. I have two stepsiblings and a foster brother, but we usually don't use the qualifiers unless it's really necessary to communicate that we don't share genes or the same parents. "I am going to my brother's wedding," I'll say. "I can't wait to see my sister's kids." My mom would get phone calls from coaches or art teachers or friends' parents who would ask, "Are you [insert kid]'s mom?" "Well, sort of," she'd answer cheerfully. Growing up this way convinced me that family can be made in lots of ways. While other girls may have dreamed about one day feeling their baby's kicks, by high school I was firmly convinced of the benefits of adoption, at least as they appeared to my seventeen-year-old self: no sharing your body for the better part of a year, no need for a totally new wardrobe, no interruption to your workout routine. You're going along pretty much as normal until one day, voilà! You get to snuggle your kid. Something like how many men experience having children, I guess.

It's also how many people experienced adoption in the American past. The *Oxford English Dictionary* traces the word "adoption" back to the fourteenth century, when it had roughly the same meaning it does today: the practice of legally or informally taking a person into a relationship that did not previously exist.[59] In the United States, the "legal" part of that practice was largely an innovation of the first half of the nineteenth century, around the same time Americans were settling on the importance of the nuclear family and of knowing which kids belonged to which parents. Before that, courts and communities cared surprisingly little about formalizing the relationship between a child and whatever adult planned to raise them. Bethiah Lothrop, for example, became a mother in seventeenth-century Massachusetts when her husband Thomas came home with an infant in his arms. The baby was the orphaned daughter of Thomas's cousin, and after her parents' death she had been passed from home to home without finding one that could keep her. The Lothrops may have taken her in out of pity or because of her desperate situation, but Bethiah would later say that they loved her as much as any parents love any infant. She and Thomas spent their evenings sitting by the fire, gazing at the baby, and thanking "the Providence of God in disposing of the child from one place to another" until she landed in their home. The Lothrops' adoption was nothing more formal than deciding to bring her home and keep her there, involving no courts, no laws, no paperwork. The situation found its way to a courtroom only years later, after Thomas was killed in King Philip's War. Relatives eager for a piece of the Lothrops' wealth appeared out of the woodwork to challenge the baby's status as his daughter. Thomas didn't leave a will, but Bethiah was insistent that the child was Thomas's rightful and intended heir. "My dear husband was a tender nursing father to it," she pleaded with a judge. "I humbly apprehend that he did as really and truly accept of that child for his adopted daughter as he accepted me for his wife." The court agreed she was the Lothrops' child simply because the Lothrops had been raising her, and gave Bethiah permission to use Thomas's estate to provide for her.[60]

Of course, the process of adoption today bears little in common with Bethiah Lothrop's path to motherhood, or with the naive notion of easy family making that I had as a teenager. For one thing, adoptions are expensive: according to the Child Welfare Information Gateway, a federal service, private domestic adoptions average between $15,000 and $45,000, and international adoptions run $20,000 to $50,000.[61] For another, the process can take years. One scholar has observed that adoption agencies are reticent to market themselves to people struggling with infertility, often out of concern that a couple still grieving their inability to become parents biologically may not be ready to fully accept an adopted child. This, paired with the IVF industry's enthusiasm for marketing itself to those couples, likely means many never consider adoption in the first place.[62] Perhaps most challengingly, the ethics of adoption have received increasing attention in recent years, raising questions about the rights of adoptees to information about their origins, the rights of birth parents, discrimination against adoptive parents based on sexuality or race, and about the potential for harm in transnational or transracial adoptions. Perhaps for these reasons, the annual number of adoptions in the United States fell 17 percent between 2007 and 2014, and has continued falling since.[63] One group of researchers has pointed out that this downward slide in adoptions tracks neatly with advances in reproductive technologies like IVF and cryopreservation.[64] When faced with similarly staggering costs, ethical complications, and a society with a long preference for biological motherhood, women facing infertility may increasingly have come to see adoption as "not quite as good as having your own"—as "second best" to having a biological child.[65]

There is some irony in the fact that IVF has become the preferred—even the *less* ethically complicated—solution for infertility. In our historical memory, it is abortion that looms large over any debate on reproductive ethics. The clinic bombings, murdered doctors, and hundreds-of-thousands-strong Marches for Life that emerged in the 1980s and gained steam in the 1990s make it impossible to imagine a hotter-button political issue, embryo-wise, than abortion. But in the early 1970s, early experiments with in vitro fertilization were at least as controversial. Creating human embryos on lab tables in serum-filled petri dishes in the hope that they could one day become human beings? It sounded, to many, like a terrible idea. Would IVF open the floodgates to other experiments with human reproduction, like cloning or designer babies? Was it a little too close to playing God? After the Supreme Court legalized abortion in 1973, the young but growing American anti-abortion movement took aim at IVF—which, they pointed out, also involved destroying human embryos—and convinced Congress to pass a ban on embryonic and fetal research in 1974. Meanwhile, scientists and doctors highlighted the risks for the children who might grow from those embryos. "What I worry about," a scientist told the *Washington Post*, "is the effect on all scientific progress if this or another experiment like it goes wrong. Has society really given us enough of a go-ahead?"[66]

After July 25, 1978, society almost unanimously did. That day, a baby girl was born at the Oldham General Hospital in Lancashire, England. Louise Brown weighed five pounds, twelve ounces, and had ten fingers, ten toes, chubby cheeks, and a wail that came from two powerful, tiny lungs. These facts have undoubtedly brought joy and relief to new parents for millennia, but in this case both her parents and the doctor who delivered her must have let go a breath they'd been collectively holding for nine months. Louise Brown was the first baby born through in vitro fertilization. News of Louise's birth quickly ricocheted around the world. "SUPERBABE," announced the *London Evening News*.[67] "It's a Girl," the *New York Daily News* celebrated with a full-page spread. "Condition 'Excellent.'"[68]

"Had there been anything at all wrong with me," Louise Brown reflected recently, "I think it would have been the end of IVF."[69] But there was nothing wrong with her, and Louise's perfection washed away American resistance to IVF almost overnight. Within days of her birth, scientists across the country were clamoring for the Department of Health, Welfare, and Education's Ethics Advisory Board, which had been established under President Jimmy Carter's administration to consider questions relating to fetal research, to lift the nationwide moratorium on IVF research. Within a year, scientists were given the green light to conduct research on embryos, "even if the embryo is then destroyed." Pierre Soupart, a researcher at Vanderbilt, received $375,000 from the National Institutes of Health to fertilize, examine, and then dispose of four hundred human embryos to "establish the genetic risk" of IVF.[70]

In vitro fertilization is wedged into a narrow spot between two of America's most closely held ideals: two hundred years of reverence for the biological nuclear family on the one hand and, on the other, the belief that human lives are inviolable well before they are born, a tenet of anti-abortion movements that has come to the forefront in the past half century. The fact that the former has largely won out over the latter in guiding public perception of IVF is revealing about how much power the nuclear biological family has over us—and how much power the expectation of having biological children has over women. Though both procedures can involve the destruction of fertilized human embryos, in a 2013 Pew survey about half of Americans said they believed abortion to be morally wrong, and only 12 percent believed the same of IVF.[71] Alabama state senator Clyde Chambliss, who sponsored the Human Life Protection Act, which banned virtually all abortions in the state to protect "the sanctity of unborn life," clarified that he had no issue with discarding IVF-produced embryos. "The egg in the lab doesn't apply," he said. "It's not in a woman. She's not pregnant."[72]

"It's much more difficult to try to explain what is objectionable about IVF," Ann Scheidler, the cofounder of the Pro-Life Action League, a national anti-abortion organization, has conceded.[73] It is far easier to explain what is objectionable about the woman seeking an abortion. Despite the fact that most women seeking abortions are already mothers—according to the CDC, six in ten women who undergo the procedure already have children—and many go on to become mothers afterward, abortion is usually framed as an attempt to avoid motherhood.[74] In contrast, "IVF doesn't question the woman's role as a mother," writes Margo Kaplan, a law professor at Rutgers.[75] The average IVF patient is in her thirties, married, college educated, well-off, white, and wants to be a mother.[76] She is, in other words, the same woman whose empty uterus has concerned those in power for more than a century and a half, whose worsening health or "constitutional reluctance to pregnancy" was said to be causing "national decline."[77] Even for those who otherwise insist on the sanctity of human life from the moment of conception, IVF's ends—turning a childless woman into a biological mother—have come to obscure, if not to fully justify, the means.

Fertility treatments have become a multibillion-dollar industry precisely because of people's desire to share genes with their children, even at great expense or physical burden. This desire is so common, and so strong, that it seems to require no explanation. But whether it needs one or not, an explanation exists: as Americans went all-in on the nuclear family in the latter half of the nineteenth century and into the twentieth, it became more important, to families and to society at large, where the child came from. It is undoubtedly true that individual women experience extraordinary pain and grief when faced with infertility, pain that warrants immense sacrifice to remedy. It is also true that the expectation that we should want and have biological children—and the belief that if we don't, we are somehow deficient—is one that history and society impose on all of us.

In their succinctly titled 1944 text, *Vaginal Hysterectomy*, a textbook about when doctors should remove a woman's uterus and how best to do it, James William Kennedy, surgeon in chief of Philadelphia's Joseph Price Hospital, and Archibald Donald Campbell, associate professor of obstetrics and gynecology at

McGill University, put to paper what women had known in their bones for centuries: "The value of the uterus is to be estimated by its probable sterility or fertility."[78] If a uterus has the potential to be fertile, they advise, doctors should do what they can to avoid removing it, the woman's pain or lack of desire for children notwithstanding. The implication: the act of pregnancy and childbirth makes a woman and her parts valuable, worth keeping. The biblical Sarah laughs in God's face when he tells her she will bear a child in her nineties, but the joke is, ultimately, on her: it is that pregnancy that earns her a place in the sacred text. When, elsewhere in Genesis, Rachel finally gives birth to her son, Joseph, her primary emotion is not joy but relief. "God," she says, "has taken away my reproach."[79] There is Hannah, who is so fulfilled by carrying and delivering Samuel that she need not even raise him, leaving him to God as soon as he is weaned. There is Brigitte Adams, who blamed herself when the gamble she took—five figures to "freeze her eggs and free her career"— didn't work out. And between them lived countless women who suffered personal anguish made worse by societal pity, suspicion, scorn, and blame.

Technology has improved, of course, since Hollick's mannequins and Graham's vibrating bed, and the fact that we can make human beings out of frozen eggs or in petri dishes at all is genuinely amazing. Even so, the success rates of infertility treatments like IVF remain relatively low. A 2019 survey of fertility clinics done by the CDC found that just about half of women under thirty-seven had a baby after multiple cycles of IVF. After age thirty-eight, success rates dropped dramatically.[80] Even so, the mere existence of IVF has neatly tied up the loose ends of the reproductive narrative we tell ourselves. With the Supreme Court decisions in *Griswold* and *Baird* (which legalized contraception for married women in 1965 and all women in 1972, respectively) and *Roe* (which held that abortion was a constitutional right from 1973 until it was overturned in 2022), we came to believe any woman could choose not to have children. With technologies like egg freezing and IVF, it looked like they could choose *to* have them at will. For women without children, this was a tectonic shift in the assumptions others made about their lives. How many women throughout the centuries, one historian has asked, were pitied as barren when they were actually choosing a life without children?[81] Today, we might ask the opposite question: How many women are assumed to be joyfully, intentionally childfree when they want nothing more than to be mothers?

IVF's promise to place babies in the arms of these women who want them desperately is not what makes it unique. Informal and formal adoption, foster parenthood, and communal parenting have been placing children in childless homes for centuries. What IVF really promises is to turn a woman into a biological mother, to restore value to her uterus. The problem is, it sometimes doesn't deliver on that promise, and its failures can leave women feeling even more broken than they might have in the past, when they had fewer options. For many women, IVF is a gift from God, or science, or both. For others, it is a source of unattainable hope that brings only climbing credit card balances and hazmat bags full of syringes from self-administered shots. For others, it's out of reach entirely, for reasons that aren't always an accident. The two-century-long quest to solve the puzzle of infertility is still only partially realized. So, if we're asking why women today aren't having children, one answer is both the most obvious and the most often ignored: they can't, or they can't because they can't access expensive reproductive technologies, or—as Brigitte Adams found out on the worst day of her life—they still can't, even if they can.

CHAPTER 6

BECAUSE WE WANT OTHER LIVES

IN 1974, A TEACHER NAMED MARCIA DRUT-DAVIS WENT ON *60 Minutes,* the long-running investigative news program on CBS that has beamed into living rooms across the United States for more than half a century. Drut-Davis was thirty-two years old, a teacher on Long Island, and married to a man named Warren who wrote songs about her on his guitar. But behind their conventional-looking life in the white middle class, Warren and Marcia had a secret they were afraid to tell anyone, even, for a long time, each other: they didn't want kids. In the early years of their marriage, the question simply hadn't come up. Their finances were precarious for a while, and they both loved their jobs. But when Drut-Davis read Ellen Peck's 1971 book *The Baby Trap,* the first treatise on the benefits of a life without children that got anywhere near the American mainstream, she had a revelation. "We need to talk," she told Warren, handing him the book. They realized they'd each been too scared to admit their deep, dark truth to the other. With *The Baby Trap* in hand, it all came flooding out. "We were like, 'Phew, no, we don't want to have children.'" A feeling of relief may have settled over their marriage, but their inner peace was quickly replaced by a new fear: telling anyone else. "We had not come out and said, 'This is our choice. We're happy with it. Be happy for us.'" That night on CBS, they said those words to the entire country.[1]

In theory, the premise of the *60 Minutes* segment was simple: film Marcia and Warren as they broke the news to his parents that they didn't plan to have children. In practice, it was a nightmare. When the couple invited them to have a serious conversation on air, Warren's parents worried that they were communists or selling drugs. They weren't, but by the end Drut-Davis wished that was their secret, because the truth went down even worse. The filming was a "two-hour ordeal," she remembered. Her father-in-law wondered aloud what they did wrong in raising Warren, how they could have created such a selfish son. At one point, her sobbing mother-in-law asked why Drut-Davis married Warren at all if she didn't plan to have his children.[2] When the segment aired, the two hours of painful conversation and careful explanations had been whittled down to just a few minutes of footage, during which Warren opens his mouth only once, to whisper something to his father. "So," Drut-Davis remembered later, "I'm the bitch."[3] The segment paired their conversation with clips of young childless couples doing the selfish, expensive things everyone thought young childless couples did: waving from the windows of their private planes and yachts, generally drowning in money and spending it on themselves. Mike Wallace, the legendary newsman who anchored *60 Minutes* for nearly four decades, ended the segment with an apology to his viewers for what they'd just witnessed. "Pardon our perversion for airing this on Mother's Day," he said. "Good night, everyone."[4]

This is when the shit, as Drut-Davis remembers, hit the proverbial fan. Her mother-in-law, recovered from her tears, turned to composing angry, offensive poetry. The morning after the CBS interview, Marcia and Warren awoke to find one of her poems stuffed under their door. "To whom will you leave all your worldly goods?" it read. "To the robbers, the junkies, just the plain hood." That poem ended: "Our children, though married, are really just friends." After the segment aired, Drut-Davis says, she was let go from her teaching job and blacklisted from even substitute teacher lists for fifteen years. The couple got death threats. Their dog got death threats. When she was invited to speak to high school seniors on Long Island about choosing when and if to have children—at the time, teen pregnancies on Long Island were rising at an alarming rate—Drut-Davis needed to have police escort her through the crowd of protestors gathered outside.[5] "The Devil's sister is speaking today," their signs read. "Keep the child-haters away." "Children are a blessing." A neighbor sent an anonymous letter expressing regret that a "Godless, baby-hating bitch" lived on the street. "You should not call yourself a woman because it's unnatural for any woman not to want kids."[6]

The intensity of the backlash took Drut-Davis by surprise. "I didn't know what pronatalism was, I didn't know what editing was. I didn't know anything until that show."[7] Pronatalism is defined in the *Oxford English Dictionary* as "advocacy or encouragement, esp. by the State, of the practice of having a large family." That "advocacy or encouragement" saturated the American postwar period, soaking life so completely that Drut-Davis didn't even recognize it when it was staring her in the face. Her mother-in-law's poetry was a particularly weird example, but in more mundane forms it was everywhere, like a Campbell's commercial with the tagline "It's not soup until Mother makes it!" "If that's true, what the hell did I make for lunch yesterday?" Drut-Davis asked her husband sarcastically.[8] Sometimes, pronatalist policies are helpful to families, like tax credits to help offset the expense of raising a child, or policies that guarantee generous maternity leave and postpartum support in countries like France or Sweden. Others—like the bans on birth control and abortion that have accompanied pronatalist efforts in the United States since the late nineteenth century, in Nazi Germany in the 1930s, and in Soviet Republics into the 1970s—have focused more on punishing those who wouldn't conform.

In the 1950s and 1960s, American women got married young, had babies young, and reversed a century-long decline in the American birth rate. After the Second World War, creating biological nuclear families became "a national obsession," as one historian has put it. "The only salvation for the nation and the self."[9] As the 1970s dawned, young women like Drut-Davis and Peck were rethinking what salvation might look like for their generation. In 1970, a group of Dutch feminists picketed a gynecological conference, lifting their coats to the cold North Sea wind to reveal a slogan scrawled in permanent marker across each of their torsos: "Baas in eigen buik," it read. "Boss of my own belly." The following year, German feminists marched in Berlin. "Should we have children, or should we have none?" they called. "The choice belongs to us alone." One historian has called them "the generation of refusal."[10]

Refusal had consequences. Drut-Davis's *60 Minutes* of fame—and the Dutch feminists, and the German feminists, and Peck's book—unearthed pronatalism's ugly underbelly. Rather than state-sponsored pressure to have children, this was rage at women who didn't. And it was a particularly vehement kind of rage reserved for the sort of women who, increasingly in the 1970s and 1980s, came to call themselves "childless by choice" or even "childfree"—women who proudly and openly didn't want children. As hard as it was to explain that you did not have children because of your job, or finances, or lack of family support, or sense of duty to the planet, or difficulty conceiving, perhaps hardest of all was to explain that you'd simply rather live a life without them.

This desire, however, is not new. Near the end of the eleventh century in Huntingdon, England, a noblewoman named Beatrix gave birth to a daughter who would grow up to want a life without children. Beatrix and her husband, Autti, named the girl Theodora, but the name didn't stick. History remembers Theodora as Christina, a name that comes from the Greek word *christós* and literally means "a Christian" or "a follower of Christ." It was clear to her parents that Christina née Theodora was special even in utero: While Beatrix was pregnant, a snow-white dove flew from the local monastery straight into the window of her bedroom. There, it folded its wings, tucked itself into Beatrix's sleeve, and proceeded to sit with the expectant mother for seven full days. Beatrix, who apparently did not move for an entire week, softly stroked the bird as it "nestl[ed] comfortably and with evident pleasure first in her lap and then in her bosom." When the bird finally flew away, Beatrix was left with a sense of certainty and peace. The child she carried, she told anyone who would listen, "would be very pleasing to God." Jesus, she pointed out, also had a dove hang around him at one point, and that bird turned out to be the Holy Spirit itself. So, really, this could only be good news. The day Theodora/Christina was born, Beatrix spent all day in church—as one does in the early stages of childbirth—and then bore "with fortitude the pains of labour for her hope in her offspring." The baby arrived, beautiful and, her mother was sure, blessed by God.

As a child, Theodora had some strange personality quirks. For example, she "beat her own tender body with rods whenever she thought she had done something that was not allowed." Each night, she talked to Jesus as she lay in bed, "just as if she were speaking to a man she could see," apparently believing that no one else could hear her. Her siblings, who probably shared her bedroom and just wanted to get some sleep, disabused her of this notion, teasing her until she figured out a quieter way to pray. At fourteen, Theodora made a formal vow of lifelong virginity. "There is none upon earth that I desire besides Thee," she told God. She would never marry, she promised, and never submit to a man's touch. And as a result, she would never have children.

Whatever promises their daughter made to God, Theodora's parents were wealthy merchants, and they likely saw their kids' marriages as opportunities to forge alliances with other families, advance their business interests, and boost their social standing. Women born into families like Theodora's generally married the man their family chose for them and assumed a traditional life: running a household, serving their husband, and having children. Some did go to convents, a common fate of the younger daughters of upper-class medieval families, once their parents ran out of the money or the will to pay dowries. Unfortunately for Theodora, Beatrix and Autti seem to have had plenty of money and no desire to see their daughter don a habit. They arranged for her to marry a young nobleman with the unpromising name of Burthred. Theodora was not pleased. "I wish to remain single," she reminded her parents, "for I have made a vow of virginity."

On her wedding night, Theodora's parents hustled Burthred into their daughter's chambers and locked the door. When they opened it the next morning, hoping to find her glowing in a decidedly non-virginal manner, they were aghast to hear that Theodora had spent the night lecturing her new husband about the virtues of chastity. When Burthred tried to consummate the marriage a second time, slipping into her room the next night to force himself on her, Theodora successfully hid behind a tapestry. Frustrated, her parents called in the local priest to convince her of the value of marriage and motherhood. Do not think, the priest instructed Theodora, "that only virgins are saved: for whilst many virgins perish, many mothers of families are saved, as we well know." "If many mothers of families are saved," Theodora retorted, "certainly virgins are saved more easily." She debated the priest, meeting his every biblical argument with her own faithful reasoning, until he gave up and returned to her parents, shrugging. Theodora ran away from home, changed her name to Christina, and spent years hiding out with local monks, wearing her parents down until they realized she was really not kidding about her vow of virginity. In the end, her father allowed her to dissolve the marriage. Freed from her earthly husband, Christina became Christina of Markyate, a bride of Jesus, the prioress at Saint Albans Abbey, a scholar, and the leader of a large group of female disciples.[11]

The record we have of Christina's life is a hagiography, a style of biography written with one very specific purpose in mind: to make the case to the Catholic Church that its subject should be sainted. Because of this, hagiographies tend to be hyperbolic, featuring acts of faith and goodness that stretch even the most generous imagination. Men tended to starve themselves, give away large sums of money, take vows of silence, or, in an attempt to emulate the prophets of the Hebrew Bible, live alone in the desert and/or be naked for long periods of time.[12] When they're about women, hagiographies often feature an early vow of virginity and then repeated and heroic efforts to defend that vow from powerful and/or sneaky men. As in Christina's case, one of the trials is often marriage, when the potential saint in question must fend off not only her own lust but also that of a man who has both a legal and a religious right to her body. To a twenty-first-century reader, hagiographies like Christina's illustrate how hard it was to avoid the traditional path of marriage and motherhood, even with the most airtight of medieval excuses, like a vow made to God. Like Drut-Davis's nine centuries later, Christina's decision to live a life without children was grieved, rejected, and bitterly resented by those around her.

For some, the life they got on the other side of that struggle was worth it. Hildegard of Bingen, for example, a twelfth-
century German Benedictine abbess, was a famed mystic, poet,
and composer who wrote everything from botanical treatises
and medical texts to *Ordo Virtutum*, one of Europe's earliest
known musical plays. She advised popes, kings, and at least one
Holy Roman emperor. Like Christina, Hildegard had been born
and educated as a noblewoman, but few women even of that status had the ear of the pope and the emperor. Hildegard's vow of
virginity, and her renunciation of motherhood and marriage, allowed her to pursue an intellectual and influential life.[13] With her
own vow of virginity, Christina also found one of the only ways
out of the traditional path available to a medieval English noblewoman. Far from regretting her choice, Christina mentored
a group of female followers—and encouraged them to make the
same one.

Motherhood holds a high status in Christianity, of course.
Since about the fourth century, Mary, the mortal woman who
carried, gave birth to, and raised Jesus, has also been referred to
in church teachings as the "Queen of Heaven." Yet religiously inclined women have, for just as long, looked to Mary's other defining trait: her virginity. Mary was the mother of Jesus, but she was
also a virgin when God chose her to carry his child, a fact that
has been confusing Sunday school classes for centuries. From the
Roman Empire to at least the American nineteenth century, religious life offered women a socially acceptable alternative to the
only other model available to them. With virginity ensuring their
uteruses would remain empty, they created a motherhood of their
own definition, one forged through charitable and religious work
on behalf of their community. "Our mission as Carmelites," Saint
Thérèse of Lisieux, a nineteenth-century French Catholic nun,
wrote in a letter to her sister, "is to form evangelical workers who
will save thousands of souls whose mothers we shall be."[14]

Like Christina, Ellen Peck collected a group of disciples whom she led through a nontraditional life. Peck was the author of *The Baby Trap*, the book that gave Marcia Drut-Davis permission to consider not having children. Like Drut-Davis, Peck also held the distinction of causing a stir on prime-time television. In 1971, Peck appeared on the *Tonight Show*, one of the most widely watched programs of the day. As she took a seat by the side of Johnny Carson's glossy wooden desk, Peck's physical appearance was striking. She was glamorous: long blond hair with Farrah Fawcett bangs, blue eyes set off by swipes of black eyeliner, and an angled jawline and cheekbones that earned her regular comparisons to Brigitte Bardot.[15] But any favor her looks earned her with viewers quickly evaporated. As the live audience booed angrily, Carson smiled gamely, and as millions of American viewers watched from their living rooms, Peck laid out her argument for intentional childlessness, or, as she called it, a childfree life.[16]

Peck was a teacher like Drut-Davis: she taught eighth grade English at Pimlico Junior High in Baltimore, Maryland. Members of the school's alumni Facebook page seem to remember her fondly, as a young, cool teacher with a propensity for miniskirts—reportedly, she taught in skirts so short that they would have violated the dress-code rules for students. "All of the guys had crushes on her!" one poster remembers. She was also apparently an excellent grammar teacher: one alum credits Peck's class with helping him win an argument with a tenth-grade teacher whom everyone remembers rather less well.[17] Peck's first book, 1969's *How to Get a Teenage Boy and What to Do with Him When You Get Him*, was a tongue-in-cheek guide to beauty, romance, and fashion for teenage girls that solidified her reputation as the coolest of older sisters. Two years later, *The Baby Trap* launched her to national fame. The first print run of ten thousand copies sold out in just ten days.[18]

In our society, *The Baby Trap* observes, "to the extent that babies are emphasized, adults are de-emphasized. To the extent that a woman is regarded as a means to an end (propagating the species) she is not seen as beautiful, vibrant, valuable, in and of herself. To the extent that a man is seen as a mere provider, he may be seen as less of a person."[19] Unfortunately, this reasonable and even useful nugget of social critique is buried under a veritable mountain of other observations that must have turned many readers off before they could get there. *The Baby Trap* begins with sixty pages of stories from Peck's international travels with her husband: picnicking on "truffle-spiced ham, fruit, brioches, and ice-cold champagne by a roadside in the south of France," "tasting the black Chambertin wine in a cave of the Burgundy country," wandering the Musée Picasso on the French Riviera and the private art galleries of "Lucerne, Paris, Geneva, Barbizon." "We met Marc Chagall," she adds, breezily.[20] Peck implies that these adventures were made possible by the money they'd saved by not having children, brushing off the idea that they might just simply be rich. You'd also have to make it past wild generalizations like "The girls I've talked to who don't have children are, almost without exception, prettier, more conversational, more aware, more alive, more exciting, more satisfied."[21] And you'd have to survive stories like the one about Lori, who was "thirty but look[ed] eighteen" and had a propensity for jetting off to the Azores with whatever married man she happened to be dating at the time. All of her married suitors, of course, had children. "Sure, it's the guys with kids," Lori explained to Peck. "The ones who don't have kids still like their wives."[22]

Ellen Peck, suffice it to say, had a particular knack for pissing people off. For example, on Mother's Day in 1972, she wrote an obituary for the institution of motherhood that ran in the *New York Times*. "Once, there were good and valid reasons to have children," she wrote. "Once, it was inevitable. Once, there was nothing else to do. Once, human survival depended on human fertility." These things were no longer true, she continued: hormonal birth control existed, there were plenty of other opportunities available to women, and the earth was groaning under what then seemed like a staggering population of four billion people. Motherhood died, Peck declared, without a hint of humor, "sometime in the early nineteen-seventies." This, and her assertion that "parenthood, today, seems to us the very opposite of adulthood," didn't win her any friends among conservatives or traditionalists, certainly. But it didn't do her any favors in feminist circles either.[23]

Many of Peck's feminist counterparts in the early 1970s wore their motherhood like a shield, believing it was their status as mothers that would make their movement palatable, respectable. The fact that many women activists throughout history were mothers, Betty Friedan wrote in *The Feminine Mystique*, disproved the stereotype that feminists were "embittered shrews."[24] For many of that era, women without children seemed like nothing more than a symptom of the problem: they were evidence of a societal failure to support women at work and at home. Far more energy went into reclaiming motherhood from the patriarchal frameworks that made it difficult—replacing male doctors and hospital deliveries with woman-centered natural birth practices, demanding the right to breastfeed in public, advocating for policies to make working motherhood possible, like paid maternity leave or universal day care—than toward the question of whether all women should be mothers, or whether they all wanted to be. In a review of *The Baby Trap* for *Ms.* magazine, Ellen Willis called Peck "arrogant" and argued that her "childfree" framing ran counter to feminist aims. The very word "childfree," Willis wrote, implied that motherhood was only for women who were too stupid to avoid it.[25]

A century of government-run and societally endorsed programs designed to limit births in communities of color—everything

from forced sterilizations to strategically placed public birth control clinics to residential schools that removed Native children
from their families to "assimilate" them into Euro-American
culture—made feminists from those communities even less
inclined than white women to throw motherhood out the
window. The right to be mothers, the right to mother, was a
central piece of their politics. In a 1969 treatise, a group of
Black women from New York's Hudson Valley argued that, far
from being the oppressive institution their white counterparts
thought it was, motherhood was the source of their power. "The
woman's body, which receives, hosts, and gives forth the future
of the species, is inherently powerful," they wrote.[26] Peck's out-
right rejection of the value of motherhood and her delight in
the glamorous benefits of a life without children ran against all
these feminist grains. When a reporter from the *Baltimore Sun*
asked Peck about her relationship to feminists at large, Peck
paused for a moment, "a slight smile on her lips." "There are
some members of the feminist movement to whom I seem," she
said, "regrettable."[27]

Peck didn't do a much better job selling her cause to the public at large. The benefits of a childless life that she identified—
specifically, better sex, more disposable income, more frequent
vacations, and the ability to build a third home on a remote
Caribbean island, as she and her husband had done—seemed
handpicked to earn her the least amount of sympathy possible.[28]
These reasons did not go over particularly well with Johnny
Carson's live audience at NBC Studios in 1971. "I thought the
audience was going to lynch her before she got out of here, because she simply said, and it was an honest opinion, that there
can be more to life than just getting married and raising babies," Carson recalled in an interview a few years later. "It was
like [she was] against motherhood, against the American flag,
Kate Smith and Lassie combined."[29]

In 1974, Peck's organization, the National Organization for Non-Parents (NON for short), hosted an elaborate ceremony for Non-Parents Day, which they decided should be celebrated on the first of August. The event took place in New York's Central Park and featured a choreographed "non-fertility ritual," danced by three women wearing head-to-toe silver spandex to the tune of a single flute. The centerpiece of the event came when the science-fiction writer Isaac Asimov carefully placed laurel wreaths on the heads of a young man and woman, crowning them "Non-Parents of the Year." The non-mother and non-father of the year were to serve as ambassadors, both to introduce upstanding nonparents to the kidded masses and to advertise how great a life without children could be to those who hadn't had them yet.

That year's non-mother was none other than Stephanie Mills, the "ex-potential parent" who had risen to fame with her graduation address of doom five years earlier. In the intervening years, Mills had authored a short book called *The Joy of Birth Control* and distanced herself from the environmental childlessness that had made her a household name. At a party on the eve of Non-Parents Day, Peck—"barefoot and ethereal in a white gown," as one guest noted—invited Mills to make a statement about the societal good that could come from non-parenthood. Mills declined. Since her graduation speech, she explained, she'd discovered that not having children simply allowed her to live the lifestyle she most enjoyed. "But couldn't you say some of those wonderful things you used to say," Peck asked, with some desperation, "one of those phrases like, 'we're breeding ourselves out of existence'?" No, Mills said.

The non-father of the year was a novelist named Dan Wakefield, a man Peck would also find disappointing. He had been hesitant to accept the award in the first place, and he told Peck that he wasn't totally convinced that non-parenthood was a thing in need of celebrating, or that nonparents were even subject to any discrimination. Wakefield's ambivalence peeked through in his acceptance speech: "I do not consider myself fit to be, say, an astronaut or a father of children," he said into the microphone the next day in Central Park, "and I do not believe that my lack of potential for success in either of these capacities makes me less of a human being." But Wakefield quickly learned what Peck, Drut-Davis, Mills, and women without children before and since already knew: lots of people did think childlessness made you less of a person. "You know what it was like, picking up the paper and reading about you being crowned Non-Father of the Year?" a friend asked Wakefield after reading an Associated Press story about the event. "It's like picking up the paper and reading that one of your dearest friends has become a Nazi." Nonparenthood, Wakefield ultimately conceded, "turns out to be a touchy subject."[30]

It was stereotypes like these that made Shirley Radl, the executive director of Zero Population Growth, seek an alliance with Ellen Peck. Radl had plenty to keep her busy in the early years of the 1970s. She was arguing for liberalizing abortion laws in state legislatures across the country and trying to hold together the threads of an environmentalist-feminist alliance that was beginning to fray. She also knew that she could talk about the dire ecological consequences of population growth all day, but she'd never get anywhere if people still called their friends Nazis for not having children. Radl herself was a mother, but she was open about the fact that she regretted becoming one. She loved her children, she would clarify, but she did not like mothering. Rather than the joy, fulfillment, and sacred sense of purpose she had been told would accompany having children, Radl found motherhood to be a source of "resentment, hostility, and rage," something that would sooner destroy a marriage than build a family. She agreed to join Peck's organization—the

National Organization for Non-Parents, or NON, for short—as its coleader. In joining forces with Peck and NON, Radl hoped to legitimize not having children as a choice in and of itself: not something that made you a Nazi, but also not just something you chose out of concern for the future or obligation to an environmentalist cause. Radl and Peck wanted to make non-parenting something you could do simply because you wanted to.[31]

With Peck and Radl at its helm, the National Organization for Non-Parents aligned itself against one enemy: not children, not parents, but the pronatalist ideology they saw everywhere in American society. Pronatalism, they argued, reduced marriages to baby-making arrangements and gave women only two possible identities: potential mother, or actual mother. In merely existing, NON made the radical claim that non-parenthood was a valid identity, and one you could share with others. Outsiders continued to hate NON, accusing it of everything from satanism to "vilifying storks."[32] But for many who joined, it was life changing. Members of NON met for drinks on what were other people's school nights, vacationed together at adults-only resorts, and validated and reaffirmed each other's choices and lifestyles. "This is the movement for which I have waited all my life," a sixty-seven-year-old woman said, standing at the microphone at NON's annual convention in 1975. "I have suffered the guilt of not giving my parents grandchildren, and I suffered the taunts of self-righteous people who thought they were doing the right thing for society by having children. What a group like this can do is lift away the guilt and self-consciousness that people feel if they don't want children."[33] Finding NON also was transformative for Marcia Drut-Davis and her husband, Warren. "We no longer considered ourselves a childless couple," Drut-Davis writes in her memoir. "We were a childfree family."[34]

For Drut-Davis, Peck, and many of NON's members, this small change in vocabulary had an outsize effect. The word "childless" implied deficiency, that their households were not families, that they were lacking something as women. "Childfree" emerged as an alternative early in the 1970s. No one seems to know quite who coined it, but *The Baby Trap* is peppered with the term, as were the pamphlets and marketing materials NON produced to further its cause. By the middle of the decade, it was appearing in academic publications, often in place of clunkier, qualified terms like "voluntarily childless" or "childless by choice."[35] Replacing "childless" with "childfree" was the key, NON's leaders and members believed, to normalizing and even celebrating lives that didn't include parenting. If "childless" implied a person's pitiable lack, "childfree" sounded like something you'd choose—maybe even an improvement on the original, like how sugar-free gum is the kind that won't rot your teeth. The semantic sleight of hand that transformed a childless couple into a childfree family was transformative for those who greeted "childfree" as a term they could own.

Even so, NON's membership remained sparse and extremely niche. It had just over two thousand members globally when the organization officially disbanded in 1982. Virtually all of them were white, at least middle-class, married, and heterosexual.[36] For many of NON's members, "childfree" meant something extremely specific: a life chosen out of an unlimited buffet of available options, and one arrived at with equal parts joy and relief. Do you want to be the Cleavers, or do you want to drink champagne on the Riviera? Anguish had no home there, whether it came from infertility or difficulty finding a partner or professional priorities or finances that made having children impossible. Neither did other kinds of nontraditional thinking, strangely enough. Unlike the movements for women's liberation, civil rights, labor protections, social justice, or environmentalism that roiled American society in the 1960s and 1970s, the National Organization for Non-Parents wasn't looking for major societal change. They didn't want to blow up domesticity, or reorder gender roles in the home, or fundamentally alter American systems of privilege and injustice. Childfree activists like Peck largely limited their critique to mandatory parenthood, arguing for the right to be respectable middle-class and upper-middle-class people arranged in nuclear families—just without the children that status usually required.[37]

In many ways, it is NON's small *c* conservatism, not its celebration of not having kids, that makes it notable in the longer sweep of American history. In the eighteenth century, a woman named Ann Lee also founded a movement around non-procreation, but her aims were anything but conservative. She wanted to burn everything down. Lee was born into a working-class family in Manchester, England, in 1742. At sixteen years old, she joined a niche sect of Quakers known as the Shaking Quakers, who shook and writhed in ecstasy as they prayed. Shaking, they believed, was the result of the Holy Spirit purging sin from their bodies. But Lee took things one step further: she taught a small but growing group of followers that the real way to achieve perfect holiness, perfect purity, was to give up all sexual relations, including marital sex and procreative sex. Lee taught her followers they "must forsake the marriage of the flesh, or you cannot be married to the Lamb, nor have any share in the resurrection of Christ; for those who are counted worthy to have part in the resurrection of Christ neither marry nor are given in marriage."[38] Lee would later be known to her followers and to history as Mother Ann Lee, but she had no interest in being a mother in the biological sense—and she thought others should reconsider the whole institution as well.

From a very young age, Lee found sexuality repulsive, her own most of all, and desperately lobbied her father to allow her to remain single and childless, not entirely unlike Christina of Markyate had done. England had gone through the Protestant

Reformation in the seven centuries between these two women's lifetimes, so being a Catholic nun wasn't on the table for Lee. But like her eleventh-century counterpart, Lee wanted to be a woman of God and a spiritual leader, preaching the virtue of life-long celibacy not just for nuns, but for everyone. That idea went over about as well with Lee's father as it had with Christina's, and Lee found herself married at the age of nineteen to a man named Abraham Stanley. The marriage was, not surprisingly, unhappy: Ann and Abraham hated each other. Things were made worse by the sexual relations Lee was duty bound to participate in, and by their consequences. She survived four grueling, dangerous pregnancies and deliveries, but all of her children died in infancy. The physical and emotional trauma caused by her attempts at reproduction only made her more confident that her take on sex was right: It was not just gross, or unclean, or displeasing to God. It also destroyed women's bodies, threatened their lives, and limited their options.[39]

British authorities repeatedly arrested Lee and imprisoned her for various religious offenses, from breaking the Sabbath with "dervishlike dancing and crying out in strange tongues," to disregarding the Anglican Church's strict prohibition on women preaching, to good old-fashioned blasphemy.[40] Once, Lee claimed, she'd confounded the arresting authorities by speaking at them for four hours in seventy-two different tongues. In a vision, a burning tree directed Lee to move her church to America, where offbeat flavors of Christianity had freer rein. Lee, her husband Abraham, and seven of her most loyal followers landed in New York City in 1774. Abraham abandoned the group once they arrived, but Lee was undaunted. With her remaining followers, she set out for leased land near Albany, where they quickly distinguished themselves among the many fledgling denominations and communal experiments that speckled the late-eighteenth-century American religious landscape.[41]

One factor that set Lee's community of Shakers apart was the principle of full gender equality. She taught her followers that the lesson of the story of Adam and Eve was not, as many held, that women were weak, disobedient, helpless in the face of their desire, and desperately in need of a steady male hand. Lee preached instead that God had forgiven Adam and Eve equally for the sin of being human, and that equal forgiveness had earned them equal standing in God's eyes. It was this belief that led to Lee's disapproval of marriage. The institution resulted in the "ownership" of a wife by her husband, which Lee believed was in direct contradiction to God's stated desire for gender equality. To reach salvation, Shaker doctrine held, men had to overcome their "feelings of superiority and possessiveness," and women their "inferiority and submissiveness." Shaker communities had both women and men in positions of authority and power.[42]

Shakers had a policy of strict celibacy and lived by a set of elaborate rules designed to maintain it. Shaker women and men were forbidden from speaking to each other one-on-one or walking together alone, and children could not bathe without adult supervision. If they passed each other on the stairs, women were commanded to step aside, not out of deference, but to prevent their bodies from brushing up against men's. "When ye are together, and in any way begin to feel your natures excited," their rules cautioned, "withdraw immediately from each other's presence, and war against that filthy spirit."[43] With such strict rules about sex, of course, new Shakers could not be made. The only way to grow the community was to recruit them.

"Come join us! You can't have sex, children, or an intimate relationship!" might not sound like a terribly good sales pitch, but Lee and the Shakers initially didn't have trouble gaining recruits. They were particularly good at attracting women, even and especially women in early adulthood, those years when having marital sex and children were the primary things society expected them to do. Shakers under twenty years old were equally split along gender lines. But in the twenty to forty-five age bracket, prime childbearing and mothering years, women outnumbered men almost three to one. Shaker communities, it seems, were havens for Lee's kindred spirits: women of childbearing age who wanted an alternative. Far from being a deterrent, the total ban on having children—and freedom from many of the domestic tasks that accompanied motherhood—may have been an appealing feature of Shaker life for many women who joined.[44] According to some estimates, at its peak in the early 1860s there were four thousand to six thousand Shakers living in approximately twenty communities in the Northeast and Midwest. By 1900, though, their numbers had dropped to 855, and most of them were elderly. Conversions couldn't keep up with the march of time, and ultimately the Shakers' aversion to making new members started to catch up with them.[45]

A century after the Shakers had their heyday, in the early 1970s, a new genre of separatist communities went one step further than eliminating sex: they eliminated men entirely. The feminist upheavals of the 1960s had opened the eyes of many women in the American mainstream to gender inequality and oppression. They also convinced some women that a society whose culture and laws sought to uphold that inequality and oppression was not one they'd like to live in anymore. Lesbian separatists set up Women's Land communities across the United States and Canada, buying houses and sprawling rural properties where all women were welcome and men, even sometimes male children, were decidedly not. The Gutter Dykes lived in Berkeley; the Radicalesbians in New York City; the Furies Collective in Washington, DC; the Gorgons in Seattle. A large swath of land in southwestern Oregon was purchased to form the Oregon Women's Land Trust. One group founded the New York Lesbian Food Conspiracy, a women-only co-op in Manhattan. A group

of van-driving vegans called themselves the Van Dykes, a sur-
name they hoped all American lesbians would eventually adopt,
and spent the 1970s hopping from community to community,
mapping out Women's Land's North American borders. "We
were everywhere," Lamar Van Dyke told a reporter in 2009. "We
found Women's Land in North Carolina, Florida, Texas, Arkansas, New Mexico, Arizona, a lot of Women's Land in California and Oregon. You could actually go all around the country
from Women's Land to Women's Land. . . . It was a whole world."
At the movement's peak, one scholar of lesbian history has estimated, there were "thousands" living on Women's Land spaces
across the United States.[46]

Lesbian separatism represented a radical new era for women's
movements in the United States. When Betty Friedan founded
the National Organization for Women in 1966, she was clear
that the group's goal was to revise "the conditions that prevent women from easily combining marriage and motherhood
and work." This "was (and remains!) a revolutionary vision," the
writer Rebecca Traister has observed, "yet there was no hint of
recognition that not every woman's life would (or should) include
marriage"—specifically, marriage to a man—"and children, in
that order."[47] It was also strategic: there was political safety in the
message that women still wanted to be wives and mothers, that
they just *also* wanted careers. Women who didn't want marriage
and motherhood, then, were a threat. In 1969, Friedan reportedly
called lesbians within the movement "the lavender menace"—a
reference to the "red menace," a Cold War term used as short-
hand for communism and the threat it posed to American society.
Lesbians' presence within the women's movement, she believed,
gave opponents everything they needed to dismiss their political
claims. They weren't asking for political and legal equality, or
for support for working mothers, opponents could say. They just
hated men.[48]

But groups like the Furies and the Radicalesbians believed eschewing sexual and romantic relationships with men was not a threat to women's causes. To the contrary, they saw it as necessary for the political coherence of the feminist movement. In 1970, members of the Radicalesbians stormed the stage at NOW's Second Congress to Unite Women, wearing purple T-shirts with the words "lavender menace" silkscreened on their chests. They held signs with slogans like "We are all lesbians!" and "Lesbianism is a women's liberation plot." Being a lesbian was "not a matter of sexual preference," a 1972 statement from the Furies Collective explained, "but rather one of political choice, which every woman must make if she is to become woman-identified and thereby end male supremacy."[49] Today, we generally understand sexuality as an innate part of a person's identity, but for some feminists of the 1970s, pursuing sexual and romantic relationships only with other women was a way of living your politics. "The lesbian," wrote Jill Johnston in her 1973 book *Lesbian Nation*, "is the woman who unites the personal and the political in the struggle to free ourselves. . . . By this definition, lesbians are the vanguard of the resistance."[50]

Being the vanguard required more than just swearing off men. A woman who joined a Women's Land or other lesbian separatist community did so at the cost of biological motherhood, unless she had children before joining. Insemination with donor sperm, which today makes it possible for women to have biological children without having sex with men, was all but legally impossible in the United States until 1973—when a federal law clarified that sperm donors did not have parental rights—and rare until the early 1990s.[51] But for some who joined, opting out of motherhood was, in some ways, part of the point: dispensing with sacred institutions, questioning what was expected of them, and disregarding societal norms. As Lamar Van Dyke puts it, "We were off doing whatever we wanted."[52]

In addition to offering support and validation to a particular type of person without children, in its early years the National Organization for Non-Parents also succeeded in attracting an enormous amount of attention. For an organization with three thousand members at its peak, NON got enviable media real estate: hundreds of feature stories everywhere that mattered, from *Cosmopolitan* and *Glamour* to *Time*, *Newsweek*, the *New York Times*, the *New Yorker*, *60 Minutes*, and the *Today Show*. Unfortunately, much of it was negative. "At long last," a stridently satirical piece in the *Boston Globe* proclaimed, "an organization has been founded to make the child-free adult a social hero." Mother's and Father's Day, the author went on sarcastically, were to be "amalgamated into one holiday called Chumps' Day."[53] In the pages of *Time* magazine, even a writer who was sympathetic to NON's cause lamented their "juvenile" and "frequently childish espousal of childlessness." "The cultural bias against it is so strong," the writer acknowledged, "that husbands and wives cannot choose nonparenthood freely; they know they will be branded selfish, shallow, and neurotic." It was just a shame, the writer continued, that the best NON could come up with was the slogan "none is fun," and that Peck "disparages motherhood mostly because it gets in the way of the glamour of a free life."[54]

With its public relations strategy in trouble, NON hired Carole Baker to replace Peck in the organization's leadership in 1974. Baker had two teenage sons, and her presence was intended to broaden and soften NON's public reputation, as well as make it more palatable to funders who could help them spread their message. In 1976, Baker approached the Rockefeller Brothers Fund, a philanthropic organization that had a track record of giving grants to organizations working on the environment and overpopulation. NON wanted to take its fight against pronatalism national, Baker told a roomful of Rockefeller representatives. Educating Americans that parenthood was an option, not a mandate, would improve the lives of nonparents, she said, *and* help to slow the population growth that many still thought was cause for concern. The Rockefeller Brothers Fund shared NON's concerns about the negative effects of pronatalism, but the group's tactics gave them pause. "When it comes to children and family," they wrote in a memo to Baker after the meeting, "Americans do not yet have the kind of sense of humor that permits disrespect for time-honored traditions." The fund would support NON's efforts to combat pronatalism, they wrote, but only if the organization agreed to make major changes, including a branding overhaul and an effort to create "a more professional image for itself." Baker agreed to all their terms. NON was "ready to leave the 'flag waving' behind," she assured them, referring specifically to the spandex-clad anti-fertility dance they had put on in Central Park, "and to maintain an earnest, academic, and unbiased approach."[55]

Money from the Rockefeller Brothers Fund allowed NON to run a series of television and radio commercials aimed at exposing the unconscious ways pronatalism sneaks into everyday life, using the slogan "You <u>Do</u> Have a Choice." In one of the ads, a realtor shows a house to a young couple. As the realtor describes how one room would make a sweet nursery, another a functional playroom, the couple starts to imagine his-and-hers home offices. If they didn't plan to have children, the realtor snaps, he could "show them a condominium downtown." In another, a couple sits in tense silence after what viewers are supposed to understand was an ugly fight. The husband says tentatively, "Maybe things would be better around here if we had a baby." The image freezes, and an ominous voice-over intones, "Probably not."[56] In a third, a newlywed couple returns home from their honeymoon to find that a baby carriage has creepily materialized in their living room. "With all the pressure we get to be parents," a voice-over says, "it's easy to forget we ever had a choice in the first place." In 1978, the board voted to change their name from the National Organization for Non-Parents to the National Alliance for Optional Parenthood, inviting all people, regardless of their parental status, to become supporters. "We're not against children. Don't think that," Baker told reporters, again and again. "We just want couples to be allowed the choice of having babies or not."[57]

That NON—or in its new, clunkier iteration, NAOP—would go all-in on choice in its mid-1970s rebranding is not particularly surprising. The right to abortion access had just been won on arguments in favor of "freedom of personal choice." It's nearly impossible to imagine now, but that framing played almost as well with some conservatives as it did with feminists, at least initially. A week after the Supreme Court released its decision in *Roe v. Wade*, the *Baptist Press*—the "News Service of the Southern Baptist Convention," as it terms itself, the mouthpiece of the largest Protestant denomination in the United States—published an article explaining the ruling to its readers. "There is no official Southern Baptist position on abortion, or any other such question," the newspaper clarified. But it added approvingly that "the decision to obtain an abortion or to bring pregnancy to full term can now be a matter of conscience and deliberate choice rather than one compelled by law."[58] Another piece in the *Baptist Press* that week featured an interview with Linda Coffee, one of the attorneys who presented the case in favor of abortion rights before the Supreme Court. Coffee was raised a Southern Baptist, and she encouraged readers to view *Roe* through the conservative lens of freedom and choice. Coffee explained that the ruling would allow for more constitutional freedom than she, as a Christian, would personally choose to exercise.[59] For an organization looking to expand its audience, it was hard to do better than language endorsed by the Southern Baptists *and* Planned Parenthood.

As we know all too well, this moment of alignment didn't last. The National Alliance for Optional Parenthood officially disbanded in 1982—fittingly, on August 1, the date it had declared Non-Parent's Day. The group's last newsletter blamed financial troubles for its demise, but shaky finances were likely a symptom of a much bigger problem: not having kids is a hard sell as a political platform in the best of times, and these were the Reagan eighties, when the only thing valued more than individual freedom was "traditional" American values. Peck's glamor and unapologetic rejection of motherhood, Baker's public relations savvy, and NON's support for a particular sort of living without children couldn't find purchase in a country where the nuclear family had become a patriotic ideal.

Still, NON's activism—even when widely criticized—did change the game, if only by getting words like "childfree" and "nonparents" published in newspapers and in front of people's eyeballs as they drank their morning coffee. In a culture that saw, and largely continues to see, parenthood as a necessary step in becoming an adult, public recognition of the choice to eschew parenthood was hugely consequential for those who felt they'd made it. For the rest of us, though, NON's legacy is more complicated. Even today, NON's definition of childfreedom captures just a small slice of people who are not parents. Surveys done by the CDC indicate that only about 6 percent of people are "intentionally childless" in the way NON imagined it—that is, they actively made the choice not to have children and built their lives around that choice.[60] For the rest of us, our childlessness was arrived at through factors out of our control, like infertility, or *because* of the rest of the lives we have built: prioritizing getting a graduate degree, establishing a career, finding the right partner, saving for a house or retirement, caring for an aging parent, paying off student loans, working multiple jobs to make ends meet. The childfree movement's emphasis on choice—the choice to be childfree!—allows us to ignore all of the factors that can make that choice feel not very free at all.

Being childfree was never really Karen Malone Wright's choice. In 2010, Wright was happily married and professionally successful, living in her hometown of Cleveland, Ohio, with twenty years of experience in corporate communications and a thriving career in digital marketing. She was also over fifty, had no children, and was an only child, and she found herself grieving the big, boisterous family she'd always hoped she would have. Nothing she could find on the internet spoke to her experience: Blogs by empty nesters her age fit her no better than those by prospective adoptive parents or the childfree by choice. Infertility blogs didn't either. They felt "too sad," full of women actively grieving a loss and nursing a hope Wright had long since let go of. Since she couldn't find a community that felt right, she decided to make one that did. The following year, Wright launched the NotMom, an online resource and community that has since spun out into a regular conference, a podcast, and a hub of meetup groups across the country. The NotMom's tagline is "By Choice or By Chance," and the group takes its motto seriously. "We embrace women who never wanted children," their website reads, "those who once hoped for them, and those who have never given birth but may care for stepchildren or young relatives. We are on different paths, on the same road."[61] The keynote speaker at the 2013 NotMom Summit in Cleveland, a Case Western University ob-gyn named Marjorie Greenfield, was struck by the wide range of participants: young and old, joyfully childfree by choice and in the throes of grief after abandoning IVF, talking, crying, eating lunch together.[62] If NON was an exclusive club, the NotMom is the big-tent version of not having children. It has room for people who are childfree and childless and people who don't identify with either because they find the idea of basing an identity on their reproductive status boring or condescending or reductive—which might be one reason they found motherhood unappealing in the first place.

In a piece for *HuffPost* in 2014, actress Jennifer Aniston expressed this kind of frustration—frustration with how women are defined solely and primarily by the kids they have or don't. "For the record, I am *not* pregnant. What I am is *fed up*," Aniston wrote. Aniston's 2008 divorce from Brad Pitt, and her subsequent failure to have children, spawned the "sad Jen" meme, which became one of the most durable in internet history, despite overwhelming evidence that she has been living her best life all along. Aniston wrote she was fed up with the idea that her reproductive status is anywhere near the most interesting thing about her. "We don't need to be married or mothers to be complete. We get to determine our own 'happily ever after' for ourselves."[63]

It might be overly obvious to point out that eleventh-century nuns, Shakers, lesbian back to landers, and Jennifer Aniston don't have all that much in common with each other. But what they do share is this: all of them wanted lives that were incompatible with traditional expectations like marriage, kids, and nuclear families. Theirs was not simply a choice not to have children. It was a choice to live a life that not having children made possible.

Simone de Beauvoir died in 1986 after a long battle with pneumonia, just eight hours shy of the sixth anniversary of her lifelong partner Jean-Paul Sartre's death. Obituaries around the world called her "prolific," "brilliant," "provocative," and a "fundamental philosopher" of the women's rights movement.[64] She was buried next to Sartre in the Montparnasse Cemetery in Paris, consenting in death to what she could or would not in life: lying with him for the rest of time.[65] As death rounded out the sharp edges of her intellect, contradictions, and politics, she became not just a wife but a mother. Articles and obituaries published around the world proclaimed her the mother of the women's movement, even the mother of all liberated women. The founders of the Centre Audiovisuel Simone-de-Beauvoir, an audiovisual archive of women's art and political movements in Paris, declared in a statement, "We are all orphans now."[66] Seven months before her death, an interviewer had asked Beauvoir what she thought of being considered a mother figure by feminists and feminist movements around the world. "The analogy is erroneous," the philosopher said, laughing, "because people don't tend to listen to what their mothers are telling them."[67]

CONCLUSION

AND, IF YOU'LL FORGIVE ME FOR ASKING, WHY SHOULD WE?

The electrician sings "Easy Love" in the kitchen
while fixing my light

Sea ice around Antarctica reaches a record low
and now, on the news, a man rushes down the streets
of Kyiv, his toddler in his arms. The word war enters
every room. Earth warms. In Texas, a child grows
bright with grief. Everything threatens to burst.

In the morning, my belly asks again for a baby.
I leak with longing. No one has told my body
yet about the world. All she hears is the sound
of someone in the other room,

still singing.

—Joy Sullivan, from *Instructions for Traveling West*

In 1976, Eppie Lederer, the woman behind the pseudonymous advice columnist Ann Landers, received a letter that made even her, by then the seasoned recipient of America's most burning questions, pause. "It was a simple enough letter," Landers wrote in a follow-up column published in *Good Housekeeping* that summer. "A young couple about to be married wrote to ask for guidance. They were undecided. They just couldn't make up their minds whether or not to have a family." So many of their friends seemed to resent their children, the letter writer observed. Their friends envied their freedom, their finances. One couple they knew got a tubal ligation *and* a vasectomy after their second child was born, just to make absolutely sure they'd never have another. "All this makes me wonder, Ann Landers. Is parenthood worth the trouble? Jim and I are very much in love. Our relationship is beautiful. We don't want anything to spoil it. All around us we see couples who were so much happier before they were tied down with a family." Landers put the question to her vast readership: "If you had it to do over again, would you have children?" Ten thousand replies poured in from across the United States, and—to Landers's "horror"—70 percent of them said no.[1]

No one has ever been able to replicate these results—buyer's remorse on the order of seven in ten parents wishing they could return their children to the store—and, to my knowledge, no one has even been able to give a satisfactory answer about why Landers's question returned such a high level of parental regret. *Newsday* reran the survey later that year, asking its readers the same question. "91% Would Have Children," the headline read when they published their results, adding, "(Take That, Ann Landers)."[2] In a 2013 Gallup poll, just around 7 percent of American parents said they would not have children if they could do it all over again.[3] So it's definitely not 70 percent of parents who regret having children (take that, Ann Landers), but it's also not zero.

The Norwegian sociologist Thomas Hansen has pointed out that there's a logical flaw in the three major stereotypes—or, as he calls them, "folk theories"—about people without children: (1) that children make people happy, ergo people without children are less happy than parents; (2) that people without children live lonely, empty lives, ergo they are less happy than parents; and (3) that people without children have prioritized pleasure and freedom, time with friends, romance, good food, nice houses, and travel over parenthood. The last stereotype, he observes dryly, "seems to suggest a pretty happy group." There's research to support that too. For at least thirty years, studies have repeatedly shown that people without children are happier than parents in the United States and in many developed countries.[4] More recent research has shown that parents are not only less happy when their children are young and the demands of time, energy, and money are greatest, as might seem logical. American empty nesters also report lower levels of happiness than older nonparents. Researchers studying American adults could find no type of parent—with or without custody; biological, adoptive, or step; of young or adult children—who reported a greater sense of well-being than nonparents. In the United States, parents report themselves to be 12 percent less happy than people without children. This is the biggest happiness gap between parents and nonparents in the developed world.[5]

To be clear, this is *not* because of the actual children. Children may be exhausting, but they are also joyous, curious, adorable, energetic beings that represent our future and enliven our present. Parents credit parenthood with giving them purpose, a sense of satisfaction, an identity, and meaningful social relationships.[6] Parents may report lower levels of happiness than nonparents, but other studies have suggested that people who have children have a greater sense of purpose or meaning and are more satisfied with their lives.[7]

The problem is not the children. The problem is the society parents have to parent in. "The emotional rewards of having children," a group of researchers recently explained, "are over-shadowed by the stress associated with contemporary parent-hood." Specifically, the emotional rewards are overshadowed by the stress of parenting in countries that don't have policies that support parents, like subsidized childcare that allows parents to work and generous paid time off that allows parents to spend time with their kids. These two policies alone—affordable child-care and paid time off for illness and vacation—have the power to fully erase the happiness gap between parents and nonparents, even in the absence of other supportive policies like maternity leave and guaranteed health insurance. In France, Finland, Nor-way, and Sweden, countries that have these policies and more, parents are happier than nonparents by as much as 8 percent. "The policy context of nations explains up to 100% of the par-enthood disadvantage" in happiness, the researchers concluded.[8]

In spite of widespread concern across the political spectrum about America's declining birth rate, we've done little to correct the policies that make parenting an unhappy endeavor. Nearly half of American women do not qualify for the Family and Medi-cal Leave Act, a 1993 law that guarantees twelve weeks of *unpaid* maternity leave.[9] According to the Bureau of Labor Statistics, just 23 percent of American workers qualify for paid parental leave of any length.[10] In late 2021, with Democrats holding the House, Senate, and White House, lawmakers failed to pass a law that would have provided a meager four weeks of paid maternity leave for many, but still not all, working women. For compar-ison's sake, according to data from the World Policy Analysis Center at UCLA, the global average for government-mandated paid maternity leave is twenty-nine weeks.[11] If you've ever ad-opted a puppy, you'll know that dogs, mammals that reach young adulthood in the span of a single year, are generally not taken from their mothers until they're eight weeks old.

And it's not just maternity leave. Health care, for us and our children, still comes and goes with employment, and its quality and cost hinge entirely on the generosity of our employers. Elder care really exists only if you can pay for it, meaning that many of us have found ourselves caring for aging parents, financially and otherwise, before we ever had a chance to contemplate children.[12] The US Supreme Court's 2022 decision to overturn *Roe v. Wade* allowed more than half of states to sharply curtail women's ability to terminate a pregnancy should something terrible happen to her or the child, making pregnancy and birth all the riskier in a country that already ranks well behind most developed nations in maternal mortality.[13] Our jobs come home with us on the phone in our pocket, demanding our time and attention during the evenings and on weekends. Wages have been stagnant for decades, and the rising costs of childcare and housing and student loan payments grow ever harder to cover. School shootings are so prevalent in the United States that districts across the country regularly hold active-shooter drills—drills that, according to researchers at Georgia Tech, cause trauma of their own. Anxiety, depression, and other symptoms of poor mental health are more common in children who go through them.[14] Oh, and then there's the climate, which barely makes headlines even when, as in the summer of 2021, enormous wildfires in the American and Canadian West blackened skies from Chicago to New York City to the White Mountains of New Hampshire, or as in the summer of 2022, when smoke from tundra fires across Alaska stretched from Fairbanks to Nome and heavy rains wiped out entire towns in Kentucky and Missouri. In light of our failure to account for the pressures, anxieties, and dangers of modern life, it's possible to argue that the decision to opt out of parenthood is perfectly rational. The decision to *have* children might be the one more in need of explanation.

"There's this expectation that we must justify our choice. People ask, 'Why not?'" Guen Douglas is a Canadian-born tattoo artist who owns a studio in Berlin, where she lives with her partner and a brown-spotted dachshund named Ludwig. She illustrates children's books on the side. Douglas is one of forty women profiled in We Are Childfree, a series of portraits and life stories of women without children compiled by the British photographer Zoë Noble. "Why don't we ask the other question?" Douglas went on. "'Why are you choosing to have a child?' That's the bigger question. Do you have the resources and emotional ability? Or is it just a shot in the dark because you feel you're supposed to? With our friends, we see that a lot of women have children because it's next on their checklist. The world is overpopulated. We have a climate crisis. If someone says they don't want kids, it should be like, 'Cool,' move on."[15]

But we struggle to move on, not least because the nuclear family is served to us as the only possible model of what it means to be a family: a married mother and father with biological children whom they raise mostly without help. Commonly used terms like "broken family" or "blended family"—like the one I grew up in— or "extended family" make sense only if the definition of family is something unbroken or unblended or limited. This is the kind of family we see on television and in movies and on social media platforms like Instagram, where the business of motherhood, a for-profit venture with a picture-perfect family as its most valuable product, has reached its highest expression. "Instagram is pure PR for the nuclear family," Kathryn Jezer-Morton has observed. "It totally erases how much childcare has always been shared within communities—and how much families have always relied on each other to raise their kids." Jezer-Morton is a doctoral student in sociology at Concordia University in Montreal.

Her dissertation documents what she calls the "mamasphere," the ever-expanding universe of women who build businesses, sometimes very lucrative ones, by featuring their homes, their marriages, and their children on social media. In the context of that business, Jezer-Morton explains, "it's easier to control the imagery if it includes only the nuclear family. Like, you're not going to ask your neighbour Janine who looks after the kids twice a week to put her hair in barrel curls so she can appear polished in a picture, you know?" The result is "a completely ahistorical representation of family life in most of the mamasphere"—and one, I might add, that viewers are meant to aspire to.[16]

But the isolation of family units also exists in people's actual offline, messy, and totally non-Instagram-worthy lives. The American retreat into the nuclear family over the past two centuries has been reinforced in our lifetimes, in part because the demands of modern life have reduced everyone's bandwidth. In one recent survey, more than one in five millennials said they didn't have a single friend beyond their partner or immediate family members, a number far higher than among boomers or Gen X. One in three said they found making new friends difficult. A common reason? "I'm too busy for friendships."[17] For parents in particular, friendships have been sacrificed on the altar of family survival, of getting everyone through the day fed, clothed, and with at least some of their material and emotional needs met. "You're stuck with your family, and you'll prioritize your spouse," Julie Beck wrote in *The Atlantic*. When our capacity gets stretched, it's friendships—that is, relationships sustained not by law or blood but by mutual and consistent gifts of time, attention, care, and presence—that "take a hit."[18] Building relationships that extend past our front doors takes time and emotional energy, and too many of us have too little of both.

"Community is wonderful," says Casper ter Kuile, a fellow at Harvard Divinity School. "But," he adds, community "is also *awful."* Kuile's research focuses on the rise of spirituality among young people. There is a growing pattern of people maintaining religious beliefs while abandoning organized religious communities for a variety of reasons: because of unwelcoming or discriminatory congregations, or because they've moved too frequently to have roots anywhere, or because they just need to sleep in on Sunday mornings to recover from grueling workweeks.[19] A Gallup poll in 2020 found that just 47 percent of Americans were members of churches, synagogues, or mosques—the first time in eighty years of polling that belonging to a religious organization would put you in the minority in America.[20] It's a pattern that extends far beyond church. In the 1950s, nearly one-third of American workers belonged to labor unions, organizations that served as social hubs for their members. In 2021, just over 10 percent of workers belonged to a union—about the same percentage of the workforce that are independent contractors or "gig workers," unmoored not just from a union but from any workplace or colleagues at all. Donations to charity have gone up significantly over the past two decades, but the percentage of people actually doing volunteer work in their communities has plummeted—a pattern that suggests people still feel obligated to their communities but are less willing or able to engage with them, or that they're so disconnected from their neighbors that they might not even know how to help. Breaking bread with others is one of life's simplest and most sustaining pleasures, and yet by some estimates Americans eat more than half of their meals alone.[21] It's a vicious cycle: one reason we don't have time and emotional energy to build community is because we don't have the communities or external support systems that—in other times and other places—might have helped to give us a break.

Community is hard. Building it, maintaining it. Community requires you to care about other people you have no legal or genetic reason to care about, maybe people you don't even know or don't really like. (Re)creating a community that lifts burdens off of parents and shares the work and joy of children requires some people to care about children they didn't birth. It requires people without children of their own to *actively* care, to show up consistently, in real, time-intensive, and material ways, for our friends with kids or the kids in our community. It requires parents to care about their neighbors, barrel curls or no, to allow them a real role in the responsibilities and joys that come with having children. It requires people with children to stop telling their childless friends, "You'll never understand," and instead say, "I'll do my best to explain it to you." And it requires all of us to invest in and support infrastructure and policies and institutions that help families of all kinds, whether or not we have kids of our own. It's what people have always done when times were hard: build kin and care for each other. We just have to want to.

At the end of January 2020, I signed a contract with Seal Press to publish a book about women without children in American history, about the "vibrance and variety," as I put it, of the choices they made, the lives they lived, and the things they accomplished. Within six weeks, I was instead consumed by trying to find toilet paper on the internet, relearning how to teach in a virtual classroom, and attending video birthday parties from my little household pod. I had a knot of fear and loneliness in my stomach that whole spring, especially as I tried to help my students navigate crises of every kind. But however hard my pandemic was, it was nothing compared to the one the parents I knew were having. Without even the meager support they receive in the best of times, they were barely making it through each day.

The last two years were, for me, an education on how little we care for mothers, families, and children, however much we protest otherwise. We've ended up at this bizarre political impasse, where the case that provided an opportunity for the US

Supreme Court to overturn *Roe*—ostensibly in defense of babies
and children—originated in Mississippi, a state that has proven
itself to be very bad at caring for the babies and children who
have already been born. Mississippi's infant mortality rate is the
worst in the nation. According to the nonprofit Save the Children, nearly one in four minors in the state experiences hunger.[22]
Governor Tate Reeves tweeted that once *Roe* fell, the state would
commit itself to taking care of mothers and children.[23] Why do
you have to wait for abortion laws to change, one commenter
asked, before you can help people?

The years I spent writing this book have softened me, especially toward the mothers and parents in my life. I originally
wanted to write about the value and accomplishments of women
without children in part because I wanted us to get more credit.
I was someone who would get annoyed, even angry, at the things
that fall onto people without kids, women in particular, especially at work: cleaning up after events alone after parents left
for day care pickups and dinner, finding my job harder because
of someone's maternity leave, picking up the slack when childcare arrangements fell through. Not having children, I'll admit to thinking, bitterly and more than once, doesn't mean I'm
not busy, or tired, or that I don't have anything important to
do. But as I researched and wrote, as I watched parents around
me struggle, I realized this kind of thinking is not just ungener-
ous and unkind, though it certainly is both of those things. It is
also dangerous, because it slips so easily into other, bigger, more
consequential things: *Why should my tax dollars fund that public
school, that program for at-risk youth, that housing project for struggling families, that early childhood initiative? I didn't choose to have
kids—you did.*

Women in the past, women in the pages of this book, taught
me that this kind of thinking—my time versus yours, your kids
versus my lack of them, my choices versus yours—is not the only

option. Watching parents struggle in our present has convinced me it cannot be. The way we've pulled back from each other has isolated all of us, and it's created a divide between mothers and women without children—a divide that would make sense only if our lives were lived entirely apart from each other's. But they aren't. We must think of the next generation as a project that demands work from all of us, not an individual one that parents must shoulder alone, if we have any hope of making it out of the crises that are coming for all of us: environmental, political, cultural. I wince when I think about how close I came to writing a book that took a side in what Sheila Heti called the "civil war" between mothers and non-mothers. If there are trenches—and it sure as hell looks like there are—we're in them together. We might as well have each other's back.

This book started with a question: Why aren't American women having children? The answer isn't simple. As we've seen, it's got history, and a lot of it. And childlessness in the present—by choice, by fate, or somewhere in between—is not something we can fix, even if we could pinpoint its precise constellation of causes, even if we agreed that it is necessary or even beneficial *to* fix it in the first place. The reasons women give today for not having children aren't new, and they aren't excuses. They're the result of clear-eyed stocktaking about the state of the world around them. We *do* work more, move more, and have fewer and looser community ties than Americans did in the past. The demands of modern parenting *have* ratcheted up: mothers today spend nearly twice as much time providing childcare for their children than they did fifty years ago, despite the fact that they are also much more likely to work outside the home.[24] It *is* harder to get pregnant today than it was thirty, seventy, one hundred years ago, not just because maternal age is rising (at least in part due to the pressures of modern life) but also because of environmental factors that have made all of us, but particularly men, less fertile.[25] Globally, historically, fertility *has* fallen when educational and professional opportunities open up to women. The earth *does* need fewer humans on it—fewer people burning oil and making trash and eating meat raised half a world away— if we want any hope of the future looking something like the present. We *do* have more freedom to pick which path we want to walk in life—and with more paths to choose from, there are more we leave behind.

In my more cynical moments, I think the right question is not "Why are American women not having children?" but "Why"— or, perhaps, *how on earth*—"would we?" In my more hopeful ones, the question is more productive: What are we going to do about it? How can we make fewer new lives, as our resource-strapped planet and time- and cash-strapped existences demand, without denying ourselves the joy, hope, and energy children offer? Can we imagine a future where the difference between having and not having children isn't so stark, where more than two adults are involved in raising any given child, where motherhood doesn't mean being crushed by work and life, and where nonmotherhood doesn't mean you are irrelevant in raising the next generation? "What if," the theorist Donna Haraway asks, "making a new baby became truly an act of joy and material, daily responsibility for an enlarged community?" This, Haraway writes, would require thinking beyond "my own body's babies."[26]

I often run on Chicago's Lakefront Trail, a paved bike and footpath that traces the edge of Lake Michigan for eighteen miles, from Edgewater Beach on the city's North Side all the way south to the Seventy-First Street Beach. One route takes me through Jackson Park, a Frederick Law Olmsted–designed patch of green space that served as the site of the 1893 World's Columbian

Exposition, across a patch of reclaimed prairie so wild that coyotes the size of German shepherds frolic in the snow in the winter, and through a tunnel to the lakefront at Promontory Point. The Point is a man-made peninsula cut into Lake Michigan, a landfill held in place by a limestone step revetment constructed in the 1920s and 1930s that now hosts a popular picnic area with fire pits and, in my humble opinion, the best swimming spot on the third coast. Standing on the Point's westernmost tip, you can see the towers of Chicago's downtown skyline to the north, and, more faintly, the smokestacks and giant factories that are Gary, Indiana, to the south.

I'll usually stop at a row of benches there, to retie a shoe or stretch out my creaky right hip or stare, usually in existential exhaustion, at the faraway horizon where the great lake meets the sky. One bench bears a small metal plaque dedicated to "Our Beloved Danny Boy," who died in October 2019 at the age of fifteen. It takes my breath away each time I stop there, the quiet grief in this beautiful, sacred-to-me place hitting me like a punch in the gut. More often, though, I visit Nancy Olivi's bench, just south of Danny's. "Nancy Olivi raised 10,000 kids," the plaque reads. "She was a teacher." Olivi was born and raised in the southwestern corner of Chicago and worked as a Chicago Public Schools teacher for more than thirty-seven years. When she died at the age of seventy in 2017, Olivi's obituary in the *Chicago Tribune* mentioned no sons or daughters, but notes that she was survived "by the thousands of children she poured [herself] into."[27]

In 2015, Donna Haraway helped organize a panel at the annual meeting of the Society for Social Studies of Science to talk about how we all can pour more of ourselves into children we didn't give birth to. 4S, as it's known for short, is a professional organization for the historians, sociologists, economists, and anthropologists who study the history and present of science and technology. Academic conferences are a genre of weekend travel like no other: hundreds, sometimes thousands of scholars wearing dorky lanyards take over a hotel in a seemingly random city—for this particular meeting, Denver—to rub shoulders with luminaries in their field, to make connections with book editors and publishers, and to drink far too much and far too late at the lobby bar with friends from graduate school who are now scattered at institutions across the country. Sometimes, though it has never seemed to me the primary purpose of such events, they even go to panels, where scholars share research on curated topics and invite feedback from audience members. Remarkably, the panel Haraway helped to organize convinced some two hundred attendees to put down their beers and cut short their coffee dates. The ballroom where it was held, rooms that are often freezing, echoey, and nearly empty at conferences like these, was standing room only.

In the conference booklet, the panel's description asked, "Can we develop anti-colonial, anti-imperialist, anti-racist, STS[Science and Technology Studies]-informed feminist politics of peopling the earth in current times, when babies should be rare yet precious?" Translated from the academese: Can we rethink family? If we truly valued the children we did bring into the world, caring for them and investing in their futures and lives at the level of community and society, could we make fewer of them, make their lives better, and lessen the burden on our planet? Could we do it without the racism and coercion that is all but synonymous with the term "population control"? Could we do it without reducing the joy and meaning parents get from their children—or, by spreading the burden and the number of people who share in that joy, could we increase it?

In spite of the body heat generated in that packed hotel ballroom, these questions have a way of leaving everyone cold. American conservatives, defenders of the traditional family as both an ideal and a right, tend to see population as a problem "out there."

"American fertility is falling!" they say. If we're pointing fingers, point them at India, central and southern Africa, the global
south, places where fertility is still relatively high. For some on
the political left, the merest suggestion of making fewer people rings any number of "history repeating itself" alarm bells:
sterilizations of the mentally ill, the poor, prisoners, Jews, Black
Americans, Indigenous people; American and international aid
given only if developing nations implement sterilization regimes;
eugenic policies that encouraged some births and limited others;
governments stripping women at home and abroad of bodily and
reproductive autonomy. "I have been screamed at after lectures
by my feminist colleagues of many years, told I can no longer
call myself a feminist," Haraway has said, "for arguing in public
that the weight of human numbers on a global scale, however
broken down by analysis of structured inequalities [and] oppo-
sition to ongoing racist population control programs . . . is an
outrage." But what if the goal was not just fewer babies, but more
community, more friends who count as family, more people we
call our kin? We need bumper stickers, Haraway has suggested:
"Make Kin Not Babies."[28]

The divide we understand to be so real between mothers and
non-mothers is one that was built for us long ago, and it was
built for a purpose: to limit women's socially acceptable options
to motherhood and the domestic sphere, and to mark as deviant those who dared to do other things. Mothers' options and
identities are constrained by this framework, no less than they
are for women without children. In a society that wants to divide
us, maybe the most radical thing we can do is turn to each other,
invite each other into our homes and our lives and our families.
If we want to change our society for the better, Sam Adler-Bell
wrote recently in New York magazine, "we must make this offer—
of interdependence in exchange for shared liberation—again and
again, in different places, to different people, in different ways

and hope that it begins to make sense."[29] On the "Make Kin Not Babies" bumper sticker, it's the "not babies" part that gets all the attention. I think that's warranted, considering the dark paths "not babies" initiatives have walked in recent history and in our deeper past. But since American women are making fewer babies anyway, it seems to me that the imperative to "make kin"—that is, to open our families and hearts and commitments to children we didn't birth, to people who didn't birth our children, and to the young people who represent all our futures—is where we should focus our energy.

"Nancy Olivi raised 10,000 kids," her plaque reads. "She will be missed."

Photo by author.

ACKNOWLEDGMENTS

I owe a deep debt of gratitude to Target, which provided extensive in-person and virtual therapy throughout the entire book-writing process. Simply walking through Target's automatic doors is enough to give me a full-body feeling of calm: if the apocalypse happens while I'm in here, I think, I'll have everything I could ever need. This is a thought I've had to have more often lately. Ellie and Jake—and, briefly but significantly, Daisy—also provided essential emotional support. Much of this book was written on my couch (chairs are unacceptable, as they don't have room for three) with a sleeping pug leaning against each of my thighs.

My dear friend Bathsheba Demuth told me repeatedly and with great patience how on earth someone writes a book, reminded me almost daily to eat lunch, and always texted me at the precise moment the wheels were falling off with the most inspiring of questions: "So, what are we buying today?" Many credit cards were harmed in the making of this book. For the past fifteen years, she and Alex Labinov have shown me what it means to have chosen family. I will always be grateful.

Don Fehr was a champion of this project from day one, when I was at my most unsure. He offered encouragement, humor,

kindness, and wisdom at every stage, and, critically, made it possible for me to pretend I knew what I was doing. To Emma Berry,
Claire Potter, Madeline Lee, Lara Heimert, Liz Dana, and everyone at Basic/Seal: thank you for taking a chance on me, and for
your warmth, enthusiasm, and commitment to shepherding this
book through a global pandemic, economic chaos, personal trag-
edies and joys, moves, and years of working from home. Editing
someone else's book is an act of immense generosity, and—even
though I and this book sort of fell into her lap—I could not have
asked for a better editor than Emma. Thanks to her, this book is
better than I could have made it on my own. Stephanie Palazzo,
Rebecca Altman, and Kathleen Belew were the wisest and kind-
est of "book doulas," holding my hand as this manuscript made
its way out of my head and into the world.

I owe a huge debt of gratitude to the brilliant poets Kate Baer
and Joy Sullivan for allowing me to use their work as this book's
two epigraphs. Their poetry captures the complexities and contradictions of existing in the world as a woman—being a mother,
not being a mother, longing to be one, and kind of sometimes
wishing you weren't—far more viscerally than I ever could.
Sullivan's much-needed reminder—that "joy is not a trick"—
may have to be my next tattoo. It is an honor to have both of
their words here alongside mine. Thanks are also due to Joanna
MacKenzie, who renewed my belief in serendipity, possibly even
in fate, and definitely in good people.

It is a regular source of amazement for me that I have found
myself teaching in the History Department at the University of
Chicago, where I am surrounded by colleagues who are as kind
as they are intellectually terrifying. My job, and therefore this
book, would not exist without their support. I am even more
grateful to UChicago's history students, for their intelligence,
curiosity, enthusiasm, and commitment to making a better world
than the one they've been given—and for keeping me up-to-date

on the really important issues, like what kind of jeans I should be wearing if I don't want to look old. The kids are all right, y'all, and I'm lucky to spend so much time with them.

My mom continued to pick up the phone even though I insisted on calling much too early in the morning, usually while on a run and with considerable traffic noise and wind in the background, and often complained and/or panicked and then hung up without asking much about her. She is my mother, and she is also my friend. For this, I am astonishingly fortunate.

A list of friends and family too long to name supported and loved on me unceasingly throughout the book-writing process: they sent encouraging texts and Starbucks gift cards, kept calling when I didn't call back, fed me dinner, shared baskets of curly fries, and were remarkably willing to drink wine with me on weeknights. Stephanie Davis texted "Good morning!" to me every single morning, a daily, cherished reminder that I was not and am never alone. Alice Goff and Ariana Strahl made me a gin and tonic on a Tuesday in November 2021 that may actually have saved everything. It is a well-known truth that behind every great woman there are many other, far greater women who answer her texts at all hours of the day and night. Thank you to all of mine.

Finally, I owe so much of this, as I do much of most things, to my husband Bob, who dutifully repeated, "Your book is not bad," every time I declared that it was for more than three years. His partnership and support make everything possible. Happy birthday! I am the one who is lucky.

NOTES

Author's Note

1. Sheila Heti, *Motherhood* (New York: Henry Holt, 2018), 157–158.
2. Adele E. Clarke, "Introduction," in *Making Kin Not Population*, eds. Adele E. Clarke and Donna Haraway (Chicago: Prickly Paradigm Press, 2018), 30–31.

Introduction: We're Not Having Children

1. Sheila Heti, *Motherhood* (New York: Henry Holt, 2018), 90.
2. I'm thinking specifically of the episode titled "Cherry" of the 2018 HBO miniseries *Sharp Objects*, but there are many, many other examples.
3. *House of Cards*, season 4, episode 12, "Chapter 51," directed by Jakob Verbruggen, Netflix, March 4, 2016.
4. Meredith Hale, "5 Things People Without Kids Just Don't Understand," *Scary Mommy*, September 29, 2015, www.scarymommy.com/5-things-people -without-kids-just-dont-understand/; Natalie Stechyson, "I Didn't Lose Friends After Having Kids. I Just Moved On," *HuffPost*, September 16, 2019, www.huffpost.com/archive/ca/entry/losing-friends-after-kids_ca_5d76ab bee4b0752102312651; "Can Mothers and Childless Women Ever Truly Be Friends? Two Writers Explain Why They Believe These Relationships Rarely Work Out," *Daily Mail*, October 11, 2017, www.dailymail.co.uk /femail/article-4971826/Can-mothers-childless-women-truly-friends.html.
5. J. Christopher Herold, *The Age of Napoleon* (New York: Mariner Books, 2002), 434.
6. Linda K. Kerber, *Women of the Republic: Intellect and Ideology in Revolutionary America* (Chapel Hill: University of North Carolina Press, 1980), 11.
7. Myra Bradwell v. State of Illinois, 83 U.S. 130 (1873), 141.
8. The video has since been deleted. Quoted in Dayna Evans, "Ivanka Trump Says a Woman's Most Important Job Is Being a Mother," *The Cut*,

October 3, 2016, www.thecut.com/2016/10/ivanka-trump-says-a-womans
-most-important-job-is-motherhood.html.

9. White House, "Remarks by the First Lady at Tuskegee University
Commencement Address," news release, May 9, 2015, https://obamawhite
house.archives.gov/the-press-office/2015/05/09/remarks-first-lady-tuskegee
-university-commencement-address.

10. Amy Chozik, "Hilary Clinton and the Return of the (Unbaked) Cookies," *New York Times*, November 5, 2016, www.nytimes.com/2016/11/06/us
/politics/hillary-clinton-cookies.html.

11. Anastasia Berg, "Now Is as Good a Time as Ever to Start a Family,"
New York Times, April 30, 2020, www.nytimes.com/2020/04/30/opinion
/coronavirus-pregnancy.html; Tom Whyman, "Why, Despite Everything,
You Should Have Kids (If You Want Them)," *New York Times*, April 13,
2021, www.nytimes.com/2021/04/13/opinion/baby-bust-covid-philosophy
-natalism.html.

12. Ross Douthat, "More Babies, Please," December 1, 2012, www.nytimes
.com/2012/12/02/opinion/sunday/douthat-the-birthrate-and-americas
-future.html.

13. Senator Mike Lee, "Remarks on the Green New Deal," March 26, 2019,
www.lee.senate.gov/2019/3/remarks-on-the-green-new-deal.

14. Quoted in Caroline Vakil, "JD Vance Takes Aim at Culture Wars,
Childless Politicians," *The Hill*, July 23, 2021, https://thehill.com/homenews
/senate/564646-jd-vance-takes-aim-at-culture-wars-and.

15. Keith Wagstaff, "Is Francis the Most Liberal Pope Ever?," *The
Week*, January 9, 2015, https://theweek.com/articles/461664/francis-most
-liberal-pope-ever; Stephanie Kirchgaessner, "Pope Francis: Not Having
Children Is Selfish," *The Guardian*, February 11, 2015, www.theguardian
.com/world/2015/feb/11/pope-francis-the-choice-to-not-have-children-is
-selfish.

16. Quoted in "Pope Francis Says Choosing Pets Over Kids Is Selfish," BBC News, January 5, 2022, www.bbc.com/news/world-europe
-59884801.

17. Amy Blackstone, *Childfree By Choice: The Movement Redefining Family
and Creating a New Age of Independence* (New York: Dutton, 2019), 25–26.

18. Adrienne Rich, *Of Woman Born: Motherhood as Experience and Institution* (1986; repr., New York: W. W. Norton, 1995), 11.

19. Quoted in Frank F. Furstenburg, Sheela Kennedy, Vonnie C. McCloyd,
Ruben G. Rumbaut, and Richard A. Setterstein Jr., "Growing Up Is Harder
To Do," *Contexts* 3, no. 3 (August 2004): 35.

20. See Stanlie M. James, "Mother*ing*: A Possible Black Feminist Link to
Social Transformation," in *Theorizing Black Feminisms: The Visionary Prag-
matism of Black Women*, eds. Stanlie M. James and Abena P. A. Busia (New
York: Routledge, 1993), 34–54.

21. bell hooks, "Revolutionary Parenting," in *Feminist Theory: From Margin to Center* (New York: Routledge, 2016), 133–147.

22. Lawrence Stone, *The Family, Sex and Marriage in England, 1500–1800* (New York: Harper & Row, 1977), 7–9.

23. Elaine Tyler May, *Barren in the Promised Land: Childless Americans and the Pursuit of Happiness* (New York: Basic Books, 1996), 12.

24. Brady E. Hamilton, Joyce A. Martin, and Michelle J. K. Osterman, "Births: Provisional Data for 2021," National Center for Health Statistics, Vital Statistics Rapid Release report no. 20, May 2022, www.cdc.gov/nchs/data/vsrr/vsrr020.pdf.

25. Jo Jones and Paul Placek, *Adoption: By the Numbers* (Alexandria, VA: National Council for Adoption, 2017), ii; Katherine Wiles, "International Adoptions Dropped by Nearly Half During 2020. But COVID-19 Only Helped to Accelerate a Years-Long Decline," *MarketWatch*, November 10, 2021, www.marketwatch.com/story/international-adoptions-dropped-by-nearly-half-during-2020-but-covid-19-only-helped-to-accelerate-a-years-long-decline-11636496504.

26. According to data from the Pew Research Center, as of 2018, 55 percent of millennial women had experienced at least one live birth. Amanda Barroso, Kim Parker, and Jesse Bennett, "As Millennials Near 40, They're Approaching Family Life Differently Than Previous Generations," Pew Research Center, May 27, 2020, www.pewresearch.org/social-trends/2020/05/27/as-millennials-near-40-theyre-approaching-family-life-differently-than-previous-generations.

27. Anna Brown, "Growing Share of Childless Adults in U.S. Don't Expect to Ever Have Children," Pew Research Center, November 19, 2021, www.pewresearch.org/fact-tank/2021/11/19/growing-share-of-childless-adults-in-u-s-dont-expect-to-ever-have-children.

28. According to data from the World Bank, "Fertility Rate, Total (Births per Woman)—East Asia and Pacific," https://data.worldbank.org/indicator/SP.DYN.TFRT.IN?locations=Z4.

29. "Fertility Statistics," Eurostat Statistics Explained, March 2021, https://ec.europa.eu/eurostat/statistics-explained/index.php?title=Fertility_statistics#live_births_per_woman_in_the_EU_in_2019; East-West Center, "The Influence of Family Policies on Fertility in France" (policy brief no. 7, United Nations Expert Group Meeting on Policy Responses to Low Fertility, November 2–3, 2015).

30. Hamilton, Martin, and Osterman, "Births: Provisional Data for 2021."

31. Sabrina Tavernise, Claire Cain Miller, Quoctrung Bui, and Robert Gebeloff, "Why American Women Everywhere Are Delaying Motherhood," *New York Times*, June 16, 2021, www.nytimes.com/2021/06/16/us/declining-birthrate-motherhood.html.

32. The Pew Research Center defines millennials as people born between 1981 and 1996. Michael Dimock, "Defining Generations: Where Millennials End and Generation Z Begins," Pew Research Center, January 17, 2019, www.pewresearch.org/fact-tank/2019/01/17/where-millennials-end-and-generation-z-begins.

33. Anna Louie Sussman, "The Sexual-Health Supply Chain Is Broken," *The Atlantic*, June 8, 2020, www.theatlantic.com/international/archive/2020/06/coronavirus-pandemic-sex-health-condoms-reproductive-health/612298.

34. Laura D. Lindberg, Alicia VandeVusse, Jennifer Mueller, and Marielle Kirstein, "Early Impacts of the COVID-19 Pandemic: Findings from the 2020 Guttmacher Survey of Reproductive Health Experiences," Guttmacher Institute, June 2020, www.guttmacher.org/report/early-impacts-covid-19-pandemic-findings-2020-guttmacher-survey-reproductive-health#.

35. Quote from Dr. Meera Shah, chief medical officer of Planned Parenthood Hudson Peconic, in AP, "Abortion Demand Rising Amid Pandemic," CBS News, April 14, 2020, www.cbsnews.com/news/abortion-demand-rising-amid-pandemic.

36. Lindberg et al., "Early Impacts of the COVID-19 Pandemic."

37. Quoted in Natalie Gontcharova, "Yes, the 'COVID Baby Bust' Is Real—Unless You're Rich," *Refinery29*, March 3, 2021, www.refinery29.com/en-us/2021/03/10320247/covid-pregnancy-baby-bust.

38. Jennifer Nelson, *Women of Color and the Reproductive Rights Movement* (New York: New York University Press, 2003), 3.

39. Theodore Roosevelt, "On American Motherhood," delivered to the National Congress of Mothers, March 13, 1905, in Melody Rose, *Abortion: A Documentary and Reference Guide* (Westport, CT: Greenwood Press, 2008), 24.

40. Donna Haraway, "Making Kin in the Chthulucene: Reproducing Multispecies Justice," in *Making Kin Not Population*, 68.

41. Linda Gordon, *Women's Body, Women's Right: Birth Control in America* (New York: Grossman, 1976), 332.

42. Dorothy E. Roberts, *Killing the Black Body: Race, Reproduction, and the Meaning of Liberty* (New York: Vintage Books, 1999), 90; Clarke and Haraway, *Making Kin Not Population*, 55.

43. Jane Lawrence, "The Indian Health Service and the Sterilization of Native American Women," *American Indian Quarterly* 24, no. 3 (Summer 2000): 400.

44. Maya Manian, "Immigration Detention and Coerced Sterilization: History Tragically Repeats Itself," ACLU News & Commentary, September 29, 2020, www.aclu.org/news/immigrants-rights/immigration-detention-and-coerced-sterilization-history-tragically-repeats-itself.

45. Mary Harris and Laurie Bertram Roberts, "What Happens to the Pro-Choice Movement Now," October 26, 2020, in *What Next*, podcast, https://slate.com/transcripts/cUdVYoFoWGcvWEo5alFkUVRoKzhRbUdDL2E1eEdRQk85RDB2ZXhUS1VDZz0=.

46. Gladys Martinez, Kimberly Daniels, Anjani Chandra, "Fertility of Men and Women Aged 15–44 Years in the United States: National Survey of Family Growth, 2006–2010," *National Health Statistics Reports*, no. 51 (April 12, 2012): 4.

47. Tomas Frejka, "Childlessness in the United States," in *Childlessness in Europe: Contexts, Causes, and Consequences*, eds. Michaela Kreyenfeld and Dirk Konietzka (Cham, Switzerland: Springer, 2017), 169.

48. Kristen J. Wilson, *Not Trying: Infertility, Childlessness, and Ambivalence* (Nashville, TN: Vanderbilt University Press, 2014), 25.

49. Lauren Bauer, Sara Estep, and Winnie Yee, "Time Waited for No Mom in 2020," Brookings, July 22, 2021, www.brookings.edu/blog/up -front/2021/07/22/time-waited-for-no-mom-in-2020. Data taken from 2020 American Time Use Survey, published by the US Bureau of Labor Statistics, July 22, 2021.

50. Hooleeya M-N (@hooleeya), "But also, there's a reason I chose not to have kids and while being stuck at home for weeks during a pandemic wasn't explicitly one, it isn't far off.," Twitter, March 16, 2020, https://twitter.com /hooleeya/status/1239714705947660291.

51. Natalie Zemon Davis, "'Women's History' in Transition: The European Case," *Feminist Studies* 3, no. 3/4 (Spring–Summer 1976): 90.

52. This is paraphrased from Emma Brockes, "Sheila Heti: 'There's a Sadness in Not Wanting the Things That Give Others Their Life's Meaning,'" *The Guardian*, May 25, 2018, www.theguardian.com/books/2018/may/25 /sheila-heti-motherhood-interview.

53. "The Ghost Ship That Didn't Carry Us," Dear Sugar, *The Rumpus*, April 21, 2011, https://therumpus.net/2011/04/dear-sugar-the-rumpus -advice-column-71-the-ghost-ship-that-didnt-carry-us.

54. See Jenny Brown, *Birth Strike: The Hidden Fight over Women's Work* (Oakland, CA: PM Press, 2019).

55. Tavernise et al., "Why American Women Everywhere Are Delaying Motherhood."

56. Michel-Rolph Trouillot, *Silencing the Past: Power and the Production of History* (Boston: Beacon Press, 1995), 24.

Chapter 1. Because We've Always Made Choices

1. George Washington Dixon, *Trial of Madame Restell, Alias Ann Lohman, for Abortion and Causing the Death of Mrs. Purdy* (New York, 1841), 3; Clifford Browder, *The Wickedest Woman in New York: Madame Restell, the Abortionist* (Hamden, CT: Archon Books, 1988), 42.

2. Marvin Olasky, "Advertising Abortion in the 1830s and 1840s: Madame Restell Builds a Business," *Journalism History* 13, no. 2 (Summer 1986): 49–50.

3. A. Cheree Carlson, *The Crimes of Womanhood: Defining Femininity in a Court of Law* (Urbana: University of Illinois Press, 2009), 112–113, 120.

4. Leslie J. Reagan, *When Abortion Was a Crime: Women, Medicine, and Law in the United States, 1867–1973* (Berkeley: University of California Press, 1997), 8–9.

5. Madame Restell, *The Wonderful Trial of Caroline Lohman, Alias Restell, with Speeches of Counsel, Charge of Court, and Verdict of Jury* (New York: Burgess Stringer & Co., 1847), 17.

6. Rickie Solinger, *Pregnancy and Power: A Short History of Reproductive Politics in America* (New York: New York University Press, 2005), 55.

7. Reagan, *When Abortion Was a Crime*, 8–14.

8. James Mohr, *Abortion in America: The Origins and Evolution of National Policy* (New York: Oxford University Press, 1978), 50.

9. Janet Farrell Brodie, *Contraception and Abortion in Nineteenth-Century America* (Ithaca, NY: Cornell University Press, 1994), 227.

10. Discussed in William D. Haggard, "Abortion: Accidental, Essential, Criminal," address before the Nashville Academy of Medicine, August 4, 1898; see also Carroll Smith-Rosenberg, *Disorderly Conduct: Visions of Gender in Victorian America* (New York: Oxford University Press, 1986), 221.

11. Daniel K. Williams, *Defenders of the Unborn: The Pro-Life Movement Before Roe v. Wade* (New York: Oxford University Press, 2016), 13.

12. Dale Cockrell, *Demons of Disorder: Early Blackface Minstrels and Their World* (New York: Cambridge University Press, 1997), 96–98; Dixon, *Trial of Madame Restell*, 5.

13. Multiple classified advertisements, *New York Herald*, December 10, 1841.

14. Dixon, *Trial of Madame Restell*, 3.

15. Carlson, *Crimes of Womanhood*, 118–120.

16. Sarah Gristwood, *Elizabeth and Leicester: The Truth About the Virgin Queen and the Man She Loved* (New York: Viking Penguin, 2007), 125.

17. Kate Clifford Larson, *Bound for the Promised Land: Harriet Tubman, Portrait of an American Hero* (New York: Random House, 2004), 260.

18. Josef Ehmer, "The Significance of Looking Back: Fertility Before the 'Fertility Decline,'" *Historical Social Research/Historische Sozialforschung* 36, no. 2 (2011): 24.

19. John M. Riddle, *Eve's Herbs: A History of Contraception and Abortion in the West* (Cambridge, MA: Harvard University Press, 1997), 54; Aine Collier, *The Humble Little Condom: A History* (Buffalo, NY: Prometheus Books, 2010), 29; Timothy Taylor, *The Prehistory of Sex: Four Million Years of Human Sexual Culture* (New York: Bantam Books, 1996), 86–87; David Michael Feldman, *Birth Control in Jewish Law: Marital Relations, Contraception, and Abortion as Set Forth in the Classic Texts of Jewish Law* (Northvale, NJ: J. Aronson, 1998), 169–170.

20. Soranus of Ephesius, *Soranus' Gynecology*, trans. Owsei Temkin (Baltimore: Johns Hopkins University Press: 1991), 60–66.

21. Ludwig Edelstein, *The Hippocratic Oath: Text, Translation, and Interpretation* (Baltimore: Johns Hopkins Press, 1943), 6; Hippocrates of Cos, "Nature of the Child," in *Hippocrates*, trans. Paul Potter, vol. 10 (Cambridge, MA: Harvard University Press, 2014), 36–37.

22. Taylor, *The Prehistory of Sex*, 88–91.

23. Ehmer, "The Significance of Looking Back," 27.

24. Gen. 38:9 (NRSV); These (and more!) can be found in Gigi Santow, "Coitus Interruptus and the Control of Natural Fertility," *Population Studies* 49, no. 1 (March 1995): 35–37.

25. Simon Szreter and Eilidh Garrett, "Reproduction, Compositional Demography, and Economic Growth: Family Planning in England Long Before the Fertility Decline," *Population and Development Review* 26, no. 1 (March 2000): 57.

26. Ann Taylor Allen, *Feminism and Motherhood in Western Europe, 1890–1970: The Maternal Dilemma* (New York: Palgrave Macmillan, 2005), 11.

27. Judith Walzer Leavitt, *Brought to Bed: Childbearing in America, 1750–1950* (New York: Oxford University Press, 1986), 19.

28. Margaret Marsh and Wanda Ronner, *The Empty Cradle: Infertility in America from Colonial Times to the Present* (Baltimore: Johns Hopkins University Press, 1996), 92.

29. Peggy Cooper Davis, "Neglected Stories and the Lawfulness of Roe v. Wade," *Harvard Civil Rights–Civil Liberties Law Review* 28, no. 299 (1993): 375.

30. See Carol Anderson, *White Rage: The Unspoken Truth About Our Racial Divide* (New York: Bloomsbury, 2017).

31. Solinger, *Pregnancy and Power*, 63–65.

32. Alice Kessler-Harris, *Out to Work: A History of Wage-Earning Women in America* (New York: Oxford University Press, 2003), 98.

33. Lillie Devereux Blake, testimony of September 18, 1883, in US Education and Labor Committee, *Report of the Committee of the Senate Upon the Relations Between Capital and Labor* (Washington, DC: Government Printing Office, 1885), 597, https://hdl.handle.net/2027/pst.000006655358.

34. Mary Alden Hopkins, "Birth Control and Public Morals: An Interview with Anthony Comstock," *Harper's Weekly*, May 22, 1915 (archived by Pluralism and Unity Project, Michigan State University), www.expo98.msu.edu/people/comstock.htm.

35. Amy Werbel, *Lust on Trial: Censorship and the Rise of American Obscenity in the Age of Anthony Comstock* (New York: Columbia University Press, 2018), 15.

36. Werbel, *Lust on Trial*, 267.

37. Amendment to the Comstock Act, ch. 186, 5 1, 19 stat. 90 (1876), 42. 3 Q.B. 360 (1868).

38. "Debated In Senate," February 20, 1873, Cong. Globe, 42nd Cong., 2nd Sess., 1525 (1873).

39. "Amended and Passed House," March 1, 1873, Cong. Globe, 42nd Congress, 2nd Sess., 2005 (1873).

40. Hopkins, "Birth Control and Public Morals."

41. Werbel, *Lust on Trial*, 90.

42. Brodie, *Contraception and Abortion*, 281.

43. Hopkins, "Birth Control and Public Morals."

44. Browder, *The Wickedest Woman in New York*, 185; Werbel, *Lust on Trial*, 306.

45. Statement by Joseph Earle Moore (Joint Army and Navy Committee, Conference of Morale Officers, Washington, DC, February 25–28, 1941); "Classified List of Social Hygiene Pamphlets—February 1944," Publications

A–D, Records of the Office of Community War Services, Record Group 215, National Archives Building, College Park, MD, cited in Madeleine L. Gaiser, "The Other 'VD': The Educational Campaign to Reduce Venereal Disease Rate During World War II" (thesis, Gettysburg College, 2016), https://cupola.gettysburg.edu/student_scholarship/475.

46. Werbel, *Lust on Trial*, 127–128.

47. Jonathan Eig, *The Birth of the Pill: How Four Crusaders Reinvented Sex and Launched a Revolution* (New York: W.W. Norton, 2014), 257, 265, 313.

48. Eisenstadt v. Baird, 405 U.S. 438 (1972), 453.

49. Centers for Disease Control and Prevention, "Achievements in Public Health, 1900–1999: Healthier Mothers and Babies," *Morbidity and Mortality Weekly Report* 48, no. 38 (October 1, 1999): 849–858.

50. Caroline S. Carlin, Angela R. Fertig, and Bryan E. Dowd, "Affordable Care Act's Mandate Eliminating Contraceptive Cost Sharing Influenced Choices of Women with Employer Coverage," *Health Affairs* 35, no. 9 (September 2016); Sue Ricketts, Greta Klingler, and Renee Schwalberg, "Game Change in Colorado: Widespread Use of Long-Acting Reversible Contraceptives and Rapid Decline in Births Among Young, Low-Income Women," *Perspectives on Sexual and Reproductive Health* 46, no. 3 (September 2014): 125–132.

51. "About Teen Pregnancy," Reproductive Health: Teen Pregnancy, Centers for Disease Control and Prevention, last modified November 15, 2021, www.cdc.gov/teenpregnancy/about/index.htm.

52. Stories about delayed care were widely reported in the weeks after the *Dobbs* decision. For example, Frances Stead Sellers and Fenit Nirappil, "Confusion Post-Roe Spurs Delays, Denials for Some Lifesaving Pregnancy Care," *Washington Post*, July 16, 2022, www.washingtonpost.com/health/2022/07/16/abortion-miscarriage-ectopic-pregnancy-care.

53. S. Philip Morgan, "Late Nineteenth- and Early Twentieth-Century Childlessness," *American Journal of Sociology* 97, no. 3 (November 1991): 779.

54. Rachel Benson Gold, "Lessons from Before Roe: Will Past Be Prologue?," *Guttmacher Policy Review* 6, no. 1 (March 2003): 8.

Chapter 2. Because We'll Be on Our Own

1. Barbara Ransby, *Ella Baker and the Black Freedom Movement: A Radical Democratic Vision* (Chapel Hill: University of North Carolina Press, 2003), 37–40.

2. Ella Baker, interview with Sue Thrasher, April 19, 1977, interview G-0008, Southern Oral History Program Collection #4007, Southern Historical Collection, Wilson Library, University of North Carolina at Chapel Hill, https://docsouth.unc.edu/sohp/G-0008/excerpts/excerpt_8569.html.

3. Ransby, *Ella Baker*, 29.

4. Charles Payne, "Ella Baker and Models of Social Change," *Signs* 14, no. 4 (Summer 1989): 886.

5. Ellen Cantarow and Susan O'Malley, *Moving the Mountain: Women Working for Social Change* (Old Westbury, NY: Feminist Press, 1980), 58.

6. Payne, "Ella Baker and Models of Social Change," 886.

7. Patricia Hill Collins, *Black Feminist Thought: Knowledge, Consciousness, and the Politics of Empowerment* (New York: Routledge, 2000), 194; Cantarow and O'Malley, *Moving the Mountain*, 59.

8. Collins, *Black Feminist Thought*, 53.

9. W. Dale Nelson, "Quayle Says He'd Support Daughter on Any Abortion Decision," Associated Press, July 23, 1992, https://apnews.com/article/c3a19b8dd82a54646b424ef6a651d2c3.

10. Ann Hartman, "Murphy Brown, Dan Quayle, and the American Family," *Social Work* 37, no. 5 (September 1992): 387–388.

11. James Danforth Quayle III, "Murphy Brown Speech," May 19, 1992 (archived by Voices of Democracy: The U.S. Oratory Project, University of Maryland), https://voicesofdemocracy.umd.edu/quayle-murphy-brown-speech-text; Andrew Rosenthal, "Quayle Attacks a 'Cultural Elite,' Saying It Mocks Nation's Values," *New York Times*, June 10, 1992, A1, www.nytimes.com/1992/06/10/us/1992-campaign-quayle-attacks-cultural-elite-saying-it-mocks-nation-s-values.html.

12. Helena M. Wall, *Fierce Communion: Family and Community in Colonial America* (Cambridge, MA: Harvard University Press, 1990), 8.

13. Collins, *Black Feminist Thought*, 55; see also James H. Sweet, *Domingos Álvarez, African Healing, and the Intellectual History of the Atlantic World* (Chapel Hill: University of North Carolina Press, 2013), 33.

14. Kim Anderson, "Affirmations of an Indigenous Feminist," in *Indigenous Women and Feminism: Politics, Activism, Culture*, eds. Cheryl Suzack, Shari M. Huhndorf, Jeanne Perreault, and Jean Barman (Vancouver: University of British Columbia Press, 2010), 83.

15. Sacha C. Engelhardt, Patrick Bergeron, Alain Gagnon, Lisa Dillon, and Fanie Pelletier, "Using Geographic Distance as a Potential Proxy for Help in the Assessment of the Grandmother Hypothesis," *Current Biology* 29 (2019): 652–653; Jonathan Lambert, "Living Near Your Grandmother Has Evolutionary Benefits," NPR, February 7, 2019, www.npr.org/sections/goatsandsoda/2019/02/07/692088371/living-near-your-grandmother-has-evolutionary-benefits.

16. Biography of Le Play in *Fifty Key Sociologists: The Formative Theorists*, ed. John Scott (New York: Routledge, 2007), 70.

17. Oxford English Dictionary cites the first use of the term from Malinowski's 1924 text *Psyche*, *Oxford English Dictionary* online, s.v. "nuclear family," accessed June 29, 2021.

18. William M. Fowler, *The Baron of Beacon Hill: A Biography of John Hancock* (Boston: Houghton Mifflin, 1980), 10–11, 13–14.

19. Marsh and Ronner, *The Empty Cradle*, 18.

20. 100,000 pounds sterling in 1764 is equivalent to well over $19 million today. Eric W. Nye, "Pounds Sterling to Dollars: Historical Conversion

of Currency," accessed November 18, 2020, www.uwyo.edu/numimage
/currency.htm.

21. Fowler, *The Baron of Beacon Hill*, 49.

22. Tamara K. Hareven, "The History of the Family and the Complexity of Social Change," *American Historical Review* 96, no. 1 (February 1991): 104.

23. Wall, *Fierce Communion*, 14.

24. Lawrence Stone, *The Family, Sex and Marriage in England, 1500–1800* (New York: Harper & Row, 1977), 6.

25. Carroll Smith-Rosenberg, "The Female World of Love and Ritual: Relations Between Women in Nineteenth-Century America," *Signs* 1, no. 1 (October 1975): 1–29.

26. Marsh and Ronner, *The Empty Cradle*, 17.

27. Mary Ann Mason, *From Father's Property to Children's Rights: The History of Child Custody in the United States* (New York: Columbia University Press, 1994), 39.

28. Wall, *Fierce Communion*, 97–98.

29. Robert Wells, *Revolutions in Americans' Lives: A Demographic Perspective on the History of Americans, Their Families, and Their Society* (Westport, CT: Greenwood Press, 1982), 50–51.

30. Stone, *The Family*, 4; Wall, *Fierce Communion*, 127; Marsh and Ronner, *The Empty Cradle*, 10–11, 17–19.

31. Ransby, *Ella Baker*, 64–65.

32. Payne, "Ella Baker and Models of Social Change," 887.

33. Aprele Elliott, "Ella Baker: Free Agent in the Civil Rights Movement," *Journal of Black Studies* 26, no. 5 (May 1996): 595.

34. Quoted in Juan Williams, *Eyes on the Prize: America's Civil Rights Years, 1954–1965* (New York: Penguin, 2013), 180.

35. Raymond Arsenault, *Freedom Riders: 1961 and the Struggle for Justice* (New York: Oxford University Press, 2006), 153–157.

36. Payne, "Ella Baker and Models of Social Change," 888.

37. Baker, interview with Sue Thrasher, April 19, 1977; Payne, "Ella Baker and Models of Social Change," 888; see also Ransby, *Ella Baker*, 120.

38. Ransby, *Ella Baker*, 34, 145.

39. Ransby, *Ella Baker*, 145.

40. Baker, interview with Sue Thrasher, April 19, 1977.

41. Ransby, *Ella Baker*, 254–255.

42. See, for example, Gretchen Livingston, "For Most Highly Educated Women, Motherhood Doesn't Start Until the 30s," Pew Research Center, January 15, 2015, www.pewresearch.org/fact-tank/2015/01/15/for-most-highly-educated-women-motherhood-doesnt-start-until-the-30s.

43. Niara Sudarkasa, "Reflections on Motherhood in Nuclear and Extended Families in Africa and the United States," in *Extended Families in Africa and the African Diaspora*, eds. Osei-Mensah Aborampah and Niara Sudarkasa (Trenton, NJ: Africa World Press, 2011), 46, 51.

44. Carol B. Stack, *All Our Kin: Strategies for Survival in a Black Community* (New York: Basic Books, 1974), xiii.

45. Stack, *All Our Kin*, 60–62, 66.

46. Stack, *All Our Kin*, 74–75, 85.

47. Patricia Hill Collins, "The Meaning of Motherhood in Black Culture and Black Mother-Daughter Relationships," *Sage* 4, no. 2 (Fall 1987): 4; Collins, *Black Feminist Thought*, 195.

48. Andrea G. Hunter, "Counting on Grandmothers: Black Mothers' and Fathers' Reliance on Grandmothers for Parenting Support," *Journal of Family Issues* 18, no. 3 (May 1997): 265; Collins, *Black Feminist Thought*, 192–198.

49. George C. Williams, "Pleiotropy, Natural Selection, and the Evolution of Senescence," *Evolution* 11, no. 4 (December 1957): 407–408.

50. John Hajnal, "European Marriage Patterns in Perspective," in *Population in History: Essays in Historical Demography*, eds. D. V. Glass and D. E. C Eversley (New Brunswick, NJ: Transaction Publishers, 1965), 101.

51. Jan Luiten van Zanden, Tine De Moor, and Sarah Carmichael, *Capital Women: The European Marriage Pattern, Female Empowerment, and Economic Development in Western Europe, 1300–1800* (New York: Oxford University Press, 2019), 5, 21–25, 38–40.

52. Josef Ehmer, "The Significance of Looking Back: Fertility Before the 'Fertility Decline,'" *Historical Social Research/Historische Sozialforschung* 36, no. 2 (2011): 24.

53. Marsh and Ronner, *The Empty Cradle*, 19.

54. From a contribution titled "Home" in *Ladies Magazine*, May 1830, quoted in Kirk Jeffrey, "The Family as Utopian Retreat from the City," *Soundings* 55, no. 1 (Spring 1972): 28.

55. Stone, *The Family*, 7.

56. Heman Humphrey, *Domestic Education* (Amherst, MA, 1840), 16, quoted in Jodi Vandenberg-Daves, *Modern Motherhood: An American History* (New Brunswick, NJ: Rutgers University Press, 2014), 23.

57. Lewis Henry Morgan, *Systems of Consanguinity and Affinity of the Human Family* (Washington, DC: Smithsonian, 1871), xxii.

58. Kim TallBear, "Making Love and Relations Beyond Settler Sex and Family," in *Making Kin Not Population*, eds. Adele E. Clarke and Donna Haraway (Chicago: Prickly Paradigm Press, 2018), 148.

59. Anderson, "Affirmations of an Indigenous Feminist," 83.

60. TallBear, "Making Love," 146–148.

61. Leith Mullings and Alaka Wali, *Stress and Resilience: The Social Context of Reproduction in Central Harlem* (New York: Kluwer Academic/Plenum Publishers, 2001), 1–3.

62. Mullings and Wali, *Stress and Resilience*, 3–6; Collins, *Black Feminist Thought*, 196; Ruha Benjamin, "Black Afterlives Matter," in *Making Kin Not Population*, 61.

63. Leith Mullings, *On Our Own Terms: Race, Class, and Gender in the Lives of African American Women* (New York: Routledge, 1997), 93.

64. Mullings and Wali, *Stress and Resilience*, 29.

65. Collins, *Black Feminist Thought*, 196, 198.

66. Ellen Cantarow and O'Malley, *Moving the Mountain*, 61.

67. Edward Randolph Carter, *The Black Side: A Partial History of the Business, Religious and Educational Side of the Negro in Atlanta, Ga.* (Atlanta, 1894), 35–36.

68. Collins, *Black Feminist Thought*, 195.

69. "CSPH: A Rich History," Carrie Steele-Pitts Home, www.csph.org /history.

70. W. E. B. Du Bois, ed., *Some Efforts of American Negroes for Their Own Social Betterment* (Cambridge, MA: Harvard University Press, 1898), 60–61.

71. Rick Badie, "Ollivette Eugenia Smith Allison, 86: 'Great Mother' at the Carrie Steele-Pitts Home," *Atlanta Journal-Constitution*, June 8, 2010, www.ajc.com/news/local/ollivette-eugenia-smith-allison-great-mother -the-carrie-steele-pitts-home/hUXT003kHFF1syqx9QqccI.

72. "CSPH: A Rich History."

73. Andrew Karch, *Early Start: Preschool Politics in the United States* (Ann Arbor: University of Michigan Press, 2013), 66–69, 81.

74. Karch, *Early Start*, 82–83; "Veto of the Economic Opportunity Amendments of 1971," S. Doc. 92-48, 92nd Cong., 1st Sess. (1971), 3 (archived by the American Presidency Project, University of California, Santa Barbara).

75. Quoted in Stanlie M. James, "Mothering: A Possible Black Feminist Link to Social Transformation," in *Theorizing Black Feminisms: The Visionary Pragmatism of Black Women*, eds. Stanlie M. James and Abena P. A. Busia (New York: Routledge, 1993), 44.

Chapter 3. Because We Can't Have It All

1. Helen Gurley Brown, *Sex and the Single Girl* (New York: Bernard Geis, 1962), 257.

2. Jennifer Scanlon, *Bad Girls Go Everywhere: The Life of Helen Gurley Brown* (New York: Oxford University Press, 2009), 15–22.

3. Scanlon, *Bad Girls Go Everywhere*, 119, 178.

4. "'Cosmo' Editor Helen Gurley Brown Dies at 90," NPR, August 13, 2012, www.npr.org/transcripts/158712834.

5. Taken from Dwight Garner's review, "Biography of Helen Gurley Brown, the Original Carrie Bradshaw," *New York Times*, April 21, 2009, www.nytimes.com/2009/04/22/books/22garn.html.

6. Scanlon, *Bad Girls Go Everywhere*, 106.

7. Jennifer Szalai, "The Complicated History of 'Having It All'," *New York Times Magazine*, January 2, 2015.

8. Wendy Wasserstein, act 2, scene 3, in *Isn't It Romantic* (New York: Nelson Doubleday, 1984), 66.

9. Quoted in William Safire, "The Way We Live Now: 3-18-01: On Language; Having It All," *New York Times*, March 18, 2001, www.nytimes.com

/2001/03/18/magazine/the-way-we-live-now-3-18-01-on-language-having
-it-all.html.

10. Scanlon, *Bad Girls Go Everywhere*, 184–185.

11. Helen Gurley Brown, *Having It All: Love, Success, Sex, Money* (New York: Simon & Schuster, 1982), 90–91.

12. Szalai, "The Complicated History of 'Having It All.'"

13. Anne-Marie Slaughter, "Why Women Still Can't Have It All," *The Atlantic*, July/August 2012.

14. Laurel Wamsley, "Michelle Obama's Take on 'Lean In'? 'That &#%! Doesn't Work'," NPR, December 3, 2018, www.npr.org/2018/12/03/67289 8216/michelle-obamas-take-on-lean-in-that-doesn-t-work.

15. Carrie L. Lukas, *The Politically Incorrect Guide to Women, Sex, and Feminism* (Washington, DC: Regnery, 2006), 141.

16. Quoted in Danielle Paquette, "Mike Pence Has Mocked Working Moms: 'Sure, You Can Have It All.'" *Washington Post*, July 19, 2016, www .washingtonpost.com/news/wonk/wp/2016/07/19/mike-pence-has-mocked -working-moms-sure-you-can-have-it-all.

17. See, for example, Sheryl Sandberg, *Lean In: Women, Work, and the Will to Lead* (New York: Knopf Doubleday, 2013).

18. "Kim Kardashian's Business Advice: 'Get Your F**king Ass Up and Work'," *Variety*, video, 5:54, March 9, 2022, www.youtube.com/watch?v =XX2izzshRmI&t=353s.

19. Rebecca Onion, "The 'Women Can Have It All' Narrative Around Amy Coney Barrett Is a Trap," *Slate*, October 1, 2020, https://slate.com/news -and-politics/2020/10/amy-coney-barrett-and-the-women-can-have-it-all -trap.html.

20. Lisa Belkin, "Judging Women," *New York Times*, May 10, 2010, www .nytimes.com/2010/05/23/magazine/23FOB-wwln-t.html.

21. Margaret Marsh and Wanda Ronner, *The Empty Cradle: Infertility in America from Colonial Times to the Present* (Baltimore: Johns Hopkins University Press, 1996), 32.

22. See Jan de Vries, *The Industrious Revolution: Consumer Behavior and the Household Economy, 1650 to the Present* (New York: Cambridge University Press, 2008), esp. chapter 5; Lenore Davidoff and Catherine Hall, *Family Fortunes: Men and Women of the English Middle Class, 1780–1850* (New York: Routledge, 1987), 182.

23. De Vries, *The Industrious Revolution*, 237.

24. Stephanie Coontz, *The Way We Never Were: American Families and the Nostalgia Trap* (New York: Basic Books, 2016), 31.

25. Bureau of Labor Statistics, "Employment Characteristics of Families— 2020," Bureau of Labor Statistics, news release, April 21, 2021, www .bls.gov/news.release/pdf/famee.pdf.

26. "The Harried Life of the Working Mother," Pew Research Center, October 1, 2009, www.pewresearch.org/social-trends/2009/10/01/the -harried-life-of-the-working-mother.

27. See Dan A. Black, Natalia Kolesnikova, Seth G. Sanders, and Lowell J. Taylor, "Are Children 'Normal'?" *Review of Economic Statistics* 95, no. 1 (March 2013): 21–33.

28. Deirdre Bair, *Simone de Beauvoir: A Biography* (New York: Touchstone, 1990), 60.

29. Bair, *Simone de Beauvoir,* 155–158.

30. Louis Menand, "Stand by Your Man," *New Yorker,* September 18, 2005, www.newyorker.com/magazine/2005/09/26/stand-by-your-man.

31. Judith Butler, "Sex and Gender in Simone de Beauvoir's Second Sex," *Yale French Studies* no. 72 (1986): 35–49.

32. Simone de Beauvoir, *The Second Sex,* trans. Constance Borde and Sheila Malovany-Chevallier (New York: Vintage, 2011), 283.

33. Beauvoir, *The Second Sex,* 556, 565, 524–536.

34. Beauvoir, *The Second Sex,* 181.

35. Alice S. Rossi, *The Feminist Papers: From Adams to De Beauvoir* (Boston: Northeastern University Press, 1988), 673–674.

36. Simone de Beauvoir, *The Prime of Life,* trans. Peter Green (Cleveland, OH: Meridian, 1966), 66–67, quoted in Ann Taylor Allen, *Feminism and Motherhood in Western Europe, 1890–1970: The Maternal Dilemma* (New York: Palgrave Macmillan, 2005), 232.

37. "A Conversation with Simone de Beauvoir," in Betty Friedan, *"It Changed My Life": Writings on the Women's Movement* (Cambridge, MA: Harvard University Press, 1998), 399.

38. Carolyn Morell, *Unwomanly Conduct: The Challenges of Intentional Childlessness* (New York: Routledge, 1994), 63.

39. Robin J. Ely, Pamela Stone, and Colleen Ammerman, "Rethink What You 'Know' About High-Achieving Women," *Harvard Business Review,* December 2014, https://hbr.org/2014/12/rethink-what-you-know-about-high-achieving-women.

40. See, for example, Alice Clark, *Working Life of Women in the Seventeenth Century* (New York: A. M. Kelly, 1968); Ivy Pinchbeck, *Women Workers and the Industrial Revolution, 1750–1850* (London: George Routledge & Sons, 1930); Lawrence Stone, *The Family, Sex and Marriage in England, 1500–1800* (New York: Harper & Row, 1977); Martha Howell, *Women, Production, and Patriarchy in Late Medieval Cities* (Chicago: University of Chicago Press, 1987).

41. This "golden era" is (somewhat sarcastically) sketched out by Friedrich Engels, *The Condition of the Working Class in England* (New York, 1887), 16–17.

42. E. P. Thompson, *The Making of the English Working Class* (New York: Pantheon Books, 1964), 416.

43. De Vries, *The Industrious Revolution,* 11.

44. See, e.g., Louise Tilly and Joan Scott, *Women, Work, and Family* (New York: Routledge, 1989).

45. Davidoff and Hall, *Family Fortunes,* 312–313.

46. Sarah Stickney Ellis, *The Women of England: Their Social Duties, and Domestic Habits* (1839), 463, quoted in Davidoff and Hall, *Family Fortunes*, 315.

47. Jeanne Boydston, *Home and Work: Housework, Wages, and the Ideology of Labor in the Early Republic* (New York: Oxford University Press, 1990), 144–145.

48. Elizabeth Cady Stanton to Susan B. Anthony, Seneca Falls, December 1, 1853, www.rochester.edu/sba/suffrage-history/susan-b-anthony-and -elizabeth-cady-stanton-their-words.

49. "Elizabeth Cady Stanton Dies at Her Home," *New York Times*, October 27, 1902.

50. Dolores Hayden, *The Grand Domestic Revolution: A History of Feminist Designs for American Homes, Neighborhoods, and Cities* (Cambridge, MA: MIT Press, 1982), 3.

51. Megan McDonald Way, *Family Economics and Public Policy, 1800s– Present* (New York: Palgrave Macmillan, 2018), 152.

52. "The Brandeis Brief," submitted to the Supreme Court of the United States, October 1907, in regard to *Muller v. Oregon*, 208 U.S. 412 (archived by Louis D. Brandeis School of Law Library), https://louisville .edu/law/library/special-collections/the-louis-d.-brandeis-collection /the-brandeis-brief-in-its-entirety.

53. Muller v. Oregon, 208 U.S. 412 (1908).

54. Section 213 of the Economy Act of 1932 is discussed in detail in Lois Scharf, *To Work and to Wed: Female Employment, Feminism, and the Great Depression* (Westport, CT: Greenwood Press, 1980), 45–53; see also John Thomas McGuire, "'The Most Unjust Piece of Legislation': Section 213 of the Economy Act of 1932 and Feminism During the New Deal," *Journal of Policy History* 20, no. 4 (November 4, 2008): 516–541.

55. *Journal of Proceedings of the Sixty-Second Session of the Wisconsin State Legislature*, vol. 3 (Madison, WI: Democrat Printing Company, 1935), 2403, https://books.google.com/books?id=mZJsAAAAMAAJ&lpg=PA2403& dq=married%20women%20work&pg=PA2403#v=onepage&q=married %20women%20work&f=false.

56. Elaine Tyler May, *Barren in the Promised Land: Childless Americans and the Pursuit of Happiness* (New York: Basic Books, 1995), 81; Dorothy Sue Cobble, *The Other Women's Movement: Workplace Justice and Social Rights in Modern America* (Princeton, NJ: Princeton University Press, 2004), 215.

57. Patricia A. McBroom, *The Third Sex: The New Professional Woman* (New York: W. Morrow, 1986), 23, 236–238.

58. US Bureau of Labor Statistics, "Women in the Labor Force, 1970– 2009," *Economics Daily* (blog), January 5, 2011, www.bls.gov/opub/ted/2011 /ted_20110105.htm?view_full.

59. US Bureau of Labor Statistics, "Employment Characteristics of Families Summary," news release, April 20, 2022, www.bls.gov/news.release /famee.nr0.htm.

60. Gretchen Livingston, "Is U.S. Fertility at an All-Time Low? Two of Three Measures Point to Yes," Pew Research Center, May 22, 2019, www .pewresearch.org/fact-tank/2019/05/22/u-s-fertility-rate-explained; Claire Cain Miller and Liz Alderman, "Why U.S. Women Are Leaving Jobs Behind," *New York Times*, December 12, 2014, www.nytimes.com/2014/12/14 /upshot/us-employment-women-not-working.html.

61. May, *Barren in the Promised Land*, 12; Tomas Sobotka, Vegard Skirbekk, and Dimiter Philipov, "Economic Recession and Fertility in the Developed World," *Population and Development Review 32*, no. 2 (June 2011): 270.

62. Robert Boyd, "Racial Differences in Childlessness: A Centennial Review," *Sociological Perspectives 32*, no. 2 (Summer, 1989): 185 (Figure 2).

63. Boyd, "Racial Differences in Childlessness," 188–189.

64. Alexis Yamokoski and Lisa A. Keister, "The Wealth of Single Women: Marital Status and Parenthood in the Asset Accumulation of Young Baby Boomers in the United States," *Feminist Economics* 12, no. 1–2 (January/April 2006): 167–194.

65. Morell, *Unwomanly Conduct*, 19.

66. S. Philip Morgan, "Late Nineteenth- and Early Twentieth-Century Childlessness," *American Journal of Sociology* 97, no. 3 (November 1991): 803; Ronald B. Rindfuss, S. Philip Morgan, and Gray Swicegood, *First Births in America: Changes in the Timing of Parenthood* (Berkeley: University of California Press, 1988), 87.

67. Bill Chappell, "U.S. Births Fell to a 32-Year Low in 2018; CDC Says Birthrate Is in Record Slump," NPR, May 15, 2019, www.npr .org/2019/05/15/723518379/u-s-births-fell-to-a-32-year-low-in-2018-cdc -says-birthrate-is-at-record-level.

68. Child Care Aware of America, *The U.S. and the High Cost of Child Care: An Examination of a Broken System*, 2019, 39, www.childcareaware.org /our-issues/research/the-us-and-the-high-price-of-child-care-2019.

69. Claudia Goldin, Sari Pekkala Kerr, Claudia Olivetti, and Erling Barth, "The Expanding Gender Earnings Gap: Evidence from the LEHD-2000 Census," *American Economic Review* 107, no. 5 (2017): 110.

70. Sabrina Tavernise, Claire Cain Miller, Quoctrung Bui, and Robert Gebeloff, "Why American Women Everywhere Are Delaying Motherhood," *New York Times*, June 16, 2021, www.nytimes.com/2021/06/16/us/declining -birthrate-motherhood.html.

71. Ann Chemin, "France's Baby Boom Secret: Get Women into Work and Ditch Rigid Family Norms," *The Guardian*, March 21, 2015, www.the guardian.com/world/2015/mar/21/france-population-europe-fertility-rate; Jenny Brown, *Birthstrike: The Hidden Fight Over Women's Work* (Oakland, CA: PM Press, 2019), 17, 26.

72. Steffen Kröhnert (rendered phonetically as Stephan Gruenert), interviewed by Rachel Martin, "Germany Frets About Women in Shrinking Work Force," *Morning Edition*, National Public Radio, May 24, 2006, www .npr.org/templates/story/story.php?storyId=5427278.

Chapter 4. Because of the Planet

1. Stephanie Mills, "Mills College Valedictory Address," in *American Earth: Environmental Writing Since Thoreau,* ed. Bill McKibben (New York: Library of America, 2008), 470. Cited in Thomas Robertson, *The Malthusian Moment: Global Population Growth and the Birth of American Environmentalism* (New Brunswick, NJ: Rutgers University Press, 2012), 1, 162.

2. Edward Valauskas, "FM Interviews: Stephanie Mills," *First Monday* 7, no. 6 (June 2002): https://doi.org/10.5210/fm.v7i6.965.

3. City of Phoenix, "Phoenix Growth," www.phoenix.gov/budgetsite /Documents/2013Sum%20Community%20Profile%20and%20Trends.pdf.

4. "Phoenix Rainfall Index," National Weather Service, accessed July 2, 2021, www.weather.gov/psr/PRI.

5. "Population by County, 1860–2000," Bay Area Census, accessed July 2, 2021, www.bayareacensus.ca.gov/historical/copop18602000.htm.

6. For a history of the 1991 Oakland Hills Tunnel Fire, see Gregory Simon, *Flame and Fortune in the American West: Urban Development, Environmental Change, and the Great Oakland Hills Fire* (Berkeley: University of California Press, 2017).

7. Paul Ehrlich, *The Population Bomb* (New York: Ballantine Books, 1968), 1.

8. Derek Hoff, *The State and the Stork: The Population Debate and Policy Making in US History* (Chicago: University of Chicago Press, 2012), 178–179.

9. Robertson, *The Malthusian Moment,* 162.

10. Robertson, *The Malthusian Moment,* 153, 165.

11. Nick Watts et al., "The 2019 Report of the Lancet Countdown on Health and Climate Change: Ensuring that the Health of a Child Born Today Is Not Defined by a Changing Climate," *The Lancet* 394, no. 10211 (November 16, 2019): 1836–1878.

12. William Petersen, *Malthus: The Founder of Modern Democracy* (Cambridge, MA: Harvard University Press, 1979), 21.

13. Robert Mayhew, *Malthus: The Life and Legacies of an Untimely Prophet* (Cambridge, MA: Belknap, 2014), 58.

14. Mayhew, *Malthus: The Life and Legacies,* 60–62.

15. Elinor Accampo, *Blessed Motherhood, Bitter Fruit: Nelly Roussel and the Politics of Female Pain in the Third Republic France* (Baltimore: Johns Hopkins University Press, 2006), 4.

16. Thomas Malthus, *An Essay on the Principle of Population,* vol. 1 (1809), 2–4, 16.

17. Mayhew, *Malthus: The Life and Legacies,* 85.

18. Percy Bysshe Shelley, "A Philosophical View of Reform," in *The Complete Works of Percy Bysshe Shelley,* vol. 7 (London: Gordian, 1829), 51.

19. Friedrich Engels, "Outlines of a Critique of Political Economy," in *Economic and Philosophic Manuscripts of 1844,* by Karl Marx, trans. Martin Milligan (New York: International Publishers, 1964), 219, 199.

20. J. Dupâquier, A. Fauve-Chamoux, and E. Grebenik, eds., *Malthus: Past and Present* (Orlando, FL: Academic Press, 1983), 258.

21. F. D'arcy, "The Malthusian League and Resistance to Birth Control Propaganda in Late Victorian Britain," *Population Studies* 31, no. 3 (November 1977): 433.

22. Charles Knowlton, *The Fruits of Philosophy: An Essay on the Population Question*, continental edition (Rotterdam: Van Der Hoven and Buys, 1877; digitized 2013 by the National Library of the Netherlands), 14.

23. Juan Martinez-Allier, *The Environmentalism of the Poor: A Study of Ecological Conflicts and Valuation* (Cheltenham, UK: Edward Elgar Publishing, 2009), 47–48.

24. Martinez-Allier, *The Environmentalism of the Poor*, 51–53.

25. Annie Besant, *Annie Besant: An Autobiography* (1893), 81.

26. F. H. Amphlett-Micklewright, "The Rise and Decline of English Neo-Malthusianism," *Population Studies* 15 (July 1961): 39–40.

27. Amphlett-Micklewright, "The Rise and Decline of English Neo-Malthusianism," 39–40.

28. "Annie Besant Cremated," *New York Times*, September 22, 1933, www .nytimes.com/1933/09/22/archives/annie-besant-cremated-theosophist -leaders-body-put-on-pyre-on-river.html.

29. *Mabel Emily Besant-Scott (née Besant)*, unknown photographer, circa 1878, albumen carte-de-visite, 3½ x 2⅜ in. (90 mm x 61 mm), National Portrait Gallery, London, www.npg.org.uk/collections/search/portrait /mw189854.

30. Donald J. Bogue, "Population Growth in the United States," in *The Population Dilemma*, ed. Philip M. Hauser (Englewood Cliffs, NJ: Prentice-Hall, 1963), 92.

31. Hoff, *The State and the Stork*, 178.

32. Paul Sabin, *The Bet: Paul Ehrlich, Julian Simon, and Our Gamble over the Earth's Future* (New Haven, CT: Yale University Press, 2013), 21.

33. Robertson, *The Malthusian Moment*, 135.

34. Robertson, *The Malthusian Moment*, 135–136.

35. Sabin, *The Bet*, 12.

36. Paul R. Ehrlich and Anne H. Ehrlich, "The Population Bomb Revisited," *Electronic Journal of Sustainable Development* 1, no. 3 (2009): 63.

37. Ehrlich, *The Population Bomb*, 3.

38. Hoff, *The State and the Stork*, 179–180; Susan Staggenborg, *The Pro-Choice Movement: Organization and Activism in the Abortion Conflict* (New York: Oxford University Press, 1991), 164.

39. Dennis Hodgson and Susan Cotts Watkins, "Feminists and Neo-Malthusians: Past and Present Alliances," *Population and Development Review* 23, no. 3 (September 1997): 475–478.

40. Robert G. Weisbord, *Genocide?: Birth Control and the Black American* (Westport, CT: Greenwood, 1975), 129.

41. Hoff, *The State and the Stork*, 180.

42. Staggenborg, *The Pro-Choice Movement*, 163.

43. Robertson, *The Malthusian Moment*, 173.

44. Hoff, *The State and the Stork*, 180.

45. Robert Rienow, *Moment in the Sun: A Report on the Deteriorating Quality of the American Environment* (New York: Dial Press, 1967), 3.

46. Sabin, *The Bet*, 18–20.

47. Robertson, *The Malthusian Moment*, 160.

48. Robertson, *The Malthusian Moment*, 10, 159.

49. Sabin, *The Bet*, 39.

50. "O and All the Little Babies in the Alameda Gardens, Yes," in *Ecotactics: The Sierra Club Handbook for Environment Activists*, ed. John G. Mitchell (New York: Pocket Books, 1970), 81.

51. Ehrlich, *The Population Bomb*, 140–141.

52. Paul Ehrlich, "Are There Too Many of Us?" *McCall's*, July 1970, 104, quoted in Robertson, *The Malthusian Moment*, 158.

53. Sabin, *The Bet*, 39.

54. "Fertility Rate, Total (Births per Woman)—United States," World Bank, https://data.worldbank.org/indicator/SP.DYN.TFRT.IN?locations=US.

55. Prajakta Gupte, "India: 'The Emergency' and the Politics of Mass Sterilization," *Education About Asia* 22, no. 3 (Winter 2017): 40, 43.

56. Robertson, *The Malthusian Moment*, 188, 193–194.

57. Hodgson and Watkins, "Feminists and Neo-Malthusians," 484; Robertson, *The Malthusian Moment*, 11, 190–191.

58. Walter E. Howard, "The Population Crisis Is Here Now," *BioScience*, September 1969, reprinted in Wes Jackson, *Man and the Environment*, 2nd ed. (Dubuque, IA: William C. Brown, 1973), 189, 191; Robertson, *The Malthusian Moment*, 191.

59. See, for example, Linda Gordon, *Women's Body, Women's Right: Birth Control in America* (New York: Grossman, 1976), 393, 398, 401.

60. See, "Garrett Hardin," Southern Poverty Law Center, www.splcenter.org/fighting-hate/extremist-files/individual/garrett-hardin.

61. Dan Wakefield, "Highlights of a NON-Event," *New York*, September 9, 1974, 34.

62. Naomi Oreskes and Erik M. Conway, *Merchants of Doubt: How a Handful of Scientists Obscured the Truth on Issues from Tobacco Smoke to Global Warming* (New York: Bloomsbury, 2010), 170.

63. Philip Shabecoff, "Global Warming Has Begun, Expert Tells Senate," *New York Times*, June 24, 1988, 1.

64. Bathsheba Demuth, "Against the Tide: The Trump Administration and Climate Change," in *The Presidency of Donald J. Trump: A First Historical Assessment*, ed. Julian E. Zelizer (Princeton, NJ: Princeton University Press, 2022), 183.

65. See Pulitzer Prize–finalist reporting by David Hasemyer and John H. Cushman Jr., "Exxon Sowed Doubt About Climate Science for Decades by Stressing Uncertainty," *Inside Climate News*, October 22, 2015.

66. Quoted in Talia Buford, "Thousands Rally to Protest Keystone," *Politico*, February 17, 2013, www.politico.com/story/2013/02/thousands -rally-in-washington-to-protest-keystone-pipeline-087745#ixzz 2LDwj7Myp.

67. Caroline Hickman, Elizabeth Marks, Panu Pihkala, Susan Clayton, R. Eric Lewandowski, Elouise E. Mayall, Britt Wray, Catriona Mellor, and Lise van Susteren, "Young People's Voices on Climate Anxiety, Government Betrayal and Moral Injury: A Global Phenomenon," *The Lancet* (preprint, September 7, 2021): 6, Figure 3, https://ssrn.com/abstract=3918955.

68. Meehan Crist, "Is It Ok to Have a Child?" *London Review of Books* 42, no. 5 (March 5, 2020): www.lrb.co.uk/the-paper/v42/n05/meehan-crist /is-it-ok-to-have-a-child.

69. Sarah Blaffer Hrdy, *Mother Nature: A History of Mothers, Infants, and Natural Selection* (New York: Pantheon Books, 1999), 314.

70. Charles Mann, *1491: New Revelations of the Americas Before Columbus* (New York: Vintage, 2006), 125.

71. Mary Annaïse Heglar, "Climate Change Isn't the First Existential Threat," *Zora*, February 18, 2019, https://zora.medium.com/sorry-yall-but -climate-change-ain-t-the-first-existential-threat-b3c999267aa0.

72. See, for example, Morris Silver, "Births, Marriages, and Business Cycles in the United States," *Journal of Political Economy* 73, no. 3 (1965): 237–255.

73. Ann Taylor Allen, *Feminism and Motherhood in Western Europe, 1890– 1970: The Maternal Dilemma* (New York: Palgrave Macmillan, 2005), 9; Hrdy, *Mother Nature*, 316.

74. Quoted in Alan Yuhas, "Don't Expect a Quarantine Baby Boom," *New York Times*, April 8, 2020, www.nytimes.com/2020/04/08/us/coronavirus -baby-boom.html.

75. *Fox & Friends*, February 26, 2019, archived by Media Matters for America, www.mediamatters.org/embed/222969.

76. Tom Whyman, "Why, Despite Everything, You Should Have Kids (If You Want Them)," *New York Times*, April 13, 2021, www.nytimes .com/2021/04/13/opinion/baby-bust-covid-philosophy-natalism.html; see also Anastasia Berg, "Now Is as Good a Time as Any to Start a Family," *New York Times*, April 30, 2020, www.nytimes.com/2020/04/30/opinion /coronavirus-pregnancy.html.

Chapter 5. Because We Can't

1. Emma Rosenblum, "Later, Baby," *Bloomberg Businessweek*, April 21, 2014, 44–49.

2. Ariana Eunjung Cha, "The Struggle to Conceive with Frozen Eggs," *Washington Post*, January 27, 2018, www.washingtonpost.com/news /national/wp/2018/01/27/feature/she-championed-the-idea-that-freezing -your-eggs-would-free-your-career-but-things-didnt-quite-work-out.

3. "IVF Is Big Business," *Pediatrics* 93, no. 3 (March 1994): 403.

4. Lucy van de Viel, "The Speculative Turn in IVF: Egg Freezing and the Financialization of Fertility," *Critical Studies of Contemporary Biosciences* 39, no. 3 (2020): 306–326.

5. Cha, "The Struggle to Conceive with Frozen Eggs."

6. Ada C. Dieke, Yujia Zhang, Dmitry M. Kissin, Wanda D. Barfield, and Sheree L. Boulet, "Disparities in Assisted Reproductive Technology Utilization by Race and Ethnicity, United States, 2014: A Commentary," *Journal of Women's Health* 26, no. 6 (June 2017): 605–608; James F. Smith, Michael L. Eisenberg, David Glidden, Susan G. Millstein, Marcelle Cedars, Thomas J. Walsh, Jonathan Showstack, Lauri A. Pasch, Nancy Adler, and Patricia P. Katz, "Socioeconomic Disparities in the Use and Success of Fertility Treatments: Analysis of Data from a Prospective Cohort in the United States," *Fertility and Sterility* 96, no. 1 (July 2011): 97, Table 1; Kristin J. Wilson, *Not Trying: Infertility, Childlessness, and Ambivalence* (Nashville, TN: Vanderbilt University Press, 2014), 6–7.

7. Margarete J. Sandelowski, "Failures of Volition: Female Agency and Infertility in Historical Perspective," *Signs* 15, no. 3 (1990): 475–499, quoted in Margaret Marsh and Wanda Ronner, *The Empty Cradle: Infertility in America from Colonial Times to the Present* (Baltimore: Johns Hopkins University Press, 1996), 246.

8. Gen. 30:1 (NRSV).

9. Gen. 16:1 (NRSV).

10. 1 Sam. 1:1–8, 1:14–16 (NRSV).

11. 1 Sam. 1:20–28 (NRSV).

12. Marsh and Ronner, *The Empty Cradle*, 12.

13. Elaine Tyler May, *Barren in the Promised Land: Childless Americans and the Pursuit of Happiness* (New York: Basic Books, 1995), 42–43. Quote from the Diary of Sally Hitchcock Bliss, entry from February 15, 1829, American Antiquarian Society, Worcester, MA.

14. "What Is Infertility?," Infertility FAQs, Centers for Disease Control and Prevention, accessed September 15, 2020, www.cdc.gov/reproductive health/infertility/index.htm.

15. Quoted in Christine Overall, *Ethics and Human Reproduction: A Feminist Analysis* (Winchester, MA: Allen and Unwin, 1987), 141.

16. Marsh and Ronner, *The Empty Cradle*, 12–15, 42; Michael J. Call, *Infertility and the Novels of Sophie Cottin* (Newark: University of Delaware Press, 2002), 56.

17. H. Celcon, "The First Century of Mechanical Electrotherapy," *Physiotherapy* 87, no. 4 (April 2001): 209.

18. Marsh and Ronner, *The Empty Cradle*, 21.

19. Lydia Syson, *Doctor of Love: James Graham and His Celestial Bed* (Surrey, UK: Alma Books, 2008), 418–419, 181, 9–11, 203.

20. Harvey Graham, *Eternal Eve: The History of Gynecology and Obstetrics* (Garden City, NJ: Doubleday, 1951), 371–374.

21. Syson, *Doctor of Love*, 9.

22. Rickie Solinger, *Pregnancy and Power: A Short History of Reproductive Politics in America* (New York: NYU Press, 2007), 59.

23. Frederick Hollick, *The Marriage Guide: Or, Natural History of Generation* (New York: T. W. Strong, 1860), 301.

24. May, *Barren in the Promised Land*, 43. Quote is from Alexander Hamilton, *A Treatise on the Management of Female Complaints* (New York: Samuel Campbell, 1792), 108–109.

25. Details and quotes from this episode are from A. D. Hard, "Artificial Impregnation," *Medical World* 27 (April 1909): 163–164, https://catalog.hathitrust.org/Record/000060888.

26. Elizabeth Yuko, "The First Artificial Insemination Was an Ethical Nightmare," *The Atlantic*, January 8, 2016, www.theatlantic.com/health/archive/2016/01/first-artificial-insemination/423198.

27. C. L. Egbert, "Regarding Artificial Impregnation," *Medical World* 27 (June 1909): 253, https://catalog.hathitrust.org/Record/000060888.

28. Earnest Bartow, "Impregnation and Religion," *Medical World* 27 (July 1909): 305, https://catalog.hathitrust.org/Record/000060888.

29. Hard, "Artificial Impregnation."

30. Marsh and Ronner, *The Empty Cradle*, 29.

31. See, for example, Thomas W. Carter, "The Morbid Effects of Tight Lacing," *Southern Medical and Surgical Journal* 2, no. 7 (July 1846): 405.

32. James Cassedy, *Medicine and American Growth, 1800–1860* (Madison: University of Wisconsin Press, 1986), 173.

33. George J. Engelmann, "The Increasing Sterility of American Women," *Journal of the American Medical Association* 27 (October 5, 1901): 893.

34. George Engelmann, "The American Girl of Today," *Transactions* 25 (1900): 4–21, quoted in Marsh and Ronner, *The Empty Cradle*, 86.

35. May, *Barren in the Promised Land*, 73. Quote from "Our Duty to Posterity," *The Independent*, January 4, 1909, 269–271.

36. Edward A. Ross and Roy E. Barber, "Slow Suicide Among Our Native Stock," *Century Magazine*, February 1924, 507–508.

37. Theodore Roosevelt, "On American Motherhood," address before the National Congress of Mothers, March 13, 1905, in Melody Rose, *Abortion: A Documentary and Reference Guide* (Westport, CT: Greenwood Press, 2008), 27.

38. Ross and Barber, "Slow Suicide Among Our Native Stock," 504.

39. Series A 6-8, "Annual Population Estimates for the United States: 1790 to 1970," in *Historical Statistics of the United States: Colonial Times to 1970* (Washington, DC: US Department of Commerce, 1975), www.census.gov/history/pdf/histstats-colonial-1970.pdf.

40. Ross and Barber, "Slow Suicide Among Our Native Stock," 504.

41. Karen Norrgard, "Human Testing, the Eugenics Movement, and IRBs," *Nature Education* 1, no. 1 (2008): 170.

42. T. G. Thomas, *A Practical Treatise on the Diseases of Women* (Philadelphia: Lea Brothers, 1891), 35, quoted in Margarete Sandelowski, "Failures of

Volition: Female Agency and Infertility in Historical Perspective," *Signs* 15, no. 3 (1990): 486.

43. Paul A. Lombardo, ed., *A Century of Eugenics in America: From the Indiana Experiment to the Human Genome Era* (Bloomington: Indiana University Press, 2011), 1–7; see also Jason S. Lantzer, "The Indiana Way of Eugenics: Sterilization Laws, 1907–1974," in the same volume.

44. George B. H. Swayze, "Reluctant Pregnancy," *Medical Times*, November 1909, 321, quoted in May, *Barren in the Promised Land*, 72.

45. C. G. Child, *Sterility and Conception* (New York: Appleton, 1931), 12–13.

46. Swayze, "Reluctant Pregnancy," quoted in May, *Barren in the Promised Land*, 72.

47. Charlotte Kroløkke, "ART in the Sun: Assembling Fertility Tourism in the Caribbean," in *Critical Kinship Studies*, eds. Charlotte Kroløkke, Lene Myong, Stine Willum Adrian, and Tine Tjørnhøj-Thomsen (Lanham, MD: Rowman & Littlefield, 2016), 149–152.

48. Simon P. Newman, *A New World of Labor: The Development of Plantation Slavery in the British Atlantic* (Philadelphia: University of Pennsylvania Press, 2013), 54–68, 75.

49. Kroløkke, "ART in the Sun," 153, 162.

50. "State Laws Related to Insurance Coverage for Infertility Treatment," National Conference of State Legislatures, March 12, 2021, www.ncsl.org /research/health/insurance-coverage-for-infertility-laws.aspx.

51. J. Farley Ordovensky Staniec and Natalie J. Webb, "Utilization of Infertility Services: How Much Does Money Matter?" *Health Services Research* 42, no. 3 (June 2007): 976.

52. Smith et al., "Socioeconomic Disparities in the Use and Success of Fertility Treatments," 97, Table 1.

53. Dieke et al., "Disparities in Assisted Reproductive Technology Utilization," 605–608.

54. B. Lunenfeld and A. van Steirteghem, "Infertility in the Third Millennium: Implications for the Individual, Family and Society: Condensed Meeting Report from the Bertarelli Foundation's Second Global Conference," *Human Reproduction Update* 10, no. 4 (2004): 321.

55. Marcia C. Inhorn and Pasquale Patrizio, "Infertility Around the Globe: New Thinking on Gender, Reproductive Technologies and Global Movements in the 21st Century," *Human Reproduction Update* 21, no. 4 (March 2015): 414.

56. Measure DHS+, *Infecundity, Infertility, and Childlessness in Developing Countries*, DHS Comparative Reports no. 9 (Calverton, MD: ORC Macro, 2004), 1, www.who.int/publications/m/item/infecundity-infertility -and-childlessness-in-developing-countries---dhs-comparative-reports -no.-9.

57. Kristin L. Rooney and Alice D. Domar, "The Relationship Between Stress and Infertility," *Dialogues in Clinical Neuroscience* 20, no. 1 (March 2018): 41.

58. Gayle Leatherby, "Other Than Mother and Mothers as Others," *Women's Studies International Forum* 22, no. 3 (May 1999): 360.

59. *Oxford English Dictionary* online, s.v. "adoption."

60. Helena M. Wall, *Fierce Communion: Family and Community in Colonial America* (Cambridge, MA: Harvard University Press, 1990), 99.

61. "Planning for Adoption: Knowing the Costs and Resources," Child Welfare Information Gateway, November 2016, www.childwelfare.gov /pubs/s-cost.

62. Elizabeth Bartholet, *Family Bonds: Adoption and the Politics of Parenting* (New York: Houghton Mifflin, 1993), 30–31.

63. Chuck Johnson and Megan Lestino, *Adoption by the Numbers: A Comprehensive Report of U.S. Adoption Statistics* (Alexandria, VA: National Council for Adoption, 2017), ii.

64. Nicholas K. Park and Patricia Wonch Hill, "Is Adoption an Option? The Role of Importance of Motherhood and Fertility Help-Seeking in Considering Adoption," *Journal of Family Issues* 35, no. 5 (2014): 602.

65. Allen Fisher, "Still 'Not Quite as Good as Having Your Own'? Toward a Sociology of Adoption," *Annual Review of Sociology* 29 (2003): 351–354.

66. Victor Cohn, "U.S. Scientists Urge More Study Before Test-Tube Babies," *Washington Post*, July 27, 1978.

67. "SUPERBABE: Meet Louise, the World's First Test Tube Arrival," *London Evening News*, July 27, 1978.

68. "1st Test Tube Baby Is Born—It's a Girl; Condition 'Excellent,'" *New York Daily News*, July 26, 1978.

69. Ciara Nugent, "What It Was Like to Grow Up as the World's First 'Test-Tube Baby,'" *Time*, July 25, 2018, https://time.com/5344145/louise -brown-test-tube-baby.

70. Robin Marantz Henig, *Pandora's Baby: How the First Test Tube Babies Sparked the Reproductive Revolution* (New York: Houghton Mifflin, 2004), 130, 134, 136, 205.

71. "Abortion Viewed in Moral Terms: Fewer See Stem Cell Research and IVF as Moral Issues," Pew Research Center, August 15, 2013, www .pewforum.org/2013/08/15/abortion-viewed-in-moral-terms/#morality -of-using-in-vitro-fertilization.

72. Quoted in Jennifer Wright, "Why Anti-Choice People Are Okay with IVF," *Harper's Bazaar*, June 14, 2019, www.harpersbazaar.com/culture/politics /a27888471/why-anti-choice-people-against-abortion-are-okay-with-ivf.

73. Emma Scornavacchi, "The Glaring Exception in the Coming Battle Over Reproductive Rights," *New Republic*, August 8, 2018, https://newrepublic .com/article/150545/glaring-exception-coming-battle-reproductive-rights.

74. Katherine Kortsmit, Michele G. Mandel, Jennifer A. Reeves, Elizabeth Clark, H. Pamela Pagano, Antoinette Nguyen, Emily E. Petersen, and Maura K. Whiteman, "Abortion Surveillance—United States, 2019," *MMWR Surveillance Summaries* 70, no. SS-9 (2021):1–29, http://dx.doi.org/10.15585 /mmwr.ss7009a1.

75. Scornavacchi, "The Glaring Exception in the Coming Battle Over Reproductive Rights."

76. Alicia Armstrong and Torie C. Plowden, "Ethnicity and Assisted Reproductive Technologies," *Clinical Practice* 9, no. 6 (November 1, 2012): 651–658.

77. May, *Barren in the Promised Land*, 72.

78. James William Kennedy and Archibald Donald Campbell, *Vaginal Hysterectomy* (Philadelphia: F.A. Davis, 1944), 133.

79. Gen. 30:23 (NRSV).

80. Centers for Disease Control and Prevention, *2019 Assisted Reproductive Technology Fertility Clinic Success Rates Report* (Washington, DC: U.S. Department of Health and Human Services, 2021), 26, www.cdc.gov/art /reports/2019/pdf/2019-Report-ART-Fertility-Clinic-National-Summary -h.pdf.

81. This point is borrowed and expanded from Carolyn Morell, *Unwomanly Conduct: The Challenges of Intentional Childlessness* (New York: Routledge, 1994), 56.

Chapter 6. Because We Want Other Lives

1. Zoë Noble and Marcia Drut-Davis, "No Regrets, with 78-Year-Old Childfree Trailblazer Marcia Drut-Davis," March 9, 2021, in *We Are Childfree*, podcast, https://wearechildfree.com/podcast/05-marcia-drut-davis.

2. Marcia Drut-Davis, *Confessions of a Childfree Woman: A Life Spent Swimming Against the Mainstream* (self-pub., 2013), 51.

3. Noble and Drut-Davis, "No Regrets."

4. Drut-Davis, *Confessions of a Childfree Woman*, 57.

5. See Shawn G. Kennedy, "Pregnancy and the Single Girl," *New York Times*, December 12, 1976, www.nytimes.com/1976/12/12/archives/long -island-weekly-pregnancy-and-the-single-girl-the-growing.html.

6. Drut-Davis, *Confessions of a Childfree Woman*, 63; Noble and Drut-Davis, "No Regrets."

7. Noble and Drut-Davis, "No Regrets."

8. Drut-Davis, *Confessions of a Childfree Woman*, 65.

9. Elaine Tyler May, *Barren in the Promised Land: Childless Americans and the Pursuit of Happiness* (New York: Basic Books, 1995), 18.

10. Ann Taylor Allen, *Feminism and Motherhood in Western Europe, 1890–1970: The Maternal Dilemma* (New York: Palgrave Macmillan, 2005), 220, 232. See photograph at "Boss of Own Belly," Atria, https://institute-gender equality.org/frames-on-gender/countries/netherlands/boss-of-own-belly.

11. Christina of Markyate's story taken from the most recent translation of her hagiography: C. H. Talbot, ed., *The Life of Christina of Markyate: A Twelfth Century Recluse* (New York: Oxford University Press, 2019).

12. See, for example, Norman Russell, trans., *The Lives of the Desert Fathers* (Kalamazoo, MI: Cistercian Publications, 1981), which is one of my favorite books I read in college.

13. On Hildegard of Bingen, see, for example, Sabina Flanagan, *Hildegard of Bingen: A Visionary Life* (London: Routledge, 1998).

14. *Lesser Feasts and Fasts* (New York: Church Publishing Incorporated, 2019), 438.

15. See, for example, Dan Wakefield, "Highlights of a NON-Event," *New York*, September 9, 1974, 33–35.

16. Jenna Healey, "Rejecting Reproduction: The National Organization for Non-Parents and Childfree Activism in 1970s America," *Journal of Women's History* 28, no. 1 (Spring 2016): 140–142.

17. Pimlico Junior High Alumni, Facebook group, www.facebook.com /groups/48093191715/permalink/10150284397521716.

18. May, *Barren in the Promised Land*, 189.

19. Ellen Peck, *The Baby Trap* (New York: Pinnacle Books, 1972), 67.

20. Peck, *The Baby Trap*, 10–11.

21. Peck, *The Baby Trap*, 16.

22. Peck, *The Baby Trap*, 22–23.

23. Ellen Peck, "Obituary: Motherhood," *New York Times*, May 13, 1972, www.nytimes.com/1972/05/13/archives/obituary-motherhood.html.

24. Betty Friedan, *The Feminine Mystique* (New York: W. W. Norton, 2016, orig. 1962), 100.

25. Healey, "Rejecting Reproduction," 143.

26. M. Rivka Polatnick, "Diversity in Women's Liberation Ideology: How a Black and a White Group of the 1960s Viewed Motherhood," *Signs* 21, no. 3 (Spring 1996): 688.

27. Sandy Banisky, "Heavy Causes Fill Ellen Peck's Day," *Baltimore Sun*, August 12, 1975.

28. Banisky, "Heavy Causes Fill Ellen Peck's Day."

29. Quoted in Healey, "Rejecting Reproduction," 139.

30. Summary of Non-Parents' Day from Wakefield, "Highlights of a NON-Event," 33–35.

31. Healey, "Rejecting Reproduction," 134–135.

32. Narrative from Wakefield, "Highlights of a NON-Event," 35.

33. Healey, "Rejecting Reproduction," 133.

34. Drut-Davis, *Confessions of a Childfree Woman*, 46.

35. For example, Ellen Mara Nason and Margaret M. Poloma, *Voluntarily Childless Couples: The Emergence of a Variant Lifestyle* (Beverly Hills, CA: Sage Publications, 1976); R. Cooper, B. Cumber, and R. Hartner, "Decision-Making Patterns and Post-Decision Adjustment of Childfree Husbands and Wives," *Alternative Lifestyles* 1, no. 1 (1978): 71–94.

36. This is according to a NON membership survey done in 1976, cited in Healey, "Rejecting Reproduction," 132.

37. Healey, "Rejecting Reproduction," 135.

38. Rufus Bishop, Seth Y. Wells, and Giles B. Avery, *Testimonies of the Life, Character, Revelations, and Doctrines of Mother Ann Lee, and the Elders with Her: Through Whom the Word of Eternal Life Was Opened in This Day*

of Christ's Second Appearing (Albany, NY: Weed, Parsons & Co., Printers, 1888), 13.

39. D'Ann Campbell, "Women's Life in Utopia: The Shaker Experiment in Sexual Equality Reappraised—1810 to 1860," *New England Quarterly* 51, no. 1 (March 1978): 28.

40. Robert Peters, "Ann Lee," in *The Reader's Companion to American History*, eds. Eric Foner and John A. Garraty (Boston: Houghton Mifflin, 1991), 646.

41. Peters, "Ann Lee," 646–647.

42. Campbell, "Women's Life in Utopia," 24–25.

43. John D'Emilio and Estelle B. Freedman, *Intimate Matters: A History of Sexuality in America* (Chicago: University of Chicago Press, 1998), 117.

44. Campbell, "Women's Life in Utopia," 28.

45. William Sims Bainbridge, "Shaker Demographics 1840–1900: An Example of the Use of U.S. Census Enumeration Schedules," *Journal for the Scientific Study of Religion* 21, no. 4 (December 1982): 355.

46. Lilian Faderman, quoted in Ariel Levy, "Lesbian Nation," *New Yorker*, February 22, 2009, www.newyorker.com/magazine/2009/03/02/lesbian-nation.

47. Rebecca Traister, *All the Single Ladies: Unmarried Women and the Rise of an Independent Nation* (New York: Simon & Schuster, 2016), 21.

48. Susan Brownmiller, *In Our Time: Memoir of a Revolution* (New York: Dial Press, 1999), 82.

49. *The Furies: Lesbian/Feminist Monthly* 1 (January 1972): 1 (archived by Rainbow History Project, Washington, DC, www.rainbowhistory.org/Furies001.pdf).

50. Ruth Rosen, *The World Split Open: How the Modern Women's Movement Changed America* (New York: Viking, 2000), 167–173.

51. Lisa Luetkemeyer and Kimela West, "Paternity Law: Sperm Donors, Surrogate Mothers and Child Custody," *Missouri Journal of Medicine* 112, no. 3 (May–June 2015): 162.

52. Levy, "Lesbian Nation."

53. Nick von Hoffman, "Better a Goat! I'm Not Kidding," *Boston Globe*, May 14, 1972, 57, 65.

54. "Down with Kids," *TIME*, July 3, 1972, 35, https://time.com/vault/issue/1972-07-03/page/37.

55. Healey, "Rejecting Reproduction," 144–145.

56. Kathleen Hendrix, "Nonparents Seeking a New Image," *Los Angeles Times*, May 26, 1976.

57. Healey, "Rejecting Reproduction," 145.

58. W. Barry Garett, "High Court Holds Abortion to be 'a Right of Privacy,'" *Baptist Press*, January 31, 1973.

59. Robert O'Brien, "Abortion Court Decision Interpreted by Attorney," *Baptist Press*, January 29, 1973.

60. Gladys Martinez, Kimberly Daniels, and Anjani Chandra, "Fertility of Men and Women Aged 15–44 Years in the United States: National Survey of

Family Growth, 2006–2010," *National Health Statistics Reports*, no. 51 (April 12, 2012): 4.

61. "About," NotMom, www.thenotmom.com/aboutus.

62. "Testimonials," NotMom, www.thenotmom.com/testimonials.

63. Jennifer Aniston, "For the Record," *HuffPost*, July 12, 2016, www.huff post.com/entry/for-the-record_b_57855586e4b03fc3ee4e626f.

64. See, for example, "Simone de Beauvoir, Author and Intellectual, Dies in Paris at 78," *New York Times*, April 15, 1986, www.nytimes.com/1986/04/15 /obituaries/simone-de-beauvoir-author-and-intellectual-dies-in-paris-at-78 .html; Associated Press, "Feminist Author Simone de Beauvoir Dies," *Los Angeles Times*, April 15, 1986, www.latimes.com/archives/la-xpm-1986-04 -14-mn-3925-story.html; Claude Jannoud, "L'Œuvre: Une vulgarisation plus qu'une creation," *Le Monde*, April 15, 1986.

65. Kate Kirkpatrick, *Becoming Beauvoir: A Life* (New York: Bloomsbury Academic, 2019), 393.

66. *Le Monde*, April 16, 1986, 19.

67. Yolanda Astarita Patterson, "Simone de Beauvoir and the Demystification of Motherhood," *Yale French Studies* 72 (1986): 90.

Conclusion: And, If You'll Forgive Me for Asking, Why Should We?

1. Ann Landers, "If You Had It to Do Over Again, Would You Have Children?" *Good Housekeeping*, June 1976, 100–101, 215–216, 223–224; see also Margaret Marsh and Wanda Ronner, *The Empty Cradle: Infertility in America from Colonial Times to the Present* (Baltimore: Johns Hopkins University Press, 1996), 214.

2. "91% Would Have Children (Take That, Ann Landers)," *Newsday*, June 13, 1976 (archived at https://econfaculty.gmu.edu/bcaplan/newsday.jpg).

3. Frank Newport and Joy Wilke, "Desire for Children Still Norm in U.S.," Gallup, September 25, 2013, https://news.gallup.com/poll/164618 /desire-children-norm.aspx.

4. Thomas Hansen, "Parenthood and Happiness: A Review of Folk Theories Versus Empirical Evidence," *Social Indicators Research* 108 (2012): 30–31.

5. Jennifer Glass, Robin W. Simon, and Matthew A. Andersson, "Parenthood and Happiness: Effects of Work-Family Reconciliation Policies in 22 OECD Countries," *American Journal of Sociology* 122, no. 3 (November 2016): 3–4, 17.

6. K. M. Nomaguchi and M. A. Milkie, "Costs and Rewards of Children: The Effects of Becoming a Parent on Adults' Lives," *Journal of Marriage and Family* 65, no. 2 (2003): 356–374.

7. For much more on this, see Jennifer Senior, *All Joy and No Fun: The Paradox of Modern Parenting* (New York: Ecco, 2014); see also Roy F. Baumeister, Kathleen D. Vohs, Jennifer L. Aaker, and Emily N. Garbinsky, "Some Key Differences Between a Happy Life and a Meaningful Life," *Journal of Positive Psychology* 8, no. 6 (2013): 505–516.

8. Glass, Simon, and Andersson, "Parenthood and Happiness," 17, 19, 22.

9. IMPAQ International and Institute for Women's Policy Research, "Qualifying for Unpaid Leave: FMLA Eligibility Among Working Mothers," January 2017, www.dol.gov/sites/dolgov/files/OASP/legacy/files /IMPAQ-Working-Mothers.pdf.

10. Bureau of Labor Statistics, "What Data Does the BLS Publish on Family Leave?," National Compensation Survey, Chart 3, www.bls.gov/ncs/ebs /factsheet/family-leave-benefits-fact-sheet.pdf.

11. Claire Cain Miller, "The World 'Has Found a Way to Do This': The U.S. Lags on Paid Leave," *New York Times*, October 25, 2021, www.nytimes .com/2021/10/25/upshot/paid-leave-democrats.html.

12. For more, see Ada Calhoun, *Why We Can't Sleep: Women's New Midlife Crisis* (New York: Grove Press, 2020).

13. According to the World Health Organization, the United States has a maternal mortality rate equal to that of Latvia, Ukraine, and Moldova, ranking behind all of western Europe and countries like Saudi Arabia, Iran, and the Russian Federation. "Maternal Mortality Ratio (Modeled Estimate, per 100,000 Live Births)," World Bank, https://data.worldbank.org/indicator /SH.STA.MMRT?most_recent_value_desc=false.

14. "The Impact of Active Shooter Drills in Schools," Everytown Policy and Research, September 3, 2020, https://everytownresearch.org/report /the-impact-of-active-shooter-drills-in-schools.

15. Quoted in Mary Katherine Tramontana, "Female and Childfree, in Pictures," *New York Times*, May 3, 2021, www.nytimes.com/2021/05/03/style /childfree-women.html.

16. Quoted in Anne Helen Petersen, "The Ideological Battlefield of the 'Mamasphere,'" *Culture Study* (newsletter), October 20, 2021, https://anne helen.substack.com/p/the-ideological-battlefield-of-the.

17. Jamie Ballard, "Millennials Are the Loneliest Generation," YouGov America, July 30, 2019, https://today.yougov.com/topics/lifestyle /articles-reports/2019/07/30/loneliness-friendship-new-friends-poll-survey.

18. Julie Beck, "How Friendships Change in Adulthood," *The Atlantic*, October 22, 2015, www.theatlantic.com/health/archive/2015/10 /how-friendships-change-over-time-in-adulthood/411466.

19. Anne Helen Petersen, "The Great Unbundling," Culture Study (newsletter), February 10, 2021, https://annehelen.substack.com/p/the -great-unbundling.

20. Jeffrey M. Jones, "U.S. Church Membership Falls Below Majority for First Time," Gallup, March 29, 2021, https://news.gallup.com/poll/341963 /church-membership-falls-below-majority-first-time.aspx.

21. Alexandra Hudson, "*Bowling Alone* at Twenty," *National Affairs*, no. 45 (Fall 2020): www.nationalaffairs.com/publications/detail/bowling-alone-at -twenty; see also Robert Putnam, "Preface," in *Bowling Alone: The Collapse and Revival of American Community*, 20th anniversary ed. (New York: Simon & Schuster, 2000).

22. Save the Children, "Childhood in the Time of COVID," www .savethechildren.org/us/about-us/resource-library/us-childhood-report#.

23. Tate Reeves (@tatereeves), "We need to prove that being pro-life is about more than being anti-abortion. We need to commit more to the mission of supporting mothers and children. We need to continuously improve our foster care system. We need to make it even easier to adopt a child. This is the mission now," Twitter, May 4, 2022, https://twitter.com/tatereeves /status/1521992445751222272.

24. Giulia M. Dotti Sani and Judith Treas, "Educational Gradients in Parents' Child-Care Time Across Countries, 1965–2012," *Journal of Marriage and the Family* 78, no. 4 (August 2016): 1090.

25. Hagai Levine, Niels Jørgensen, Anderson Martino-Andrade, Jaime Mendiola, Dan Weksler-Derri, Irina Mindlis, Rachel Pinotti, Shanna H. Swan, "Temporal Trends in Sperm Count: A Systematic Review and Meta-regression Analysis," *Human Reproduction Update* no. 23, 6 (November–December 2017): 646–659; see also Stacey Colino and Shanna H. Swan, *Count Down: How Our Modern World Is Threatening Sperm Counts, Altering Male and Female Reproductive Development, and Imperiling the Human Race* (New York: Scribner, 2021).

26. Donna Haraway, "Making Kin in the Chthulucene: Reproducing Multispecies Justice," in Adele E. Clarke and Donna Haraway, eds., *Making Kin not Population* (Chicago: Prickly Paradigm Press, 2019), 79.

27. "Nancy Olivi, 1947–2017," *Chicago Tribune*, February 27, 2017.

28. Donna Haraway, "Making Kin in the Chthulucene," 87, 68.

29. Sam Adler-Bell, "Unlearning the Language of Wokeness," *New York Magazine*, June 10, 2022, https://nymag.com/intelligencer/2022/06 /unlearning-the-language-of-wokeness.html.

INDEX

Peggy O'Donnell Heffington teaches history at the University of Chicago, where she writes and teaches on the histories of gender, rights, and the environment. She also has lots of opinions on gummy candy. Peggy lives in Chicago with her husband Bob and two pugs, Ellie and Jake.